Nonfiction Readers' Advisory

Nonfiction Readers' Advisory

Edited by
Robert Burgin

A Member of the Greenwood Publishing Group

Westport, Connecticut • London

Library of Congress Cataloging-in-Publication Data

Nonfiction readers' advisory / edited by Robert Burgin.
    p. cm.
  Includes index.
  ISBN 1-59158-115-X (pbk. : alk. paper)
   1. Readers' advisory services—United States. 2. Public libraries—Reference
services—United States. 3. School libraries—Reference services—United States. 4. Books
and reading—United States. 5. Reading interests—United States. I. Burgin, Robert.
Z711.55.N66 2004
025.5'4—dc22   2004048642

British Library Cataloguing in Publication Data is available.

Library of Congress Catalog Number: 2004048642
ISBN: 1-591158-115-X

First published in 2004

Libraries Unlimited, 88 Post Road West, Westport, CT 06881
A Member of the Greenwood Publishing Group, Inc.
www.lu.com

Printed in the United States of America

∞™

The paper used in this book complies with the
Permanent Paper Standard issued by the National
Information Standards Organization (Z39.48–1984).

10 9 8 7 6 5 4 3 2 1

Contents

Part II:
Nonfiction Materials

Part III:
Nonfiction Readers

Part IV:
Practical Advice

Introduction

Joyce G. Saricks

Readers' advisory for fiction has enjoyed a renaissance over the last decade or so. Librarians have joined the movement to offer reader-friendly access to collections, practiced talking about books, and displayed and marketed their collections. Suddenly, fiction stands not as the poor relation, but as the backbone of our library collections, and service to fiction readers is seen by many as one of the most important services we offer today and in many cases the reason readers keep returning to the library—for suggestions of what they might enjoy reading and for the books themselves.

Frankly, those of us involved in the good fight when fiction was the underdog, of only secondary importance in any library that stood for facts and information, are amazed to hear now that nonfiction is the poor stepsister in libraries dominated by fiction and service to fiction readers. It is hard to imagine that the scales could have tipped so dramatically, but those of us who work with fiction are certainly happy to welcome information specialists into the fold—and into the ongoing conversations about reading for pleasure.

From the first, when Nancy Brown and I wrote *Readers' Advisory Service in the Public Library,* we knew instinctively that work with nonfiction would follow similar patterns. However, at the Downers Grove Public Library, we worked only with fiction and the Literature collection—the Dewey 800s—so we could never try out any of our theories on the universe of nonfiction. Over the years, I have seen our suggestions for highlighting fiction collections adopted and applied to fiction and nonfiction collections equally, in my own library and beyond.

It certainly seems logical that work with nonfiction would follow similar patterns and would probably be based on appeal and mood, as is fiction readers' advisory. The same interview gambit could be employed: What have readers enjoyed in the past, and are they in the mood for that or for something different? The interviewer would then listen to the way readers described what they enjoyed, and, as with fiction, the emphasis would be not so much on subject as on appeal. Is this a reader who speaks of fast-paced adventure and survival when describing *The Perfect Storm,* or does he talk about the intricacies of the ship, the fishing, or the technical weather details? For either reader, another multifaceted storm story, such as

Isaac's Storm, might work, but for each, there are other directions that diverge from this subject-based suggestion. Does the fan of *Seabiscuit* want more about horse racing or the Depression era, or does this reader want biographies of those who took a chance on a long shot? As with fiction, the possibilities of directions to pursue for nonfiction readers are endless.

Librarians who have been offering suggestions to fiction readers will see nonfiction readers' advisory as a logical extension of the work they already do. Reference librarians new to readers' advisory in general may be more troubled by the lack of precise answers, as well as the paucity of useful resources to turn to for assistance. Currently there seem to be few, if any, truly helpful reference tools that discuss nonfiction in a way that makes librarians aware of connections and possibilities. These will come, however, just as they did for fiction readers' advisory, in a veritable flood of useful book and online resources. The bigger step will be accepting that even these tools will not provide an exact, precise answer in the way that resources provide answers to most informational questions. That simply is not the way of readers' advisory. There are usually innumerable titles that might please the waiting reader. Our job is to identify what the reader enjoys and then make the appropriate links to suggestions, just as we do with fiction titles. "It sounds as if you enjoy the intricacies of how things work, so this title, even though it's not about the same subject, might work for you because it shares that aspect." Readers' advisors working with both fiction and nonfiction collections help readers make connections to find more materials that interest them.

Because readers' advisory with fiction has been so successful with librarians, administrators, and readers, several steps in the process of legitimatizing nonfiction readers' advisory can be skipped, and we can move forward quickly. Over the past few years, we have learned to value readers and their various reading interests. We understand the importance of annotated booklists, displays, and bookmarks that link similar titles. The following would provide immediate assistance in working with nonfiction titles and readers:

- Ways to group nonfiction titles that parallel fiction genres, along with an understanding of what makes that type of book popular and key authors and titles

- Core lists of important authors and titles within these categories

- Resources (print and Web-based) that identify popular nonfiction authors and titles and that discuss the types of books these authors write, as well as the appeal of these subjects and style

- Sure Bets—lists of titles with broad appeal that will attract readers and on which librarians can fall back when they're short of suggestions

- A network of librarians working on nonfiction readers' advisory questions and sharing information and questions on a mail list, such as Fiction_L (which is really a readers' advisory mail list and could certainly accommodate both fiction and nonfiction queries).

Perhaps the most pertinent question to ask is this: What took us so long to realize that nonfiction collections and nonfiction readers deserve the same serious consideration and effort that we have made for fiction readers over the last decade and more? My role is not to speculate on why this happened, but rather to say it is time to get on with it. What are we waiting for? It is time for librarians who work with nonfiction to join the fun.

Part I

The Case for Nonfiction

    The first section of this book makes the case for nonfiction as part of readers' advisory services. The two chapters in this section make this case by examining both the historical context and the professional and cultural context of nonfiction readers' advisory services.

    In Chapter 1, Bill Crowley discusses the historical rationale for nonfiction readers' advisory by reminding us that readers' advisory services in libraries began with a focus on nonfiction, that is, the adult education movement. Of particular importance is Crowley's argument that readers' advisory service in the American public library began as early as 1876, some fifty years before the generally accepted date of the service's origin. His analysis of how the rationale for readers' advisory services was reformulated to appeal to those in leadership roles in the profession in the 1920s is especially instructive, as is his discussion of the contemporary readers' advisory revival, beginning with the founding of the Adult Reading Round Table of Illinois in 1984. Crowley's historical account suggests solutions to current problems in the provision of readers' advisory service and provides inspiration in the stories of our professional predecessors.

Kathleen de la Peña McCook then provides in Chapter 2 a more general rationale for using nonfiction in readers' advisory work, making the case that the traditional distinction between fiction and nonfiction is simplistic and fails to capture the range of texts that nonfiction comprises. Readers respond to works of nonfiction in very personal ways, just as they respond to works of fiction, and readers' advisors need to go beyond simple distinctions like fiction and nonfiction in order to serve these readers. McCook uses her discussion with experts in readers' advisory to delineate the role of nonfiction advisory services in libraries and then argues that such services not only can support or revitalize library programming but also can provide links between libraries and other cultural heritage institutions.

Both Crowley's historical investigation and McCook's contemporary analysis suggest that attention to nonfiction in readers' advisory services can help libraries both recapture traditional educational roles and expand into partnerships with other cultural institutions. Rather than limiting what librarians do, readers' advisory—especially when both fiction and nonfiction are included—can expand the profession's scope.

Chapter 1

A History of Readers' Advisory Service in the Public Library

Bill Crowley

"The RA Moment"

There is a sometimes-overused term among educators—"the teachable moment." This concept refers to an occasion, as welcome as it can sometimes be unpredictable, when an educator brings student and subject together to achieve real learning. In the professional lives of readers' advisors, there are similar points in time when one simply knows that a person waiting at a desk, standing by a book display, or wandering through the stacks can find something suitable to read if someone will take the time to help. One librarian has movingly captured the sometimes-fleeting nature of such "RA moments":

> The busy assistant at the desk may have a chance to say but a single word. Shall that word relate to the mechanics of librarianship—the charging system, the application form, the shelf-arrangement— or shall it convey in some indefinable way the fact there here is a body of workers, personally interested in books and eager to arouse or foster such an interest in others? (Bostwick 1975, 29)

This description of "the RA [readers' advisory] moment" cannot be found in the twenty-first-century pages of *American Libraries* or *RQ*. Written by Arthur E. Bostwick, it appears in "The Love of Books as a Basis for Librarianship," a famed essay first printed in the February 1907 issue of *Library Journal* (1975, 29). Although appearing nearly a hundred years ago, Bostwick's words still constitute a particularly significant contribution to the continuing, multigeneration conversation among library professionals regarding how best to bring readers and books together and for what purpose. That exchange, in effect an ongoing effort to develop and adapt RA thinking and philosophy to the changing educational, informational, and recreational needs of succeeding generations of readers, has been going on since the early years of the American public library.

Of What Use Is RA History?

This chapter seeks to provide historical perspective, to make available to contemporary practitioners the hard-won experience of more than a century of discussion and debates by RA staff whose pioneering work long predated the achievements of the Joyce Sarickses, Mary K. Cheltons, and Ted Balcoms of our own day. In this effort I have benefited greatly from the thoughtful and well-documented considerations of readers' advisory found in such influential works as the American Library Association's *Libraries and Adult Education* (1926), John Chancellor's *Helping Adults to Learn* (1939), Jennie M. Flexner and Bryon C. Hopkins's *Readers' Advisers at Work* (1941), Robert Ellis Lee's *Continuing Education for Adults through the American Public Library: 1833–1964* (1966), and Margaret E. Monroe's *Library Adult Education: The Biography of an Idea* (1963). In revisiting and extending the timeline of the RA story, it has also been necessary to fill in the gaps *before and after* the periods covered by such classic volumes. Even in an electronic age this proved to be an unexpectedly complex process. Countless times, critical perspectives could only be discerned in the pages of aging journals, yellowing and out-of-print official reports, and hard-to-obtain monographs identified and interlibrary-loaned by my graduate assistant Heather Cannon[1] or purchased by me from online used-book dealers.

Through this extended process it became abundantly clear that the contemporary revival of RA is historically unique. In privileging works of fiction, present-day practice is reversing the traditional prestige hierarchy of books in the library world. For most of the public library's history, an educational function grounded in using nonfiction to assist readers was the intellectual gold standard of adult readers' advisory service. Matching histories, biographies, textbooks, and how-to books to a reader's self-educational interests had pride of place in the written accounts of generations of RA librarians. A commitment to such reader self-education and improvement was seen as more professional and of greater value than disseminating novels to borrowers in the communities that brought public libraries into being and continued to support them with their taxes (Fihe 1936; Monroe 1963).

Official partiality for nonfiction RA in public libraries endured despite mounting evidence affirming the value of fiction reading as well its obvious role in driving up circulation statistics (Cole 1996; Dana 1920; Shearer 1998). Impressive arguments in favor of promoting fiction were advanced as far back as 1876 by William F. Poole, who disparaged the fabrications passing "as history and biography" and stressed that the "great mass of readers prefer to take their knowledge" about the world through entertaining fiction (Poole 1993, 86). The nineteenth- and twentieth-century emphasis on nonfiction's role in advancing reader self-education tended to ignore the equally valuable function of fiction in achieving similar ends. Fortunately, contemporary RA theorist Catherine Sheldrick Ross has followed Poole's lead in emphasizing the educational value of fiction (Ross 1991, 1995), as well as providing contemporary accounts of the contributions of both fiction and nonfiction (Ross 1999) to adult self-education. Such documentation may help provide continued justification for support of the public library at a time when alternative sources of information are increasingly available.

Issues in adult reading, both the relative value to assign to fiction and nonfiction books and the complexities resulting from the public's seeming preference for "recreational" over "educational" works, have been around for hundreds of years, far predating the foundation of the public library and its offering of RA service. Fruitful ideas for generating solutions to current service problems lie in earlier accounts of the RA story. Encouraging historical perspective in twenty-first-century RA professionals can offer additional benefits. Not the least is encountering the inspiring stories of professional ancestors whose commitment, passion, and wisdom matched or exceed that of participants in contemporary debates over RA issues. In this context, it is well to recall the words of Helen E. Haines, the near-legendary figure famed as much for her nineteenth-century work with *Library Journal* as she was for later decades of leadership in teaching and writing on book selection. Haines reminded her readers that "Advising service to readers has, of course, been a vital, continuing current in the life-stream of public library development" (Haines 1950, 34). RA as Haines's "vital, continuing current," whether flowing underground and out of sight (Chelton 1993, 33) or sweeping through the contemporary library world with floodlike force (Saricks and Brown 1997, vii), has always been reshaped by the shifting balance among the public library's larger educational, informational, and recreational commitments.

Definitions and Distinctions: Defining RA

The extended history of RA—more than a century of accounts by both critics and enthusiasts alike—directly and indirectly supports the contention that contemporary readers' advisory service through the public library is best understood as an organized program promoting both fiction and nonfiction discretionary reading for the dual purposes of satisfying reader needs and advancing a culture's goal of a literate population. Even when perceived as a recreational activity, effective RA is inevitably in the service of an educational end. Depending on local policies or service traditions, the beneficiaries of RA guidance can include adults, young adults, and children.

The educational rationale for recreational reading—and by implication for assistance by library staff in selecting material to read—has been well captured by the Evanston (Illinois) Public Library Board in its *Evanston Public Library Strategic Plan 2000—2010: A Decade of Outreach:*

> The Board continues to believe that promoting recreational reading is one of the most important services that the Library provides for the citizens of Evanston. We believe that reading is to the mind what exercise is to the body. People who don't read regularly and often are in great danger of not having the intellectual or emotional resources they need to deal with assignments at school or work, the challenges of everyday life, personal problems, and the huge challenge of giving meaning to their lives. In that sense reading for pleasure is a survival skill. The aim of the Library's work with children in the creation of life-long readers—in other words, the creation of recreational readers. (Evanston Public Library Board of Trustees 2003, 2)

Research supporting the Evanston Public Library Board's connection of recreational reading with educational aims is discussed later in the chapter.

RA and Adult Education

For much of its history the identification of readers' advisory service with adult education was so strong that RA might be implemented or rejected not on its intrinsic value, but on whether public library directors were comfortable in seeing themselves as educators (Monroe 1963). This unease of many public librarians about equating RA with "adult education" may have reflected a valid understanding of adult psychology as well as a librarian's doubts about her or his educational skills.

More than seventy years ago, Sir Henry A. Miers described a fundamental problem with libraries, "adult education" activities, and readers. Many adults possess negative memories of classroom life, have no wish to return to it, and may resist using any library service that seems to put them in a subordinate student role. More recent researchers such as Alisa Belzer have confirmed Miers's cautions about emulating negative educational contexts where "reading in school was boring, had little to offer . . . and was simply a task . . . to get done to get by" (Belzer 2002, 111). To adapt an observation Miers made about the successful adult education efforts of his day to the contemporary public library context, a library educational activity such as RA can be consistently successful only when librarian and reader "meet on terms of equality and the discussion is conducted as a free and easy conversation designed to exercise the wits of both" (Miers 1933, 336). Miers insisted that "adult education" in libraries did not mean the "teaching of grown people" in the schoolhouse manner but required recognizing that adults value freedom of choice in learning and are best served through "the provision of opportunity, encouragement and guidance" (Miers 1933, 335–36). The results of this advice are exemplified in our own day by approaches that range from providing multiple copies of best-sellers and Web-based RA guidance through supporting library and community book discussion groups to establishing a fully staffed Readers' Advisory Department.

Recognizing that even experienced readers' advisors can be made uneasy when contemplating their work as an educational service, I avoid using the term "adult education" in this chapter except where it is historically necessary. Instead, adapting the insights of Sir Henry to the present day, the terms "readers' advisory" or "RA" will be employed with the understanding that some educational component is inevitably present when a public library staff member assists a reader in selecting an appropriate book.

The Fiction Problem

No account of the history of nonfiction and fiction RA can be complete without an examination of a fundamental paradox over reading choice that has long afflicted the English-speaking world. As Dee Garrison noted, "from 1876 to the present," fiction inevitably represents something over two-thirds of the annual total of books loaned "in an average public library" (Garrison 1979, 68n). Yet even before the creation of the public library, cultural leaders in the English-speaking world have identified the public preference for reading fiction as, by definition, the *fiction problem*. It has been a remarkably enduring issue. As late as 1988, the reading researcher Victor Nell wrote of the "universal" identification of fiction as "trash" and "the librarian's eternal plea" urging that "borrowers read more nonfiction"

(Nell 1988, 45). The intensity of the bias against fiction within a significant portion of Western culture was captured centuries ago in an essay titled "On the Good Effects of Bad Novels," written by the otherwise unidentified "(E. A. 1798, 258–62)," and published in the October 1798 issue of the *Lady's Monthly Museum.*

According to E. A., novels are

- "universally read, and universally mischievous"

- favored by "the female part of mankind," which, as a gender, was "just emerging from infancy" and thus not marked by intellectual maturity in its reading habits

- inducing people to read who would be better off had they "never read at all"

- intellectually, the equivalent of Methodism, "the most proper religion for those whose minds are weak and depraved enough to applaud it"

- rented by "circulating libraries"—commercial book-lending agencies profiting from the loan of "very stupid stories"

- good only for the one out of a hundred readers who uses fiction to acquire the reading habit and then escapes the degradation of novel reading by embracing more worthy intellectual fare

Certain cultural stereotypes asserted by "E. A." may resonate through the public library world to our own day. The first theme is a grudging acceptance of the reality that fiction reading is enormously popular. The second theme connects novel reading with women. Their very reading preference demonstrates that females are more emotional and less rational than nonfiction-reading males. The third theme, a comparison with eighteenth-century Methodism is telling. The English cultural leaders of the period tended to identify with the Church of England, the established state religion with an historic connection to the university, reason, and the world of science. Its adherents viewed the breakaway sect of Methodism as an entity substituting emotion for logical thinking, encouraging unrestrained sexuality, fomenting the division of families, and promoting such irrational "truths" as belief in witches (Johnson 1976, 365–67). Fourth and finally, for the English intellectual elite of E. A's day, institutions providing fiction in such abundance were clearly cultural negatives.

Although "On the Good Effects of Bad Novels" was published in England, it reflected deeply held transatlantic beliefs. Another such attack, "Novel Reading a Cause of Female Depravity" was "reprinted in America several times after its original London publication in 1797." Such was the bias against the novel and its readers that Harvard College, in 1803, decided, "the principle commencement address should be directed against the dangers of fiction" (Hart 1950, 53–54). This antifiction prejudice of much of America's male intellectual elite was still in force when public library development got underway in the middle of the nineteenth century.

Accepted Belief and Historical Evidence

It is standard practice to date the start of readers' advisory service in the American public library to the 1920s (Karetzky 1982, 79; Lee 1966, 57). Although there was considerable professional discussion about RA in the 1920 to 1940 period (American Library Association 1926; Jennings 1929; Monroe 1963), it is probably a mistake to credit RA's genesis to that time. Such a claim privileges a unique type of RA, one with only a twenty-year life span. It also undervalues the longer history of a lower-key RA mainstream that permeated the very nature of the public library before, during, and after the heyday of its more publicized offshoot. As discussed later in the chapter, the type of RA typical from about 1920 to 1940 was a costly, "retail" model requiring extensive human and material resources generally available only in the major city libraries of the time. As even fervent RA advocate W. E. Henry predicted in 1925, the vast majority of public libraries were little affected by the new conception of RA and continued to provide services, specifically including readers' advisory, "in much the same way and with much the same motive" as they always had (Henry 1925, 212).

1876—"Inventing" RA

Setting the date of origin for any historical movement can be a frustrating, almost arbitrary exercise. It can hardly be otherwise. Scholars have yet to come to agreement regarding the year and location of the first American public library (Shera 1976, 37–40). Efforts at historical precision can founder on such issues as shared definitions ("What exactly is a public library?" or "What really is RA?"). Developing acceptable answers for historical questions is always an interesting challenge when the documents necessary are missing, unreliable, or open to multiple interpretations. There is also such a thing as "publication bias" (Light, Singer, and Willett 1990, 30), wherein accounts that make it into print are favored over stories that are either lost (and thus unknown) or rely for verification on reports that were misplaced or destroyed over the years. If the precise date and location of the first public library cannot be agreed on, is it even possible to pinpoint the initial occasion when a public library formalized its previously informal process of providing adult patrons with advice on reading?

There is, however, an alternative tactic that may get us closer to the actual birth of RA in the public library. Through exploring more recent and available accounts, it can be possible to identify what earlier generations of RA advocates, including those working in the 1920s, acknowledged as the prior events, people, and writings that inspired their own work. For example, the October 1927 issue of the American Library Association's *Adult Education and the Library,* a journal published during the high tide of RA as reader education, claimed it was "abundantly worth while" to find inspiration in "some of the literature on libraries which appeared fifty years ago" (American Library Association 1927, 31) during the extended celebrations that marked the hundredth anniversary of American independence.

The momentous library events of the 1876 centennial year included the founding of the American Library Association, start of *Library Journal,* and publication of *Public Libraries in the United States of America: Their History, Condition, and Management* (U.S. Interior Department, Bureau of Education 1876). The latter, a massive work, provided its readers with a cornucopia of resources, including Charles A. Cutter's "Rules for a Printed Dictionary Catalogue," articles on about every conceivable aspect of library history and service, compilations of library statistics, and even a theoretical justification for "library science" translated from the original German. In their introduction to this still-influential government document, editors S. R Warren and S. N. Clark included a section titled "The Librarian an Educator" in which they presented a vision of RA as a public library educational activity so compelling that ALA reprinted it in full fifty-one years later (American Library Association 1927, 31).

As asserted by Warren and Clark—with apologies for the noninclusive language of the nineteenth century—in an observation worthy of fully reprinting in yet another century:

The influence of the librarian as an educator is rarely estimated by outside observers and probably seldom fully realized by himself. Performing his duties independently of direct control as to their details, usually selecting the books that are to be purchased by the library and read by its patrons, often advising individuals as to a proper course of reading and placing in their hands the books they are to read and pursuing his own methods of administration generally without reference to those in use elsewhere, the librarian has silently, almost unconsciously, gained ascendancy over the habits of thought and literary tastes of a multitude of readers, who find in the public library their only means of intellectual improvement. That educators should be able to know the direction and gauge the extent and results of this potential influence, and that librarians should not only understand their primary duties as purveyors of literary supplies to the people, but also realize their high privileges and responsibilities as teachers, are matters of great import to the interests of public education. (Warren and Clark 1876, xi)

From the perspective of a century and a quarter of hard-won RA experience, this description of the educational role of librarians in shaping public reading tastes through building collections and advising readers on appropriate books can serve as a cornerstone on which to build a history of RA. Editors Warren and Clark, sympathetic observers with an appreciation of the history and role of the public library, portray the advising function as an intellectual process that can involve virtually any type of reading—fiction and nonfiction alike—provided that librarians adhere to an educational ideal in their selection and dissemination of "literary supplies" to their communities. As a guide to readers' advisory service, it remains as relevant in the twenty-first century as it was in the nineteenth and twentieth.

In 1876, the very idea that librarians ought to advise readers about reading instead of forcing them to choose their own books was a subject of contention. F. B. Perkins of the Boston Public Library, in a *Public Libraries in the United States of America* chapter titled "How to Make Town Libraries Successful," argued against what we would now term "active readers' advisory." Perkins deemed it "unreasonable" for users of a library to "plague the librarian by trying to make him (or her) pick out books" instead of making their own choices (Perkins 1876, 429). To ask for a librarian's assistance in selecting reading was, for Perkins, the equivalent of returning a book in damaged condition, refusing to pay an overdue fine, or complaining when someone else has borrowed a volume one wants. It was committing a "wrong doing," "injustice," and "undeserved annoyance" and demonstrating a lack of "considerate courtesy" (Perkins 1876, 428–29). There seems to be some evidence that such an attitude is still operative in a number of contemporary public libraries (May et al. 2000).

For all his bluster against active RA, Perkins apparently embraced the most basic form of passive RA—providing a wide spectrum of reading material. In 1876, he argued that what many people considered to be " 'silly reading,' [or] 'trash'. . . must to a considerable extent be supplied by the public library" (Perkins 1876, 421). Perkins's support for the lending of such popular material was grounded in the optimistic belief—so unlike the pessimistic views of "E. A." in the previous century—that most people progressed in their reading despite any initial limitations. For Perkins, "those who begin with dime novels and story weeklies may be expected to grow into liking for a better sort of stories; then for the truer narrative of travels and adventure, of biography and history; then of essays and popular science, and so on upward" (Perkins 1876, 422). Furthermore, a full spectrum of reading material posed little harm to the more serious booklover because "No case has ever been cited where a reader, beginning with lofty philosophy, pure religion, profound science, and useful information, has gradually run down in his reading until his declining years were disreputably wasted on dime novels and story weeklies" (Perkins 1876, 421).

Dedication to the educational function of the public library, particularly in its readers' advisory aspects, powered much of the library growth of the late nineteenth century (Wilson 1910, 7). In words that foreshadow twenty-first-century exhortations, America's nineteenth-century librarians were also told of the positive impact on education of a more globalized environment (Mowry 1891, 302). Even so, reinforcement of a library educational commitment was tied directly to the reality that less than 25 percent of American children over age fourteen were still in school and relatively few adults were college graduates (Wilson 1910, 9). It is useful to keep such a learning deficit in mind when exploring the extended debate over the library's educational priorities, including whether fiction should be disseminated for own merits or continue to be used as a lure for exposing readers to the more exalted realm of nonfiction. Whatever the local service philosophy it was a task to be undertaken for the reader's own good (Garrison 1979; Molz and Dain 1999, 12) and the good of the nation because "to produce the best results the library should furnish to all the people, old and young, of average intelligence and of the highest intellectual advancements, both improvement and intellectual entertainment" (Mowry 1891, 302).

Following 1876, *Public Libraries in the United States of America* retained its influence on the library's educational model, both at home and abroad, for a number of years. Several chapters, including F. B. Perkins's already noted "How to Make Town Libraries Successful," were cited with approval a quarter-century later in a practical 1902 English manual titled *How to Form a Library*. Although supplemented by turn-of-the-twentieth-century English examples and equivalent American accounts, these 1876 *Public Libraries* chapters were considered to be near-conclusive evidence documenting the preference of the general public for fiction, as well as the librarian's resulting fear that an institution viewed as the supplier of popular novels could lose tax support granted on the basis of its "educational value" (Wheatley 1902, 81–84). In this same 1902 work is found the reluctant admission that patrons are unwilling to change their reading habits. Borrowers from the public library are simply *not* likely to be "led from the lower species of reading to the higher" because "little confirmation of this hope [is] to be found in the case of the confirmed novel readers we see around us" (Wheatley 1902, 87–88).

Even so, the dismay at fiction reading was often alleviated by its positive impact on public library use. Before and at the turn of the last century, novel reading through the public library was a reality that could be reduced only with a similar and generally unwanted decrease in circulation statistics. For Robert Ellis Lee, writing in 1966 at a time when RA was no longer a hot topic in library publications, disapproval of fiction reading might be grounded in the simple physical separation of novels from histories, biographies, and other nonfiction works in the library's stacks. It was a segregation that could reinforce the belief among certain library employees that fiction equates with recreation and nonfiction with education (Lee 1966, 26).

As Lee further asserted,

This categorization *[fiction = recreation* and *nonfiction = education]*, however, failed to take into account two factors. First, not all fiction is recreational; some is obviously of higher educational value than non-fiction. And not all nonfiction is educational; many works in this category, consisting of friendly tips and helpful hints, do not represent a contribution to knowledge or understanding of permanent worth. Second, the purposes of readers, their educational level, and their reading abilities must be taken into consideration. To paraphrase an old adage, one man's recreation is another man's education. And, conversely, one man's education is another man's recreation. (Lee 1966, 26–27)

Lee's observation, if correct, is a powerful argument for minimizing distinctions between fiction and nonfiction "story books" by locating novels next to histories and biographies and placing related nonfiction in every genre fiction book display—and vice versa. Producing inclusive fiction-nonfiction bibliographies would also be indicated, as well as similarly integrating lists developed for book discussion groups.[2]

1920 to 1940—Privileging *Nonfiction* RA

The claim that RA was a 1920s innovation has already been challenged in this chapter, but there are understandable reasons why the generation of librarians emerging into leadership at the time might insist, often in books and journals cited by later library historians, that theirs was an original contribution and unrelated to previous incarnations of RA. One must examine such claims with a certain amount of care. Defining a program, any program, as new and exciting can be effective for securing financial support from supervisors worried about being perceived as "old-fashioned" and unconnected to current professional developments. Claims of originality can also gain the commitment of younger staff who believe that their employer is resistant to necessary change or who want to make their own professional reputations.

There were developments in the years just prior to 1920 that gave hope for a greater appreciation of the public library's educational value, with a resulting increase in public support. Experience with camp libraries serving American soldiers in World War I through the American Library Association–organized *Library War Service Program* taught librarians that men would read books and, at times, even allow themselves to be guided in book selection. The possibility existed that the readers thus gained might continue to use a public library (where such libraries existed) after their demobilization. Success in such wartime RA contributed to professional belief that the "value and need of the librarian's work in collecting and interpreting books had at last gained recognition" and the "educational commitment of the public library was still a valid one and needed to be revitalized" (Lee 1966, 43–44, 46).

The story of how a public library RA responsibility dating back to 1876 (if not earlier) was reformulated to appeal to a generation of librarians coming into leadership and positions in 1920s is admittedly impressive. There were several identifiable yet commingled intellectual streams involved in the process.

First, although the American Library Association's 1920 "Enlarged Program" to greatly expand post-WWI library service in America did not generate much public support, it did have adult education aspects that caught the attention of the Carnegie Foundation for the Advancement of Teaching. Indeed, William S. Learned's famed 1924 work *The American Public Library and the Diffusion of Knowledge* was developed out of reports made in his capacity as a staff member of the Carnegie Foundation. This book stimulated a well-discussed vision of the public library as a "community intelligence service" that, at the time, was taken as a justification of its role as an educational agency (Chancellor 1939; Lee 1966). However, from a twenty-first-century perspective the public library as "community intelligence service" advocated by Learned appears to have been more informational than educational in nature. It is even possible that it may have laid the preparatory groundwork for privileging information over education and recreation in the post-1945 years. Whatever the true nature of Learned's vision, it was most certainly not recreational. Fifteen years later the book was still being hailed as "one of the first and most important discussions of the library as an agency for adult education" as ALA reprinted significant portions in John Chancellor's *Helping Adults to Learn,* in part for the guidance of younger librarians (Chancellor 1939, 206).

Second, the 1920s did see the creation of fulltime RA positions in a number of major public libraries. This development occurred before and after the publication of the ALA Commission on the Library and Adult Education's book-length report, *Libraries and Adult Education,* a work describing RA as a major component of the public library's educational role (American Library Association 1926). In a later summary of this work, Judson T. Jennings observed that "the library's contribution to adult education resolved itself into three major activities":

1. An information service regarding local opportunities for adult students

2. Service to other agencies engaged in adult education

3. Service to individual readers and students (Jennings 1929, 13)

A third catalyst for RA in public libraries, one whose components may have had an impact on the greatest number of public libraries in the period, was the American Library Association's *Reading with a Purpose* program. This was an extended effort commissioning, publishing, and disseminating a series of bibliographical essays or "reading courses" (Phelps 1927). It is of note that the 1920s term "reading courses" seems to echo the "proper course of reading" that Warren and Clark privileged in their description of how librarians served readers in 1876.

Supported in part by the Carnegie Corporation, the *Reading with a Purpose* program brought the American Library Association and participating libraries a considerable amount of publicity for sixty-seven bibliographic essays on subjects as diverse as the sciences, the life of Christ, contemporary Europe, and African Americans in the United States. Such essays, printed in hardcover or pamphlet format, provided readers with recommendations for fiction or nonfiction reading, depending on the topic covered. A complete listing of the works in the series can be found in the American Library Association Archives Holdings Database, maintained online by the University of Illinois at Urbana-Champaign library.

As bibliographical essays, even when dealing with fiction, all the publications in the *Reading with a Purpose* were nonfiction works. One such, *The United States in Recent Times* by Frederic L. Paxson, featured an introductory essay and discussed seven books meant to be read in the order presented (Paxson 1926). Other *Reading with a Purpose* reading courses examined eight to twelve recommended works (Lee 1966, 50). These pamphlets were not universally endorsed. Concern was voiced at the time that reading courses and the overall systematization of RA itself threatened to bring the "formal methods of the elementary school" into public librarianship, to the detriment of the "informal reading which educates" ("Reading Courses" 1927, 174–75). Other criticisms voiced included the assertions that the reading courses were (a) prepared by nonlibrarians with little knowledge of their proposed readers, (b) professionally embarrassing because their authorship implied that even ALA believed librarians were incapable of providing advice on reading, (c) too difficult for the average reader to use, and (d) unlikely to be finished by individuals and thus more suited for group work. About 850,000 copies of the *Reading with a Purpose* pamphlets were sold before the series was discontinued in 1933, in part because of the problems of keeping works up to date and the reality that standardized works were not always appropriate for use with a given individual (American Library Association 1928, 77; Lee 1966, 50–51).

During the 1920–1940 period, the most influential readers' advisory program was probably that of the New York Public Library (NYPL), primarily because Jennie M. Flexner, whose numerous writings and presentations helped formulate the period's RA philosophy, headed its service (Karetzky 1982, 79–80). In 1941, Flexner and Byron C. Hopkins coauthored *Readers' Advisers at Work: A Survey of Development in the New York Public Library,* for the American Association for Adult Education. Made possible by a grant from the Carnegie Corporation, the study sought to (a) examine the changes "in thinking and in attitude" within NYPL's readers' advisory program over the years, (b) trace and evaluate the effectiveness of "techniques employed in rendering" RA, and (c) record the NYPL experience as a resource for future RA practitioners and current staff members wanting to compare their "procedures with those of another library" (Flexner and Hopkins 1941, vii). As discussed later in this chapter, the hope of Flexner and Hopkins for continued relevance is surprisingly viable six decades later.

Although Flexner and Hopkins make a point of stressing how numerous libraries, organizations, and even the national broadcast and publishing media used NYPL's Readers' Advisory Service, they also went into considerable detail describing the sometimes serendipitous nature of how the prototypical user—"the able-bodied, normal man or woman, from seventeen to eighty-five"—asked for RA assistance. Such a reader determines what he or she wants to read on the basis of both predictable and unpredictable factors, such as "the season of the year, the state of the country, by his [her] demands on life, or life's demands on him [her]." These core users of RA service "come and go continually, asking for new approaches to old subjects" (Flexner and Hopkins 1941, 6). In addition to describing consistent users of the service, Flexner and Hopkins, in a clear reflection of their times, note that RA also serves "handicapped young people," "boys and men on probation to the Court," "older people, perhaps living in institutions and trying to fill empty days," and "lately, political refugees from all over the world" (Flexner and Hopkins 1941, 6).

Were this volume dedicated solely to RA history it would be feasible to explore the in-depth interviews and detailed paperwork sought by the 1941 New York Public Library from readers who found their way to the central RA office at the library's main building on Fifth Avenue and 42nd Street. In a chapter-length account, such examination is not cost-effective.

Regardless of any intrinsic value, the heavy expense of such in-depth, one-on-one service means that it is unlikely to be revived in the twenty-first century. Nevertheless, however irrelevant may be the history of NYPL's central RA office, the experience of its branches—captured by Flexner and Hopkins through September 1940 interviews with all the branch system's readers' advisers—has definite applicability to contemporary environments (Flexner and Hopkins 1941, 24–33). At that time less than half of the NYPL branches had trained readers' advisors because RA training was not mandated but had to be requested by the branch librarian (Flexner and Hopkins 1941, 24, 27). Nevertheless, in the RA friendly branches of the NYPL system, the following policies were in evidence:

- Coordination of branch RA *on a part-time basis* was usually assigned to the assistant branch librarian. One result of this delegation, due to frequent promotions to branch head, was that a developed understanding of the value of RA was acquired by more senior NYPL administers. (Flexner and Hopkins 1941, 27)

- Adult borrowing was maintained or expanded, even at times when branches without a RA commitment experienced a loss in circulation. (Flexner and Hopkins 1941, 26)

- Special RA desks and posted RA times were abandoned because requests for help occurred "most frequently as a result of floor work" during open hours. (Flexner and Hopkins 1941, 28)

- Privacy for a RA interview was almost "never available." (Flexner and Hopkins 1941, 29)

- Work with adult groups outside the library was limited because of "an insufficient book stock and an already overworked personnel." (Flexner and Hopkins 1941, 31)

- Publicity was minimized because of insufficient books and personnel to meet any increased demand by readers. (Flexner and Hopkins 1941, 31)

- Meetings of RA staff were supported for the "discussion and exchange of ideas." (Flexner and Hopkins 1941, 32)

The practical nature of NYPL's branch-level RA experience in 1940 makes it still useful today, and its implications for contemporary service are discussed in the final section of this chapter.

1940 to 1984—RA "Lost" in Adult Services: The Turn to Information

Following World War II, the American public library community privileged its informational function and diminished the philosophical commitment to its educational and recreational responsibilities. A major symbol of this conceptual transformation was the postwar Public Library Inquiry, a massive study of America's public libraries funded by a $200,000 grant from the Carnegie Corporation and carried out by the Social Science Research Council under the direction of political scientist Robert D. Leigh (1950, 3). In the report's summary volume, *The Public Library in the United States,* Leigh and the other project staff emphasized that a mainstream professional ideology existed within the public library community supporting the commitment "to serve the community as general center of reliable information and to provide opportunity and encouragement for people of all ages to educate themselves continuously" (Leigh 1950, 223). This favoring of information provision and relegating of educational activities to a second place may constitute a reaction to the expensive RA of the previous decades. According to Leigh, mid–twentieth century research suggested that the public library as an educational center was a minority view, lacking both broad-based professional support and the possibility of securing the substantial commitment of tax dollars to sustain it (Leigh 1950, 224). The inquiry dismissed the importance the public library's *recreational* role or "giving people what they want" as a distinct negative. It further asserted that librarians who viewed the public library as a "free, miscellaneous book service supported by the public for that purpose" were cleaving to a course of action that would diminish or even doom the institution in the new communications age (Leigh 1950, 223–25).

A spectrum of reasons has been advanced by authors such as Sharon Baker and Catherine Sheldrick Ross for the decline of RA in this and the previous period, including a switch in emphasis to "more technical aspects of librarianship," rise of other suppliers of adult education, discrediting of the idea that people ought to be strongly directed in their reading, and the lack of cost-effectiveness of RA service (Luyt 2001, 444). In hindsight, the idea that advising readers could be enhanced by folding RA units into larger entities termed "Adult Services Departments," defined as providing "library services for the continuing educational, recreational, and cultural development of adults" (Lee 1966, 83), proved to be a fallacy. In theory, this development would strengthen RA by making the guidance of adults in their reading a priority for all the staff in the larger unit of service. For various reasons, including both fashion and finance, this process reduced the number of public libraries with a dedicated RA staff from sixty-three in

1935 to ten in the 1940s and 1950s (Lee 1966, 83). Most likely, in those libraries that gave up a separate RA program, it also reduced the percentage of human and financial resources dedicated to helping readers' select books from 1920–1940 levels. Writing about the process in 1955, Lowell Martin was probably correct in hypothesizing that the decline in effective service to readers that followed RA's absorption by Adult Services reflected a changeover that occurred too soon, before the institutionalization of the effective routines necessary to keep the program alive without the daily zeal of staff members who had embraced RA with near-religious fervor in the 1920s and 1930s (Martin 1955, 10).

In this period the subsuming of RA into Adult Services and privileging of information in the public librarian's professional ideology did not always mean the abandonment of the public's interest in reading. Where high public library circulation totals existed, they usually reflected a heavy library commitment to purchasing works sought by borrowers for their recreational, educational, and even informational reading interests. There was even a continuing philosophical basis for the support of reading. In 1950, the same year that Robert D. Leigh's summary volume of the Public Library Inquiry (*The Public Library in the United States*) crystallized the case for prioritizing information provision through the public library, Helen E. Haines issued the second edition of her influential *Living with Books: The Art of Book Selection*. Praised as an uniquely valuable resource for the "teachers of book selection in the country's library schools" (Warren 1950, vii), this work openly proclaimed that "the province and purpose of the public library is to provide for every person the education available through reading" (Haines 1950, 15). However strongly the informational commitment of the public library might be stressed in the literature, professionals in training were still being exposed to the concept that "Standards are raised, intelligence is enlarged, perceptions are deepened, through the simple process of reading" (Haines 1950, 3).

For much of this period information services captured public library theory, even as novels, biographies, and histories were still being purchased in massive quantities for reader borrowing. By the 1980s, however, changes in external circumstances and a revived librarian interest in promoting reading would again allow readers' advisory to be taken seriously in the public library environment. Fundamentally important to this development was the 1984 organization of the Adult Reading Round Table in the Chicago metropolitan area (Balcom 2002).

1984 and the Revival of RA

In remarks to a meeting of public library administrators later printed in the November 1988 issue of *Illinois Libraries,* Ted Balcom described the ongoing resurgence of readers' advisory service as a "renewed interest in an aspect of librarianship that for many years has seemed quaint and out-moded." Balcom ascribed what he saw as a prior lack of administrative interest in RA to "more than a decade of delving into seemingly more high-powered subjects, such as automation, planning, and grantsmanship," activities that had temporarily displaced the love of books that had drawn many of his listeners into the profession (Balcom 1988, 583). A more pervasive and elemental factor may have also been active in the downplaying of RA. For decades, when ambitious new librarians were socialized into public library cultures, they were not exposed to the value of combining "reader" and "advice" at service desks, inside reference department offices, on organization charts, or in professional job descriptions. This absence undoubtedly sent a strongly negative message about the ranking in the public library status hierarchy of activities designed to connect readers with books. By default, RA activities in the mid–twentieth century seemed to be left to the circulation staff or librarians who had resisted being overly connected with the public library's fashionable identification with "information."

Although clearly subject to challenge, this chapter sets the start of the contemporary revival of RA in 1984, the year of the founding of the Adult Reading Round Table, whose leadership has long included such well-known RA advocates as Ted Balcom, Joyce Saricks, and Merle Jacob (Balcom 2002). Even so, this selection is admittedly arbitrary and does not fully reflect the timelines of the forces moving public libraries to again embrace RA. Such developments with clear implications for RA include the 1970s-era influence of the Baltimore County Public Library in encouraging libraries to respond to reader demands (Molz and Dain 1999, 28–31), increasing availability of sources of RA assistance in both hard-copy and electronic formats (St. Louis Public Library and EBSCO Publishing 2000; Smith and Mahmoodi 2000), rise in RA training by state and national library associations (Balcom 2002), offering of courses in RA in academic institutions with ALA-accredited programs (Watson 2000), and the renewed appreciation of the service voiced by such national leaders as Dr. Robert Martin, Director of the Institute of Museum and Library Services (Martin 2001).

It is of interest that the current RA revival originally prioritized fiction (Saricks and Brown 1997), perhaps recognizing that fantasy, mystery, and romance stories had been even more neglected than the stories conveyed through biography and history. As noted earlier, it thereby reversed the historic RA prejudice in favor of nonfiction. However, as the reader will find in the other chapters of this book, attempting to limit RA to fiction will increasingly appear dated, self-interested or, at best, to borrow Balcom's words, "quaint and outmoded." Based on a century and a quarter of RA experience, any and all efforts to limit the advising of readers to only part of the vast spectrum of "story books" are likely to be both unsustainable and unsatisfying.[3]

This chapter on the history of RA has reached the twenty-first century, and further discussion of contemporary developments threatens to duplicate the fine work of the other authors in this volume. From the perspective of the history of RA, it is now more appropriate to explore the emerging evidence that supports the long-held professional view that advising readers has a distinctly educational function. As will be recalled, the definition of RA offered in the first part of this chapter asserts that contemporary readers' advisory service through the public library is best understood as an organized program promoting both fiction and nonfiction discretionary reading for the dual purposes of satisfying reader needs and advancing a culture's goal of a literate population. Even when perceived as a recreational activity, effective RA is inevitably in the service of an educational end.

In developments likely to delight or astonish the shades of past generations of RA practitioners, it is becoming clear with each new study that recreational reading has a firm educational justification. The proverbial circle has been squared and the public library's provision of recreational or discretionary reading can now be seen as a firm, lasting justification of its claim for tax support on the basis that it advances the self-education of its users.

Research Support for Reading as Self-Education

The ongoing work of library and information researcher Catherine Sheldrick Ross in exploring how reading narratives—"biography, autobiography, history or fiction"—have helped women and men grow in self-knowledge and their ability to fashion a place for themselves in the world (Ross 1999, 793) has already been acknowledged. Additionally, Stephen Krashen, in *The Power of Reading: Insights from the Research* (1993), has brought together the results of reading studies from various fields that parallel and extend Ross's findings with more elite and educated readers (Ross 1999, 786). In summarizing the effects of what he terms FVR, or "free voluntary reading," Krashen, based on his review of the research, asserts,

> What the research tells me is that if children or less literate adults start reading for pleasure, . . . good things will happen. Their reading comprehension will improve, and they will find difficult, academic-style texts more comprehensible. Their writing style will improve, and they will be better able to write prose in a style that is acceptable to schools, business, and the scientific community. Their vocabulary will improve and will improve at a better rate than if they took one of the well-advertised vocabulary building courses. Also, their spelling and control of grammar will improve. (Krashen 1993, x)

Findings such as these constitute a powerful argument for community support of the public library—the quintessential local institution dedicated to providing reading materials to all qualified borrowers. When considering how best the public library might encourage such reading, the sage advice offered by Sir Henry A. Miers again comes to mind—RA is not school-like instruction but "provision of opportunity, encouragement and guidance" (Miers 1933, 335–36). With RA history and reading research thus combining to establish an educational premise for advising readers through the public library, it is appropriate to determine how the history of RA suggests that such advice should be provided.

"Returning to the Center": What the RA Past May Offer the RA Future

Robert S. Martin, director of the Institute of Museum and Library Services, in a 2001 presentation titled "Returning to the Center: Libraries, Knowledge, and Education," described the increasingly negative implications of being seen as an information agency at a time when people with "the Internet on their desktop" perceive that they have more convenient sources of information. For Martin, the problems were largely self-created. Libraries, particularly public libraries, long ago abandoned public advocacy of their educational activities and played down their recreational functions as they embraced a narrow information focus (Martin 2001, 1). Fortunate for the public library future, and of particular note for RA practitioners and supporters, is Martin's observation that "reader's advisory services have made a comeback in recent years and brought into sharp focus one way in which libraries continue to support the independent learner," thus advancing what is perhaps the oldest objective of the public library movement in the United States (Martin 2001, 1, 4).

The twentieth-century experience of RA, both the vibrant highpoints in the 1920–1940 period and gradual dwindling in the 1940–1984 era, suggests that contemporary RA does not match children's services as a program with unquestioned value in almost all public library environments. As something that can come and go, depending on finances and fashion, RA appears to be more like a public library's young adult activities. In consequence, RA practitioners and theorists need to avoid certain pitfalls and embrace specific opportunities.

For those seeking to draw both inspiration and advice from RA history, the introspective work of Jennie M. Flexner and Bryon C. Hopkins in *Readers' Advisers at Work* is a valuable resource in that it captures both the explicit and implicit history of the most storied readers' advisory activity in the 1920–1940 period—RA as delivered in NYPL's central building and participating branches. Flexner and Hopkins's research was based on the analysis of 1,250 survey responses from users of the service, review of records in the RA office, and interviews with branch library RA staff. The first point that can be drawn from their work is the appeal to readers of both fiction and nonfiction books when they are guided through a quality RA program. Sixty-plus years may have attenuated precise comparisons with present-day data, but the willingness of men and women to read both fiction and nonfiction is repeatedly encountered. The NYPL program was openly didactic in its orientation, but readers had the choice of areas for guidance in their self-education. It may come as a shock to present-day advocates of fiction-only RA to learn that female users advised by NYPL chose to be advised about reading in history and biography (15 percent) almost as much as they sought guidance for "literature" (15.6 percent), a category that consisted primarily of prose fiction (Flexner and Hopkins 1941, 41, 60). The predominant interest of males in nonfiction was also a finding that can resonate across time to the present day (Flexner and Hopkins 1941, 60).

The second lesson that can be drawn from the 1941 Flexner and Hopkins study, as well as other evidence of Flexner's views of RA, is distinctly cautionary. Simply stated, it is the reality that claiming a special status for RA as a program superior to other public library activities is self-defeating. Even Jennie Flexner herself could make this mistake. As reported by Viarda Clark Brubeck in the 1939 *Helping Adults to Learn: The Library in Action*, Flexner defined the readers' adviser as

A librarian in the broad sense of that inclusive term, released from the pressure of routine, freed from many of the necessarily hampering restrictions of the general schedule, and who has time and opportunity to devise, record, and to perfect through trial and experiment a service which is flexible, adaptable, and capable of broad expansion. (Brubeck 1939, 19)

This definition may reflect Flexner's apparently privileged status with the New York Public Library's RA operations. One wonders whether her assertions of a status free of normal library routines was well-received by other NYPL staff members whose extensive responsibilities included regular desk and other assignments that diminished their freedom of creatively experimenting with their own areas of service. It definitely failed to capture how RA was delivered part-time in those NYPL branches that voluntarily added the program to already stressed schedules. Resented RA services can be prime candidates for termination during a budget crisis or if and when a library director wants to launch a new program, looks for areas to consolidate to free up resources, and hesitates to touch reference or children's services, areas that can alternate as the dangerous "third rail" of proposed library cutbacks.

The third point, derived directly from the RA experience in NYPL's branches, is the reminder that senior administrators who have provided RA service even on a part-time basis may become lifelong RA advocates. Youth or reference librarians have been known to become directors with a continuing fondness for the programs in which they had their professional start. To achieve such a long-term effect for RA, it is imperative to minimize the temptation to operate the program with only library assistants or associates. Librarians with degrees from ALA-accredited programs remain the individuals most likely to become senior managers in all but the smallest libraries. If they have work experience in RA, they may bring positive memories of the service with them in their rise up the administrative ladder.

A fourth point from NYPL history is that RA often involves a combination of service on the fly and a lack of reader privacy at the point of service. Jennie Flexner had the luxury of making appointments with readers in a private office. In the contemporary world, short of exceptional circumstances, RA deskwork means work done at or around a public desk. The fifth point is that launching RA as a new service is going to require some level of dedicated staff and material resources. Simply adding it to existing duties, unless, for example, declines in reference questions free up the time of some reference librarians, is going to work against the popularity of the service among the staff chosen to deliver it. Point number six is the need to ensure that library resources meet user expectations. Promising effective RA service and not delivering it is far more negative than not mentioning RA at all. NYPL found that one RA staff member per branch was not enough to provide effective service and "only the branch readers' adviser who has delegated her duties to one or two specific staff members and given these persons individual training in interviewing has been able to establish effective service during the hours she is off duty" (Flexner and Hopkins 1941, 29). Point number seven is the value of networking with an ongoing continuing education component. It is one reason of the many reasons the Adult Reading Round Table has proven to be so successful in our own day.

Undoubtedly, there are quite a number of other lessons to be learned or unlearned from the NYPL experience and the larger context of a century and a quarter of documented RA history. Perhaps the most important of such message is the realization that contemporary RA practitioners and educators are not alone. Even the best among us have much to learn from our predecessors in the ongoing effort to adapt RA thinking, philosophy, and service to the constantly changing educational, informational, and recreational needs of current readers and generations of readers yet to come.

Notes

1. Sincere appreciation is expressed to Heather Cannon for her creative researching of the roots of contemporary RA.

2. Movement to include closely related nonfiction works in fiction discussions is evident, for example, in several chapters of Joyce Saricks's *The Readers' Advisory Guide to Genre Fiction* (Chicago, IL: American Library Association, 2001). Students in my Dominican University *LIS 763 Readers Advisory Services* classes are required to provide both fiction and nonfiction recommendations with their class booktalks when suggesting similar or related works to the book under discussion. Finally, the interest of some public library borrowers in "how to write (fantasy, mystery, romance, science fiction, etc.)" types of books, to find out how favorite authors achieve certain effects or even to explore the possibility of writing such books on their own, is regularly reported to me by former students now working at RA or reference desks. So, too, are accounts of the occasional readers seeking a history of Regency England or a biography of a famed man or woman, their curiosity stimulated by a well-received novel or an interest in determining, quixotically, whether a genre fiction writer got her or his "facts right."

3. In discussing the resistance of some readers' advisors to embracing history, biography, and other nonfiction stories, a noted RA leader once informed me that her own reluctance was due not to a deeply held philosophy, but to the dread of having to learn more genres.

References

American Library Association. 1926. *Libraries and adult education.* New York: McMillan (published for the American Library Association).

American Library Association. 1927. The librarian an educator. *Adult Education and the Library* 2: 31.

American Library Association. 1928. Administration and methods. *Adult Education and the Library* 3: 76–77.

American Library Association Archives Holdings Database. URL: http://web.library.uiuc.edu/ahx/ala/ccard/default.asp (Accessed March 27, 2003).

Balcom, Ted. 1988. Rediscovering readers' advisory—and its rewards. *Illinois Libraries* 70: 583–86.

Balcom, Ted. 2002. The Adult Reading Round Table: Chicken soup for readers' advisors. *Reference & User Services Quarterly* 41: 238–43.

Belzer, Alisa. 2002. "I don't crave to read": School reading and adulthood. *Journal of Adolescent & Adult Literacy* 46: 104–13.

Bostwick, Arthur E. 1975. The love of books as a basis for librarianship. In *American library philosophy: An anthology.* Selected and introduced by Barbara McCrimmon, 20–30. Hamden, CT: Shoe String Press. First published in *Library Journal* 32 (February 1907): 51–55.

Brubeck, Viarda Clark. 1939. A close view of advisory service: In a small library (Dunkirk, N.Y.). In *Helping adults to learn: The library in action.* Edited by John Chancellor, 3–9. Chicago: American Library Association.

Chancellor, John, ed. 1939. *Helping adults to learn: The library in action.* Chicago: American Library Association.

Chelton, Mary K. 1993. Read any good books lately? Helping patrons find what they want. *Library Journal* 118: 33–37.

Cole, George Watson. 1996. Fiction in libraries: A plea for the masses. *Library Journal* 121: 58. First published in 1894.

Dana, John Cotton. 1920. *A library primer.* 3d ed. Boston: Library Bureau.

E. A. 1798. On the good effects of bad novels. *Lady's Monthly Museum* (October): 258–63.

Evanston [Illinois] Public Library Board of Trustees. *Evanston Public Library strategic plan 2000-2010: A decade of outreach.* Approved October 18, 2000. URL: http://www.evanston.lib.il.us/library/strategic-plan-00.html (Accessed March 20, 2003).

Fihe, Pauline J. 1936. Have libraries lost leadership in adult education? *Library Journal* 61: 218–23.

Flexner, Jennie M., and Bryon C. Hopkins. 1941. *Readers' advisers at work: A survey of development in the New York Public Library.* New York: American Association for Adult Education.

Garrison, Dee. 1979. *Apostles of culture: The public librarian and American society, 1876–1920.* New York: Free Press.

Haines, Helen E. 1950. *Living with books: The art of book selection.* 2d ed. New York: Columbia University Press.

Hart, James D. 1950. *The popular book: A history of America's literary taste.* New York: Oxford University Press.

Henry, W. E. 1925. The A.L.A. and adult education. *Library Journal* 50: 211–12.

Jennings, Judson T. 1929. *Voluntary education through the public library.* Chicago: American Library Association.

Johnson, Paul. 1976. *A history of Christianity.* New York: Atheneum.

Karetzky, Stephen. 1982. *Reading research and librarianship: A history and analysis.* Westport, CT: Greenwood.

Krashen, Stephen. 1993. *The power of reading: Insights from the research.* Englewood, CO: Libraries Unlimited.

Lee, Robert Ellis. 1966. *Continuing education for adults through the American public library: 1833–1964.* Chicago: American Library Association.

Leigh, Robert D. 1950. *The public library in the United States.* New York: Columbia University Press.

Light, Richard J., Judith D. Singer, and John Willett. 1990. *By design: Planning research on higher education.* Cambridge, MA: Harvard University Press.

Luyt, Brendan. 2001. Regulating readers: The social origins of the readers' advisor in the United States. *Library Quarterly* 71: 443–66.

Martin, Lowell. 1955. Library service to adults. *Library Quarterly* 25: 10. Quoted in Lee, Robert Ellis. 1966. *Continuing education for adults through the American public library: 1833–1964.* Chicago: American Library Association, 83.

Martin, Robert S. 2001. Returning to the Center: Libraries, Knowledge, and Education. Paper presented to the Colorado Library Association, October 29, 2001. *IMLS: What's New: Current News.* URL: http://www.imls.gov/scripts/text/cgi?/whatsnew/current/sp102901.htm (Accessed April 2, 2003).

May, Anne K., Elizabeth Olesh, Anne Weinlich Miltenberg, and Catherine Patricia Lackner. 2002. A look at reader's advisory services. *Library Journal* 125: 40–43.

Miers, Sir Henry A. 1933. Adult education in relation to libraries. *Library Journal* 58: 333–341. Presidential address first published in the *Library Association Record* (September 1932): 265–82.

Molz, Redmond Kathleen, and Phyllis Dain. 1999. *Civic space/ cyberspace: The American public library in the information age.* Cambridge, MA: MIT Press.

Monroe, Margaret E. 1963. *Library adult education: The biography of an idea.* New York: Scarecrow Press.

Mowry, William A. 1891. The relation of the public library to education. *Library Journal* 16: 301–302.

Nell, Victor. 1988. *Lost in a book: The psychology of reading for pleasure.* New Haven, CT: Yale University Press.

Paxson, Frederic L. 1926. *Reading with a purpose: The United States in recent times.* Chicago: American Library Association.

Perkins, F. B. 1876. How to make town libraries successful. In *Public libraries in the United States of America: Their history, condition, and management*, 419–30. Washington, DC: Government Printing Office.

Phelps, William Lyon. 1927. *Reading with a purpose: Twentieth century American novels.* Chicago: American Library Association.

Poole, William F. 1993. Some popular objections to public libraries. *Library Journal* 118: 85–86. First published in 1876.

Reading courses. 1927. *Libraries* 32: 174–75.

Ross, Catherine Sheldrick. 1991. Readers' advisory service: New directions. *RQ* 30: 503–18.

Ross, Catherine Sheldrick. 1995. "If they read Nancy Drew, so what?" Series book readers talk back. *Library and Information Science Research* 17: 201–36.

Ross, Catherine Sheldrick. 1999. Finding without seeking: The information encounter in the context of reading for pleasure. *Information Processing and Management* 35: 783–99.

Saricks, Joyce. G. 2001. *The readers' advisory guide to genre fiction.* Chicago: American Library Association.

Saricks, Joyce G., and Nancy Brown. 1997. *Readers' advisory service in the public library*, 2d ed. Chicago: American Library Association.

Shearer, Kenneth. 1998. Readers' advisory services: New attention to a core business of the public library. *North Carolina Libraries* 56: 114–116.

Shera, Jesse H. 1976. *Introduction to library science: Basic elements of library service.* Littleton, CO: Libraries Unlimited.

Smith, Duncan, and Suzanne Mahmoodi. 2000. *Talking with readers: A workbook for readers' advisory.* Ipswich, MA: EBSCO.

St. Louis Public Library and EBSCO Publishing. 2000. *Readers' advisory 101: Instructor/participant guide.* Version 2.11. St. Louis, MO: St. Louis Public Library.

U.S. Interior Department. Bureau of Education. 1876. *Public libraries in the United States of America: Their history, condition, and management.* Special Report of the Department of Interior Bureau of Education. Washington, DC: Government Printing Office.

Warren, Althea. 1950. Foreword. In *Living with books: The art of book selection,* 2d ed. Edited by Helen E. Haines, vii–x. New York: Columbia University Press.

Warren, S. R., and S. N. Clark. 1876. Introduction. In *Public libraries in the United States of America: Their history, condition, and management,* xi–xxxv. Washington, DC: Government Printing Office.

Watson, Dana. 2000. Time to turn the page: Library education for readers' advisory services. *Reference & User Services Quarterly* 40: 143–46.

Wheatley, H. B. 1902. *How to form a library.* London: Elliot Stock.

Wilson, Louis Round. 1910. The public library as an educator. *Library Journal* 35: 6–10.

Chapter 2

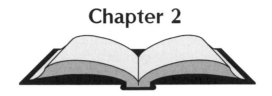

Beyond Boundaries

Kathleen de la Peña McCook

In this chapter, the overall rationale for nonfiction readers' advisory services is described by first looking at the characteristics of imaginative literature and nonfiction and the response of the reader to the text. Next, the place of library-based group support of nonfiction is characterized, followed by the expansion to nonfiction programs supported by partnerships. Finally, the nonfiction readers' advisory connection to cultural heritage institutions is established.

From Fact to Creative Nonfiction

There is some irony in discussing the rationale for nonfiction readers' advisory services from the stance that nonfiction has been overlooked. What a difference a century or so makes. At the outset of public library development in the United States, there was great controversy about the inclusion of novels in collections and much concern expressed that overindulgence in reading novels would provide readers with a false sense of reality. Arguing for the inclusion of popular reading in 1876, William Frederick Poole observed, "there is in the mental development of every person who latter attains literary culture a limited period when he craves novel-reading, and perhaps reads novels to excess; but from which, if the desire be gratified, he passes safely out into broader fields of study" (Poole 1876, 50).

Clearly, over the century since public library collection development discussions raged over the inclusion of fiction in public libraries, the proportion of imaginative literature—especially novels— has grown substantially in most public library collections. Services such as readers' advisory and book discussion groups that enhance the enjoyment of imaginative literature by the community are important aspects of most libraries' ongoing programming. Yet the thirteen "service responses" in *New Planning for Results* that public librarians use to guide overall program planning include many that primarily support the use of materials in the nonfiction portions of collections: business and career information, community referral, consumer information, general information, government information, local history, and genealogy (Nelson 2001, 145–220). In discussing nonfiction readers' advisory, it is important to distinguish fact-based services such as reference and genealogy from support for nonfiction of interest to the general reader.

The texts read by public library users may be organized into categories that at first seem to call to mind a map with two large hemispheres: imaginative literature and nonfiction. Each hemisphere contains many genre-nations. Imaginative literature genres include poetry, drama, and fiction. The fiction genre includes both what is deemed literature and then (most confusedly) genre fiction (mysteries, romances, spy novels). Nonfiction is, well, everything based on fact and organized—for libraries, at least—by classification systems where nonfiction subject headings mirror nonfiction genres: travel, science, history, geography, biography.

This Tordesillan demarcation is replete with forays across its boundaries because much nonfiction is written with great creativity. New journals such as *Fourth Genre* and *Creative Nonfiction* have expanded understanding of the possibilities of nonfiction writing. Douglas Hesse, writing of the role of creative nonfiction, has pointed out the English teacher's perplexity at the categorization of nonfiction in libraries noting, "the confusion of course, is the classic clash between form (generally the PRs and PSs [English literature and American literature, respectively]) and content (everything else)" (Hesse 2003, 238).

Once we have this "map" in mind—a map replicated in the organization of libraries and bookstores—it would seem a straightforward matter to provide advisory guidance to readers seeking support in selecting what to read in the respective hemispheres of imaginative literature and nonfiction. Yet no sooner is this map laid out than the genre skirmishes begin. Nonfiction represents a range of texts—from straightforward reporting of facts to what has been characterized as "nonfiction literature." The struggle to characterize nonfiction is made clear in Wintercrowd's 1990 monograph, *The Rhetoric of the "Other" Literature*, in which he notes:

> The greatest problem perhaps, is finding a term that covers the texts I deal with in this book [by Tom Wolfe, Hunter Thompson, Stephen Jay Gould, Truman Capote, Edward Abbey]. "The literature of facts"? But factuality is not really a central issue. "Non-imaginative literature"? Hardly, since one of my purposes is to argue that the texts I discuss are just as imaginative as the poems, stories, novels, and plays that are generally considered to constitute "imaginative" literature. (ix)

The demarcation between literature and nonfiction is breached, transcended, knocked down, and melted by the authors and their readers in a manner showing little respect or concern for good order. The readers' advisor soon realizes that classification of nonfiction often misconstrues a book's broad intent. In fact, strict adherence to classification schemes as a substitute for other advisory techniques and tools will likely mean a level of service that is less than optimal.

For example, take two recent nonfiction books intended for the general reader, *Krakatoa: The Day the World Exploded, August 27, 1883* (Winchester 2003) and *River of Shadows: Eadweard Muybridge and the Technological Wild West* (Solnit 2003). *Krakatoa* ends up classified as QE 523 (Volcanoes and Earthquakes) with subject headings, "Volcanoes-Indonesia-History" and "Krakatoa-Indonesia-History," but the book also contains much on evolution, the Wallace Line, plate tectonics, transatlantic communication, and Dutch colonialism. *River of Shadows* is classified as TR 849 (Cinematography and Motion Pictures) with subject headings, "Muybridge, Eadweard, 1830–1904," "Cinematographers-United States-Biography," "Photographer-United States-Biography," and "Chronophotography-History," but it is as much about these topics as the transformation of time and space in the post–Civil War United States.

So these two books provide concrete examples of the way that nonfiction writers transcend the strictures of both classification and subject headings and the challenge to the readers' advisor to traverse these artificial boundaries. Abbott has commented on the fact that "sometimes the shock of leaping borders and suddenly seeing your old familiar terms from a new disciplinary perspective can be salutary precisely because the differences of the fields are so great" (Abbott 2000, 260). He characterizes "narrative" as the telling of events and he characterizes "literature" as noninstrumental and disconnected from immediate use.

Although both *Krakatoa* and *Rivers of Shadows* are narratives, albeit far from linear, they both include many long sections in which the reader can ponder the transcendent nature of the impact of the physical world and technological development on humanity's progress. Ryan (1997) sees destabilization of the borderline between fiction and nonfiction as an enticing target for the postmodern mind. Although in the end she stands for the continuation of a nonfiction/fiction distinction, she posits a third category and suggests that there are texts that are true (nonfiction), texts that are mixed by presenting fiction as truth (classical fiction), and texts that are not true and invite participation (postmodern metafiction).

I would suggest a fourth category: transnonfiction—like *Krakatoa* and *Rivers of Shadow*—that exists in the same realm as metafiction. That is, such transnonfiction overlays fact with metaphysical and epistemological questions in such a way that the reader's response to the work is far different from absorption of new facts. In reading transnonfiction of this type, readers respond with the same varied interpretations of the discursive sort that characterize the culturally pluralistic reaction of readers to a relativist reaction to literary texts (Richardson 1997). Transnonfiction provides a synoptic view of various aspects of the world that engages the reader in much the same way as metafiction.

Thus nonfiction can mirror fiction in terms of the responses that are elicited from readers. That is, readers bring their own knowledge and understanding to the nonfiction they read in much the same way they do to fiction and these responses to the same text can be very different at different stages of the same reader's life. This comes to the fore when reading the nonfiction novels of authors like Truman Capote, Norman Mailer, Joan Didion, and Tom Wolfe. Writing of the nonfiction novels of these authors Anderson (1987, 180) has observed:

The story of contemporary American prose . . . is not about the rupturing or the collapsing of the envelope of language, the death of the membrane. It is about the expansion of the membrane to accommodate new realms of experience. It is about the growth of the organism of language.

The story is also about the growth of the reader of nonfiction. And it is this growth that provides the readers' advisor working with nonfiction with the raw material to develop techniques and tools to assist readers. Nonfiction, like fiction, has a broad range of manifestations in terms of its complexity and the demands made on the reader. Identifying reader–nonfiction matches requires an assessment of the reader's level of knowledge and capacity for ambiguity. A transaction takes place between the reader and

writer of nonfiction based on the knowledge that the subject of the nonfiction text can be understood outside of the text (Heyne 2001; Lehman 1997).
It is within this transaction that the readers' advisor can amplify the experience of nonfiction service by moving beyond taxonomies of genre.

Readers' Advisory Experts on Nonfiction and Public Libraries

To what degree are readers' advisors working today with nonfiction
readers, and what are the bases of their common understanding about the
role of nonfiction in public libraries? These are the focus of this volume,
but to gain some understanding to frame the issues, I was fortunate to have
had the opportunity to discuss the topic with a number of experts including
members of the Adult Reading Round Table of Illinois prior to developing
this essay.[1] An informal focus group discussion held at the Chicago Public
Library in May 2003 brought together more than forty librarians to discuss
the role of nonfiction readers' advisory services (McCook 2003b). The
focus was on library-based discussion groups.

The amount of nonfiction programming provided by in these Chicago-
area public librarians ranged from 25 percent to 70 percent. Although no
cross-tabulation by topic was conducted, the general discussion implied
that a reasonable proportion of this support was for very specific topics
such as

- Gardening

- Computer Training

- Genealogy

- Finances

- Travel

Library support for these kinds of topics would fall into the *New Planning for Results* service response categories as "formal learning support,"
"consumer information," or "business and career information." To gain a
complete understanding of the actual amount of programming divided between fact-based nonfiction and literary nonfiction would require a more
structured approach to the topic than the informal discussion group. However, the readers' advisory experts agreed that even programs that were
generally fact-based tended to generate additional interest that provided
adult services librarians with many opportunities to develop backstory.

The public library service responses that would best fit readers' advisory support for literary or creative nonfiction would be "cultural awareness" and "lifelong learning," and it is here that the focused discussion elicited productive background for the topic at hand. The expert readers' advisors had the following observations.

- Many of the "Great Books" are nonfiction. Great Books discussion clubs continue to be a popular offering at many public libraries. Programs are provided in series or by topics, and although most include fiction as well as nonfiction, nonfiction is a central focus. For instance, the topical program "And Justice for All," developed in connection with the fiftieth anniversary of the Universal Declaration of Human Rights includes Hannah Arendt's "The Perplexities of the Rights of Man," John Locke's "Of Civil Government," and Richard Rorty's "Human Rights, Rationality, and Sentimentality." These are all nonfiction selections and have enduring interest to readers.

- Many readers ask for nonfiction discussion groups that provide the same "sense of transport" as nonfiction. Books noted by these readers' advisors as providing the jumping off point for transportive discussion included Stille's *Future of the Past;* Branch's *Pillar of Fire: America in the King Years, 1963–1965;* Ehrenreich's *Blood Rites: Origins and History of the Passions of War;* and McBride's *The Color of Water: A Black Man's Tribute to His White Mother.*

- Biography, especially thoughtful biography that provided social context, was identified as particularly fruitful for nonfiction discussion. A few recent volumes noted included Stiles's *Jesse James: Last Rebel of the Civil War;* Schiff's *Vera (Mrs. Vladimir Nabokov);* Hillenbrand's *Seabiscuit: An American Legend;* and Gordon's life of Muddy Waters, *Can't Be Satisfied.*

- Books with themes of social concern continue to catalyze discussion and reader interest. A few noted were Hallinan's *Going Up the River: Travels in a Prison Nation;* Martinez's *Crossing Over: A Mexican Family on the Migrant Trail;* Campbell's *Blood Diamonds;* and Caldicott's *The New Nuclear Danger: George Bush's Military Industrial Complex.*

- Science was also a popular topic for nonfiction readers' advisory, and a number of recent books were noted as providing excellent opportunities for combining science with broader societal themes such as Wilson's *The Future of Life;* Ridley's *Genome: The Autobiography of a Species in 23 Chapters;* Kluger's *Journey beyond Selene: Remarkable Expedition Past Our Moon and to the Ends of the Solar System;* and Clapp's *The Road to Ubar: Finding the Atlantis of the Sands.*

The readers' advisors were in agreement that nonfiction discussion groups were more likely to attract a diverse male-female mix than fiction-only discussion groups. Additionally, nonfiction seemed to generate more requests for bibliographic support in the form of books that extended the ideas confronted in discussion groups. Subjects for nonfiction most in demand included books that reflect the daily life of the readers, science, travel, and biography. Although these are parallel to the fact-based topics mentioned at the outset of this section, the books identified by the readers' advisors led to extended interactions that were often more discursive that fact-based programming. The exception to this was local history that is fact-based but often provided the foundation for extended programs on matters of local culture and development.

It is not really a surprise that nonfiction has a growing appeal. The popularity of themed cable television such as the Food Channel, the Discovery Channel, the History Channel, and even the Weather Channel, is a strong indicator that large audiences exist for in-depth exploration of topics based on fact. Tie-in of books and book discussion programs to television series continues to be a strong mechanism for developing readers.

Adult Programming and the Public Library As Commons

Programs with a focus on lifelong learning are an important public library service. The 2002 U.S. Department of Education-National Center for Education Statistics study, *Programs for Adults in Public Library Outlets,* used the "Fast Response Survey System" to collect data on programs for adults based on a sample of 1,011 public libraries from fifty states and the District of Columbia. The sampling frame consisted of 16,918 public library outlets of which 8,954 were central or main library outlets and 7,120 were branch outlets. Based on this sample, 43 percent of all public libraries held book or film discussion groups; 41 percent held cultural performances; and 39 percent held recreational programs. Table 2.1 shows the distribution of adult programming type by library size.

Although these data do not give us a detailed picture of programming that is fiction versus nonfiction based, they do provide current verification that adult programs are a major service component in public libraries. Adult programs provide a strong basis for the development of nonfiction readers' advisory services. This strength often derives from the development of innovative partnerships that emphasize the library as a commons—the need for people to meet and interact with each other (McCook 2003c).

Table 1. *Adult Programming Type by Library Size*

1.	Book/Film Discussion Groups		43%
	• Urban	56%	
	• Suburban	50%	
	• Rural	34%	
2.	Cultural Performances		41%
	• Urban	60%	
	• Suburban	51%	
	• Rural	28%	
3.	Recreational (hobbies, travel)		39%
	• Urban	52%	
	• Suburban	50%	
	• Rural	29%	

An example of the kind of discussion-based programming that leads to demand for nonfiction readers' advisory service is the Research Revolution series. Research Revolution was a collaboration of the American Library Association and National Video Resources[2] sponsored by the National Science Foundation and presented in fifty libraries in 2003. The series was aimed at increasing public understanding of scientific discovery and technological transformations in the twentieth century (McCook 2003a). For each of the programs in the Research Revolution series (genetic engineering, military technology, robotics, DNA screening), librarians developed reading lists and provided books and personal advice for further investigation of the issues. The goal of the series was to enable people to deal more effectively with the new choices that rapid scientific change creates including ethical issues.

"The Sixties," a program funded by the National Endowment for the Humanities in collaboration with the American Library Association and National Video Resources, provided twenty-five libraries with documentaries and reading lists for a series of community programs on the social history of the United States. "The Sixties" explored the civil rights movement, the Vietnam War, the counterculture, and the sociopolitical environment of that decade. Displays and supplemental resources were projects for nonfiction readers' advisory.

Exhibits can also function as catalysts for nonfiction readers' advisory. The Smithsonian Institution's National Museum of National History, the U.S. Department of Agriculture, and the W. K. Kellogg Foundation teamed with the American Library Association to create a traveling exhibition, "Listening to the Prairie: Farming in Nature's Image," that examined the role of the central farming regions in the United States and the ecological, economic, and social costs of production.[3]

Another traveling program, "The Great Experiment: George Washington and the American Republic," based on a major exhibition of manuscripts, rare books, prints, engravings and artifacts from the Huntington and Pierpont Morgan Libraries and the Gilder Lehrman Institute of American History, traveled to forty libraries between September 2000 and October 2003 with funding from the National Endowment for the Humanities.

Reading and viewing discussion series have become a successful manifestation of the commons function of the public library. Buttressed by a rigorous review process from government agencies such as the National Science Foundation, National Endowment for the Humanities, and the Smithsonian, these programs help to fulfill the lifelong learning response of the public library. They provide the nonfiction readers' advisor with the foundation from which to create new programs and advise readers. The nonfiction readers' advisor can revitalize programming by connecting, for example, Chaffin's new book on John Charles Fremont, *Pathfinder,* and the digitized Library of Congress map, "The Road West." Such connections are the kind of innovation that the nonfiction readers' advisor can make with individual readers or discussion groups, and they lead quite naturally to far broader nonfiction programming.

Cultural Heritage and Nonfiction Readers' Advisory

Nonfiction readers' advisors can also act as the essential link between libraries and other institutions. The examples of discussion programs based on nonfiction also lend themselves to connections with other cultural heritage institutions. As public libraries expand the opportunities to support the reader of creative nonfiction the connections with other cultural heritage institutions becomes more immediate. Not only are taxonomies of subject less rigid, but also the library's articulation with local history societies, museums, botanical gardens, aquariums and other entities provides numerous chances to make connections of mutual interest.

The Institute of Museums and Library Services supports museums, libraries, archives, zoos, and historical societies and encourages partnerships to foster innovation and lifelong learning. This results in what Carr has characterized as "working laboratories for cognitive change, where voices can be heard expressing hopes and aspirations in the context of the possible" (Carr 2000, 117).

Who will write the library and museum partnership grants that extend these ideas? The most likely candidates are those readers' advisors who have worked with nonfiction readers and programs and developed an understanding of the availability of resources outside the libraries' walls. What kinds of projects? The Tucson-Pima Public Library has teamed with the Tucson Botanical Gardens to develop resources and support appreciation of the desert landscape; the Richmond Public Library and the Richmond Museum of History have collaborated on the "Home Front Digital Project," which reflects local history during World War II. Projects like these that enable libraries to develop connections with other cultural heritage institutions in the community will largely be the result of the work of readers' advisors who work with nonfiction.

Nonfiction readers' advisors will be ideally suited to work with the twenty-first-century learner and to develop cultural heritage collaborations that incorporate the integration of digital technologies in program development (McCook and Jones 2002). By working with nonfiction readers individually, in groups, in collaborative programs, and on interinstitutional initiatives, the nonfiction readers' advisor will be the essential link expanding public connections.

Notes

1. The Adult Reading Round Table (ARRT) of Illinois was founded in 1984 to promote readers' advisory service and fiction collections in public and school libraries. With more than two hundred librarian members in the greater Chicago area, ARRT offers workshops and lectures, a quarterly newsletter, and an annual fiction bibliography on a particular theme. *ARRT Reads: Adult Reading Round Table Homepage.* URL: http://www.arrtreads.org/ (Accessed July 9, 2003).

2. National Video Resources (NVR) is a not-for-profit organization that assists in increasing the public's awareness of and access to independently produced media, film, and video. NVR projects and partnerships enrich library programming and contribute to the lifelong learning and the commons roles of libraries. See the NVR Web site for additional background on "Research Revolution" and "The Sixties." *National Video Resources.* URL: http://www.nvr.org/ (Accessed July 13, 2003).

3. The American Library Association. Public Programs Office (ALA PPO) fosters cultural programming in libraries. See the ALA PPO site for background on "Listening to the Prairie: Farming in Nature's Image" and "The Great Experiment: George Washington and the American Republic." *ALA | Public Programs Office.* URL: http://www.ala.org/Content/NavigationMenu/

Our_Association/Offices/Public_Programs_Office/Public_
Programs_ Office.htm (Accessed July 13, 2003).

References

Abbott, H. Porter. 2000. What do we mean when we say, "narrative literature?" Looking for answers across disciplinary borders. *Style* 34: 260.

ALA | Public Programs Office. URL: http://www.ala.org/Content/
NavigationMenu/Our_Association/Offices/Public_Programs_Office/
Public_Programs_Office.htm (Accessed July 13, 2003).

Anderson, Chris. 1987. *Style as argument: Contemporary American nonfiction.* Carbondale: Southern Illinois University Press.

ARRT Reads: Adult Reading Round Table Homepage. URL: http://www.
arrtreads.org/ (Accessed July 9, 2003)

Carr, David. 2000. In the context of the possible: Libraries and museums as
incendiary cultural institutions. *RBM: A Journal of Rare Books,
Manuscripts and Cultural Heritage* 1: 117–35.

The Great Books Foundation. URL: http://www.greatbooks.org/home.
shtml (Accessed July 12, 2003).

Hesse, Douglas. 2003. The place of creative nonfiction. *College English*
65: 237–41.

Heyne, Eric. 2001. Where fiction meets nonfiction: Mapping a rough terrain. *Narrative* 9: 322–33, 343–45.

Institute of Museum and Library Services. URL: http://www.imls.gov/
(Accessed July 13, 2003).

Lehman, Daniel. 1997. *Matters of fact: Reading nonfiction over the edge.*
Columbus: Ohio State University Press.

McCook, Kathleen de la Peña. 2003a. Evaluation of library-based viewing
and discussion for the "Research revolution: Mid-program report."
New York: National Video Resources.

McCook, Kathleen de la Peña. 2003b. Nonfiction in readers' advisory service: Notes from a discussion with expert readers' advisors. Chicago
Public Library, Scholar in Residence Program. May 22, 2003. Unpublished report.

McCook, Kathleen de la Peña. 2003c. Suppressing the commons: Miscon-
strued patriotism vs. a psychology of liberation. *Reference and User
Services Quarterly* 43: 14–17.

McCook, Kathleen de la Peña, and Maria A. Jones. 2002. Cultural heritage institutions and community building. *Reference and User Services Quarterly* 41: 326–29.

National Endowment for the Humanities. URL: http://www.neh.fed.us/ (Accessed July 13, 2003).

National Video Resources. URL: http://www.nvr.org/ (Accessed July 13, 2003).

Nelson, Sandra. 2001. *New planning for results: A streamlined approach.* Chicago: American Library Association.

Poole, William F. 1876. Some popular objections to public libraries. *Library Journal* 1: 45–51.

Richardson, Brian. 1997. The other reader's response: On multiple, divided and oppositional audiences. *Criticism* 39: 31–53.

Richmond Public Library, Richmond Museum of History, and JFK University Awarded Prestigious IMLS Grant. URL: http://www.ci.richmond. ca.us/~library/IMLS.htm (Accessed July 14, 2003).

Ryan, Marie-Laure. 1997. Postmodernism and the doctrine of panfictionality. *Narrative* 5: 165–87.

Smithsonian Institution. URL: http://www.si.edu/ (Accessed July 13, 2003).

Society for the Study of Narrative Literature. URL: http://www.vanderbilt. edu/AnS/english/clayton/narrative/ (Accessed July 14, 2003).

Tucson Botanical Gardens. URL: http://www.tucsonbotanical.org/html/ desert_connections.html (Accessed July 14, 2003).

U.S. Department of Education. National Center for Education Statistics. 2002. *Programs for adults in public library outlets.* NCES 2003-010. Washington, DC: Government Printing Office.

Winterowd, W. Ross. 1990. *The rhetoric of the "other" literature.* Carbondale: Southern Illinois University Press.

Nonfiction Titles Mentioned

Branch, Taylor. 1998. *Pillar of fire: America in the King years, 1963–1965.* New York: Simon & Schuster.

Caldicott, Helen. 2002. *The new nuclear danger: George Bush's military industrial complex.* New York: New Press.

Campbell, Greg. 2002. *Blood diamonds: Tracing the deadly path of the world's most precious stones.* Boulder, CO: Westview Press.

Chaffin, Tom. 2002. *Pathfinder: John Charles Fremont and the course of American empire.* New York: Hill and Wang.

Clapp, Nicholas. 1998. *The road to Ubar: Finding the Atlantis of the sands.* New York: Houghton Mifflin.

Ehrenreich, Barbara. 1997. *Blood rites: Origins and history of the passions of war.* New York: Metropolitan/Henry Holt.

Gordon, Robert. 2002. *Can't be satisfied: The life and times of Muddy Waters.* New York: Little, Brown.

Hallinan, Joseph. 2001. *Going up the river: Travels in a prison nation.* New York: Random House.

Hillenbrand, Laura. 2001. *Seabiscuit: An American legend.* New York: Random House.

Kluger, Jeffrey. 1999. *Journey beyond Selene: Remarkable expedition past our moon and to the ends of the solar system.* New York: Simon & Schuster.

McBride, James. 1996. *The color of water: A black man's tribute to his white mother.* New York: Riverhead Books.

Martinez, Ruben. 2001. *Crossing over: A Mexican family on the migrant trail.* New York: Henry Holt.

Ridley, Matt. 2000. *Genome: The autobiography of a species in 23 chapters.* New York: HarperCollins.

Schiff, Stacy. 2000. *Vera (Mrs. Vladimir Nabokov).* New York: Random.

Solnit, Rebecca. 2003. *River of shadows: Eadweard Muybridge and the technological wild west.* New York: Viking.

Stiles, T. J. 2002. *Jesse James: Last rebel of the Civil War.* New York: Knopf.

Stille, Alexander. 2002. *Future of the past.* New York: Farrar, Strauss & Giroux.

Wilson, Edward O. 2002. *The future of life.* New York: Knopf.

Winchester, Simon. 2003. *Krakatoa: The day the world exploded, August 27, 1883.* New York: HarperCollins.

Part II

Nonfiction Materials

This second section of this book discusses readers' advisory for nonfiction from the point of view of the materials themselves. Are there nonfiction genres, and if so, what are they? Are there appeal factors for nonfiction materials, and if so, what are they? Do the same issues apply to nonfiction or informational audiovisual materials?

David Carr examines the lure of nonfiction (what he calls "crafted truth") in Chapter 3 and finds that nonfiction addresses a rich variety of readers' needs—their "curiosities and unfinished questions"—and helps them better understand their world and their roles in it. Nonfiction readers become learners through a firsthand knowledge of real situations enriched by the author's added context and background. Carr looks at a number of examples of both traditional nonfiction categories (biography, memoir, and history, for instance) as well as what he calls "deep dimensions," something more like the appeal factors that we often use in discussing fiction. As Carr points out, good nonfiction helps the reader make sense of his or her own situation and is therefore as diverse as the lives of the readers who approach it.

In Chapter 4, Ken Shearer uses the metaphor of a planet to describe the complex differences between fiction and nonfiction and the notion of appeal factors for nonfiction. Shearer's planet Bookscape ranges from a north pole, representing purely imaginary works, to a south pole, representing works of verifiable fact. The landscape between the two poles varies in its mix of imagination and verifiability and thereby reflects the rich diversity of texts with which readers' advisors deal, a richness that is not adequately captured in the simple distinction between fiction and nonfiction. Shearer then discusses how texts appeal to readers and distinguishes between appeal of style (pacing, use of language, humor, and the like) and appeal of substance (character, story line, setting, and so forth). Shearer's many examples show the rich variety of ways in which authors appeal to readers, all of which readers' advisors can exploit as they serve their users.

Finally, Michael Vollmar-Grone extends the discussion of nonfiction advisory to informational audiovisual materials in Chapter 5. Vollmar-Grone reminds us that the issue is not the format but the effectiveness of the format and that, for some users, nonprint will be the preferred format. He argues that librarians often overlook audiovisual materials because of their unfamiliarity with those formats, the lack of reference sources for these materials, and the difficulty of providing information in some formats. Vollmar-Grone then outlines guidelines for advising listeners and viewers and provides a list of resources to help advisors find materials in all formats.

Just as Part I of this book suggests ways in which the profession's scope can be broadened by recapturing traditional educational roles and expanding into cultural partnerships, Part II represents the possibilities inherent in expanding readers' advisory services to include nonfiction materials. Nonfiction—both print and audiovisual—allows us to use a broader range of materials to meet the diverse needs of our users. Just as Part I looks to the history of readers' advisory services to help us improve our future work, Part II suggests that our understanding of fiction genres and appeal factors can inform our understanding of nonfiction materials.

Chapter 3

Many Kinds of Crafted Truths: An Introduction to Nonfiction

David Carr

At the Taxidermist's Convention

As I began this chapter, *The New Yorker* arrived in the mailbox, including an essay by Susan Orlean about the 2003 World Taxidermy Championships (Orlean 2003). The chapter waited as I paused to read. Having grown up next door to Miss Marian Tenney, a skilled taxidermist, I have memories of many "lifelike" but very, very still decapitees and other creatures inhabiting her dark little house. Ms. Orlean brings Miss Tenney and her remarkable menagerie of orphaned fawns and roadkill bunnies back to me. "There were foxes and moose and freeze-dried wild turkeys; mallards and buffalo and chipmunks and wolves; weasels and buffleheads and bobcats and jackdaws; big fish and little fish and razor-backed boar" (Orlean 2003, 46).

What drew me to this essay? What demanded an irresistible immersion in a world of "millions of eyes, boxes and bowls of them; some as small as a lentil and some as big as a poached egg" (Orlean 2003, 46)? The topic of taxidermy touches the questioning memory of that awed small boy lost in my ten-times-older self. As a museum user (and as an associate professor) I am often in a world of stuffed things; so there is continuity between taxidermy and the rest of my life. And, though I will never shoot the dreadful squirrel at the birdfeeder, there is an undeniable nosiness and curiosity that makes me want to read about "animal mannequins, blank-faced and brooding, earless and eyeless and utterly bald: ghostly gray duikers and spectral pine martens and black bellied tree ducks from some other world" (Orlean 2003, 46). I want, immediately and without the least thought about my chapter deadline, to see inside the taxidermist's head, so to speak.

My topic here is the lure of nonfiction, the only literary or art form named for what it isn't. Nonfiction isn't fiction; it is "true" and it is "real." It isn't "made up." And when the fit is right between our self the reader and itself the text, nonfiction addresses our memories, our curiosities and unfinished questions, and our hopes to learn about something remarkable and real, something transforming and true, something lost and something discovered.

Reading *Home Town* Together

Over time, attempting to teach librarians to build collections has come to mean helping them understand the nature and structure of a place where thought and inquiry happen. I want my learners to understand the community as a gathering of others, human beings in various roles and lives, carrying evocative issues and crises, and managing the common array of problems to be addressed as the place grows, changes, and breathes. As my classroom's common reading experience about community, I ask my students to read Tracy Kidder's book about Northampton, Massachusetts, *Home Town* (Kidder, 1999). It is not a book about communities, but a book about *a* community, as perceived through the eyes and memories of a police officer whose senses of town and people are acute, extending beyond the domed cruiser into the array of selves, laws, and troubles he is given to observe.

Police eyes are not librarian eyes, but the nonfiction view is instructive among my students. It is a personalized view of a particular community in a specific time and place. The view is local; the issues are cultural and even national; the themes are universal. A police eye takes in the dysfunctional world, and implies its functional counterpart. By its individual perspective and specificity, this view offers a hypothetical ideal of order and function amid the everyday. Kidder's narrative evokes broad inferences about *the life of a person in the community*. Encounter by encounter, human beings present themselves and their experiences of place. Perhaps more important, *Home Town* is an evocation of the multiple hometowns, varied as possible, reflected among my students' lives. One home town becomes all home towns. Consequently, our work is grounded in memory and experience, and from that we begin to generate a professional world.

Reading this nonfiction, we see the systems, structures, roles and lives of one place become transferable surrogates for many others, including the community-like patterns, values, and understandings in corporate and academic settings, where some of my students will work. We learn about the common dimensions of a community stage because Kidder places us there, implicating us in the action. He identifies and reveals the actors in their places, and he helps us to meet their gaze. Kidder leads us through that gaze to an inductive understanding of the qualities and spirits of humans drawn together, and the collection of small joys, great sorrows, and ordinary mercies that promote the common themes of many lives.

This happens because nonfiction is grounded on evidence, not guile. We hear the thoughts of the writer in an authentic voice, not spoken through a mask. He furnishes and dresses the stage we see. As readers we come to grasp the effects of the narrative and the narrator; we occupy this text like renters above a Main Street store. From this vantage we hear the traffic, the stories of individual actors, and we see them move toward their authentic fates and destinies. Kidder is informed by grounded knowledge of what the hometown experience is, as it happens there. And we, through our experiences of hometowns, through our wonderings about the communities we have abandoned and occupied over time, and through our hopes to be of use in such towns as this, become informed as well.

We are able to draw lessons from *Home Town* because it is not *Our Town;* neither is it *Main Street*, nor *Winesburg, Ohio,* nor *Empire Falls*. The substance of nonfiction is *grounded*, given a foundation and a structure, by three abundant quantities, each of which allows us to experience as readers what we might call "grounded possibilities."

- The writer presents a world of firsthand knowledge, purposefully chosen and arranged to communicate in resonant ways between the narrator's experience and our motives for reading. We are offered confirmations of memories, explorations of situations we cannot enter, and connections to times and places that (given physical constraints) we cannot experience directly.

- The actions of the work include recognizable behaviors in real, knowable circumstances, in articulated settings and environments, amid authentic situations or challenges. We may come to understand the deep ambiguities and questions present in such circumstances, but given the trust evoked by the writing, we are also able to make observations and draw insights from them.

- The nonfiction work presents more than immediate information and environment; it communicates the more complex data comprising contexts and backgrounds. We are embedded in details and perspectives by documentation from various sources and situations, often the voices of informed others whose angles of view cause them to become surrogates or models for the reader.

Nonfiction offers empirical knowledge—grounded, gathered, and synthesized from evidence, firsthand experiences, and observations. The narrative is rendered through timely revelations of evidence. We see the writer's processes of thought and connection, and understand how logical insights may be drawn, and we are also given imaginative projections that allow us to suppose and speculate, and to go, as all learners must, beyond the information given.[1] Nonfiction can be seen as a narrative of crafted truths, telling many specific kinds of lived experiences in the world.

What Nonfiction Is

Nonfiction is empirically based writing, its themes and foci grounded in an individual author's lived experiences. These may be physical, intellectual, or emotional. But not all nonfiction fits our topic. For example, textbooks, reference works, self-help, and other how-to and hobby books; cookery and diet books; guides to parenting, keeping fit, rock-climbing or diseases; advice for business success or college admissions; and works prepared for "dummies" and "idiots" are likely to be nonfiction, but I do not consider them here. These are essentially detailed problem-solving guides. Also not included here are humorous, temporal, and faddish works or largely pictorial coffee-table collections. Overtly religious and spiritual works, partisan advice and punditry, and shallow accounts of celebrity do not appear here. However valuable and popular these book categories may be, they are excluded. The core of nonfiction as considered in this chapter is serious prose of a conscientious kind, honest works of coherent narrative, primarily characterized by integrity and authenticity. Nonfiction is crafted to communicate accurate images to the reader, so that the reader might in turn craft more complex understandings of lived experiences.

The reader experiences the honest work in several ways. Regardless of its subject matter, the nonfiction experience as it is told is typically subjective and transformative, allowing the writer to present the evolution of particular knowledge, using documentation, insider accounts, and human informants that help to create a more invited, informed, and engaged experience of reading. Over the course of the narrative, the writer learns and tells something. Given a firsthand perspective on this learning, the reader believes that, when seen through this writer's eyes and words, *the experience is credible, and it is of great interest to me.* A nonfiction imagination, different from the imagination-engaged-by-fiction, is evoked.

The imagination-engaged-by-nonfiction is required to fabricate less as the reading occurs, but must imagine and hold information and its contexts clearly in mind. The nonfiction reader must combine more forms of data than the imagination of fiction demands. In nonfiction, the logics of events and reactions may be critically important; they cannot be swept away by fictional plotting. The novelist need not always conform to a timeline, geography, or fabric of credible evidence. The nonfiction author's intention to engage and inform is overt and planned; a coherent nonfiction narrative must often present basic data and relationships to create an informed reader. The author is present as an actor and observer, embodying engagement and inviting curiosity in the reader's name. The experiences of one central life—a key informant, a representative of place and time, like the Northampton policeman—are often focal points for organizing a larger story.

Nonfiction differs from fiction in its presentation of documented experience as a written record, without fabrication. Experiences are not implicit in the private motives and dialogues of imagined characters but described in the lived lives of informants. Nonfiction does not offer the interior monologues or private perspectives of characters; the author's stance is likely to be reportorial, documenting events and assembling an entire view of the phenomenon. Nonfiction is analogous to documentary film: it is motivated by inquiry, by the need to discover and capture experiences through subjective eyes and direct relationships between the writer and the evidence. The reader's task is to follow the experiential line as it is spun.

Nonfiction Variations

A sorting of more than three hundred notable 2002–2003 titles identified simply as "nonfiction" by the *New York Times Book Review, Publishers Weekly,*[2] and other sources, shows an unsurprising cluster of conventional nonfiction types. Works of biography (18 percent), history (18 percent), and memoir (15 percent) compose 51 percent of the titles listed, by far the largest chunk of nonfiction subject matter. Works about contemporary issues (including a number of works about the events of September 11, 2001) compose 10 percent of the titles; added to works about travel (7 percent), politics, and government (6 percent), science (6 percent), and essays/reflections (6 percent), these categories compose an additional 35 percent of nonfiction titles. The remaining categories, sport (3 percent), food (actually better characterized as food memoir; 2 percent), military history (2 percent), crime (2 percent), and faith (1 percent) each compose small but not insignificant parts of the whole. These figures should not be confounded with the whole output of publishers nationally in these topics; these are "notable" books only, as identified by editors in selective venues, with anticipations of lasting value.

The broad categories are deceptive; they communicate little or nothing about the nature of their constituents. A closer look reveals the diversity of subjects appearing under the broad rubric of nonfiction in 2002–2003.

Biography

Biographies appearing during this time addressed an array of great and obvious lives, including Beethoven and Chopin; Napoleon, Khrushchev, Mussolini, and Churchill; the Adamses, Franklin, Madison, the first Roosevelt, Ike, and the second Presidents Johnson and Bush; W. C. Fields, Laurel and Hardy, and Valentino; Samuel Pepys, Lord Byron, Hart Crane, Sinclair Lewis, H. L. Mencken, Ted Hughes, and L. Frank Baum; Isadora Duncan, Christopher Wren; John Paul Jones, Jesse James, and John Maynard Keynes; and so on. These might be characterized as case studies of genius. They are heavy-duty books about the major actors and builders of their times, people swept into greatness by events and choices. Their stories have been told before and will be told again.

The list also holds unexpected, less frequently told lives, some that might be said to capture less visible experiences: works on Andrei Sakharov, Primo Levi, and Karel Capek; the trumpeter and singer Chet Baker; the letters of Zora Neale Hurston; the "tragic courtship and marriage of Paul Laurence Dunbar and Alice Ruth Moore"; the story of William Henry Sheppard, a black nineteenth-century missionary to the Congo; a group biography of the first thirteen women chosen to be American astronauts. Such "smaller" life stories can capture larger ideas of what one life can mean, and each life expresses a critical theme about its time.

Memoir

Among memoirs we observe more tightly focused and individual perspectives: the personal world seen through subjective eyes. Fully realized memoirs are accounts of rising above, overcoming defeat, and defining a self against daunting odds. When we read them we want to understand the textures and sequences of lives. Among notable memoirs published in 2002–2003, a typology emerges: the effects of war on growing up; understanding the former generation; managing the life of a parent with Alzheimer's disease; the general troubles and challenges of having parents and being parents, of being a writer, or worse, being a writer in prison, or being a writer in Chile or Ireland; or being a marine, being a stripper, and so on. Each memoir tells *what it has been like to be me.*

Among these works, several live up to the observation of Jerome Bruner (2002, 14) that "a self is probably the most impressive work of art we ever produce." More than autobiographies or personal histories, these works appear to rise to the level of "self-making" that the act of writing can engender. Judy Blunt describes her abandonment of being a Montana rancher's wife (*Breaking Clean*). The physician and writer Sherwin Nuland recounts a tough relationship with a dominant and angry father (*Lost in America*). Sue Graham Mingus describes her life with the difficult jazz genius she married (*Tonight at Noon*). Rick Moody recollects a psychiatric hospitalization (*The Black Veil*). Marjane Satrapi, in a graphic format, recounts a girl's life in Iran under both shah and ayatollah (*Persepolis*). Alexandra Fuller describes her youth in Rhodesia as it became Zimbabwe (*Don't Let's Go to the Dogs Tonight*). The value of reading about the "difficult" life is obvious; all lived experience entails challenges and crises. Illuminating such tensions and the dissonances between expectation and reality, biographies and memoirs help us to examine and understand a human story——ironically both smaller and larger than the whole life—in ways that can lead a reader toward empathy and self-understanding.

History

In contrast, objective works of history are typically defined by categories of place (*Seven Ages of Paris,* Alistair Horne), era (*Empire: The Rise and Demise of the British World Order and the Lessons for Global Power,* Niall Ferguson), war (*The Peloponnesian War,* Donald Kagan), social phenomenon (*Racism: A Short History,* George M. Fredrickson), institution (*Mr. Jefferson's University,* Garry Wills), technology (*Secret Empire: Eisenhower, the CIA and the Hidden Story of America's Space Espionage,* Philip Taubman), event (*Krakatoa, The Day the World Exploded, August 27, 1883,* Simon Winchester), revelation (*The Secret Voyage of Sir Francis Drake, 1577–1580,* Samuel Bawlf), ethics (*A Moral Reckoning: The Role of the Catholic Church in the Holocaust and Its Unfulfilled Duty of Repair,* Daniel Jonah Goldhagen), or . . . well, there are virtually no limits on the diversity, scope, or focus of historical works because history itself seems to have none.

But within history there is a steady flow of subgenres, none more prominent than military history. The notable lists of 2002 hold works that demonstrate the changes in how we can come to see events over time. Now that its generation is gone, World War I has become a focus of critical interest, for example. With its generation rapidly passing away, World War II has become emblematic of a war in which values seemed to be clear. (Unlike say, the story told in *Beyond the Mountains of the Damned: The War*

Inside Kosovo, by Matthew McAllester.) These recent war histories seem far less hardboiled and documentary than we might expect, and far more compassionate. Three examples capture what seems to stand out as personal sacrifice narratives. In these works, soldiers have names and places associated with both their fidelities and losses: *Soldiers: Fighting Men's Lives, 1901–2001,* by Philip Ziegler, about British veterans of the last century; *The Bedford Boys: One American Town's Ultimate D-Day Sacrifice,* by Alex Kershaw, about twenty-one boys from one town who died on D-Day; and *Blood for Dignity: The Story of the First Integrated Combat Unit in the U.S. Army,* by David P. Colley, recovering a momentous but neglected event from the end of World War II.

Other historical works evince empathy and compassion, touching something deeper and more resonant than history courses care to tell us. I am thinking of Philip Dray's *At the Hands of Persons Unknown: The Lynching of Black America;* Barbara Freese's *Coal: A Human History;* Anne Applebaum's work on Stalin, *Gulag: A History;* the strong work by Richard Rhodes titled *Masters of Death: The SS-Einsatzgruppen and the Invention of the Holocaust;* and Christopher Woodward's fine little book, *In Ruins,* addressing that long view of history where all grandeur vanishes. These have in common a largeness of conception—a characteristic of the best nonfiction—that assures a reader that, in encountering a specific narrative, there is also a larger embedded commentary to be found about humans, time, and the shaping events that transcend eras.

As we read, we find that we value broad observations of experience, documentation, and synthesis. We welcome the specific detail that tells. Contexts illuminate. Every fresh truth is the product of the past. The threads of events and lives are endless. Our reading of nonfiction is a way we have to understand the interconnected problems of real human experiences. Bruner says of great narrative, "It is deeply about plight, about the road rather than about the inn to which it leads" (Bruner 2002, 20). I tend to prefer the metaphor of a gossamer spiderweb, spun lines crossing and connecting, delicate strands that catch the eye in certain light, and also a sticky way of catching us off guard and making us feel that we have been in touch with another world. In our most satisfying reading experiences a writer provides a human presence, a narrative surrogate whose reach extends beyond ours, into the past, into the self—and therefore into our past and into our self as well, where many themes are already braided and waiting new evidence.

Great themes speak through us; they address our contemporary lives in formative ways. A life today becomes an instrument of a life from the past. Biography, memoir, and history allow us to see the individual life as it was lived, its experiences of becoming, and its embodiment of human values. And these lived experiences (of Jefferson, of Lewis and Clark, of Lee, of Presley) are evoked in our own. We know that a life happens not simply in itself but also in a contemporary social context, based first on the traditions and information of the past, and then on the edges of the future. Every life is lived in a realm of power and achievement, among arrays of family, spouses, lovers and children. When we consider lives and events, we also must consider the risks, fears, and critical circumstances entangling them. Telling a human history requires a sense of boundaries and unknowns; reading human history requires a sense of where the edges might lead us, in lives lived today, if a connection between lives can be made.

Contemporary Issues, Case Studies, Reflections

An even greater sense of breadth and relevance might apply to the array of works categorized as contemporary issues, politics and government, and essays on various topics, including the significant armful of first books about the events of September 11, 2001. All of these works are regarded here as one category, an amalgam of current thoughts and images. I will also throw in another catchall category that I refer to as "case studies," holding the anomalous and often odd books that focus on one limited place or thing. In this sense, *Home Town* is a case study. The case studies published in 2002 are eclectic. John McPhee writes about shad, in *The Founding Fish*. Mark Kurlansky writes *Salt*. David Halberstam writes *Firehouse*. Mark Edmundson writes *Teacher: The One Who Made the Difference*. The focus is clear: typically, the case study tells us more than we might ordinarily need or want to know about one thing. And in this set, we have works that do this for the pipe organ and the World Series of Poker; works that offer a celebration of eBay and a condemnation of SUVs; and the stories of the singing Carter Family and the Springhill Mine Disaster. Cases can also address specific and perhaps quirky themes, as with works devoted to "twelve of America's most popular songs," and "movie love in the fifties." The approach is also evident in nonbiographical works about individuals with specific visions of themselves and their culture—extremists and religionists, for example—often allowing an author to have moments of reflection, speculation, and deep immersions in social contexts.

The works identified as essays and reflections are among the most impressive for their authors alone: Susan Sontag (*Regarding the Pain of Others*), William H. Gass (*Tests of Time*), Salman Rushdie (*Step across This Line*), Jonathan Franzen (*How to Be Alone*), Verlyn Klinkenborg (*The Rural Life*), and Janet Malcolm (*Reading Chekhov*). They are also strikingly original. They capture free-ranging minds in contemplation of memory and possibility. We might turn to them because we have admired their work in other forms or publications, or we might find them to satisfy us in ways that permit us to address the unanswered questions that are ultimately about ourselves: *How might I come to understand this life? How have others reflected on it?* Such books may be the most demanding and challenging—the most incisive for heart and intellect—of all the works discussed here, and yet they may also be the most relevant to the confounded issues and darknesses of our own time. Headlines every day suggest the primary lifelong question that this kind of nonfiction, and the resurgent form known as "creative nonfiction,"[3] addresses: *How am I to think of this experience, from within this life? How am I to lead my life with this knowledge?*

It is difficult to separate politics and government from contemporary issues, so I want to present them as one group of books, but they settle into specific sets without my design. Here are four titles before me now: *What Went Wrong? Western Impact and Middle East Response* by Bernard Lewis; *Terror and Liberalism* by Paul Berman; *Warrior Politics: Why Leadership Demands a Pagan Ethos* by Robert D. Kaplan; and *"A Problem from Hell": America and the Age of Genocide* by Samantha Power. It seems to me that these are works that share a similar impulse: the regard of extreme politics by challenged mortals. Such works might serve as deeper background for our understanding of where we are now. This kind of social and cultural comprehension is clearly the purview of nonfiction, and it is not difficult to find critical social explorations—and much to discuss—among these works.

Again, the primary question of a contemporary world—a working, applied, and meaningful world of difficult experiences lived daily—arises to face us: *How am I to think of this?* And the nonfiction literature does not fail to help. In 2002, notable works appeared about bringing up children (*Raising America: Experts, Parents, and a Century of Advice about Children*, Ann Hulber), American motherhood (*A Potent Spell: Mother Love and the Power of Fear*, Janna Malamud Smith), and the family under stress (*Random Family: Love, Drugs, Trouble and Coming of Age in the Bronx*, Adrian Nicole LeBlanc). The list contains works that address the buffeting and exploitative effects of marketing on everyday experiences (*Dot.Con: The Greatest Story Ever Sold*, John Cassidy; *Pipe Dreams: Greed, Ego, and the Death of Enron*, Robert Bryce; and *Fat Land: How Americans Became the Fattest People in the World*, Greg Critser). Finally, we discover here the nonfiction that most closely resembles investigative journalism, addressing the administration of powerful decisions (*The Gatekeepers: Inside the Admissions Process of a Premier College*, Jacques Steinberg), the seizure of common discourse by experts and moralists (*The Language Police: How Pressure Groups Restrict What Students Learn*, Diane Ravitch), and the brief, everyday life of an invisible worker (*The Short Sweet Dream of Eduardo Gutiérrez*, Jimmy Breslin). This last would be a place to begin, I think.

As exemplary works about contemporary experiences, however, these titles must be seen as background to a shelf that stands apart, holding an extraordinary core of notable works about September 11, 2001. Written from a still-raw, hard, unique emotional place in our time, without the softening lenses of distance, discipline, or comparison, they exemplify the ways we hope to grasp (or at least to document) part of what happened on that day. Each of the nine books at hand constructs a different angle on that morning's attack, from its origins, to the events and the heroisms they evoked, through the aftermath, toward analysis and wistful remembrance. They are listed following that suggested order.

- *The Cell: Inside the 9/11 Plot, and Why the FBI and CIA Failed to Stop It,* John Miller, Michael Stone, and Chris Mitchell

- *Out of the Blue: The Story of September 11, 2001, from Jihad to Ground Zero,* Richard Bernstein

- *Heart of a Soldier: A Story of Love, Heroism and September 11th,* James B. Stewart

- *Among the Heroes: United Flight 93 and the Passengers and Crew Who Fought Back,* Jere Longman

- *After: How America Confronted the September 12 Era,* Steven Brill

- *American Ground: Unbuilding the World Trade Center,* William Langewiesche

- *Longitudes and Attitudes: Exploring the World after September 11,* Thomas L. Friedman

- *The Age of Sacred Terror,* Daniel Benjamin and Steven Simon

- *To Reach the Clouds: My High Wire Walk between the Twin Towers,* Philip Petit

This ordering of titles also captures how nonfiction in certain cases can allow a reader to have specific kinds of controls over an unknown that seems so unimaginable and out of proportion, so mythic and *fictional,* that only nonfiction can allow a mind to grasp its details and its individual impacts with a dimension of trust. It remains to be seen how fictions will capture that day of losses, but we have evidence in these volumes of how nonfiction documentation can matter as a way to remember and reflect, an anchor as the world moves on.

Devastating works demonstrate the myth of "closure" and resolution. Perhaps this is why we also have enduring bodies of nonfiction devoted to wars, crimes, disasters, and losses: they will always be open. Perhaps this also explains the importance in these narratives of telling individual stories that capture both heroic strength and abysmal loss. The steady flow of these literatures about our wars and losses suggests that we can never fully know enough about the human proclivity to remember, as long as we can, whatever we can. Memory is memorial of a kind, and it resides in these texts.

Other Subgenres

To conclude this sorting-out, there are five somewhat more specialized nonfiction genres to address, with different expectations and rewards. Predictably, the qualities of history, biography, and memoir also inhere among them. The first is most important: there is much accessible science writing to note, and its authors are often, well, truly authoritative. For example, consider the daunting panel of 2002 works by Ernst Mayr (*What Evolution Is*), Edward O. Wilson (*The Future of Life*), James D. Watson (*Genes, Girls and Gamow: After the Double Helix*), and Stephen Pinker (*The Blank Slate: The Modern Denial of Human Nature*). These are the Big Minds, asking and answering some of the Big Questions of our time, for the awed child at Mr. Wizard's elbow who lives inside us all. But science, more than answers, is also a reflective and innovative process, often conducted slowly, by the light of encircled geniuses warming themselves over great questions. Such illuminated processes also can make a fine story when rendered for a lay intelligence. Consider *The Eye of the Lynx: Galileo, His Friends, and the Beginning of Modern Natural History,* by David Freedberg; *The Lunar Men: Five Friends Whose Curiosity Changed the World,* by Jenny Uglow; and *Edison's Eve: A Magical History of the Quest for Mechanical Life,* by Gaby Wood. These works may be about collaboration as much as spectacular insight.

Investigative science writing frequently makes headlines and leads to public dialogue. Because some of our greatest fears involve science—the environment, technology, and disease and their combination in the possibilities of bioterrorism—works of this kind can give us essential information to calm or alarm. Three chilly 2002 examples are *The Demon in the Freezer: A True Story,* by Richard Preston (about smallpox); *Our Posthuman Future: Consequences of the Biotechnology Revolution,* by Francis Fukuyama (about genetic tinkering); and *The Empty Ocean: Plundering the World's Marine Life,* by Richard Ellis (about deep-sea overuse and abuse).[4]

Nonfiction examples devoted to food, travel, and sport, tend to be entertaining and engaging; they each capture experiences of satisfying pastimes and the cultural record. Every example of these categories is also about exploring possibilities, juxtaposing, and comparing. Among these 2002 notable books, see how easily food combines with travel and memoir: *Cooking for Mr. Latte: A Food Lover's Courtship, with Recipes,*

Amanda Hesser; *Feeding a Yen: Savoring Local Specialties, from Kansas City to Cuzco,* Calvin Trillin; *A Cook's Tour: In Search of the Perfect Meal,* Anthony Bourdain; and *The Apprentice: My Life in the Kitchen,* Jacques Pépin.

Works of travel are also about sampling the tastes of other times and places, of course, and yet they are also about looking for something else. The best of them appear to extend well beyond the constraints of travel, a term that seems almost incidental to the writer's intention. Here are four examples: *The Birds of Heaven: Travels with Cranes,* Peter Matthiessen; *Oaxaca Journal,* Oliver Sacks; *From the Land of Green Ghosts: A Burmese Odyssey,* Pascal Koo Thwe; and *Stranger on a Train: Daydreaming and Smoking around America with Interruptions*, Jenny Diski. They are travel books, perhaps, but also works of natural or social history.

And now, turning to the sports desk, we find that large compartment of our national sensibility that is always at play, involved in games of baseball (*The Teammates,* David Halberstam), golf (*First Off the Tee: Presidential Hackers, Duffers, and Cheaters from Taft to Bush,* Don Van Natta, Jr.), boxing (*The Gloves: A Boxing Chronicle,* Robert Anasi), soccer (*Futebol: Soccer, the Brazilian Way,* Alex Bellos), basketball (*Big Game, Small World: A Basketball Adventure,* Alexander Wolff)—all works about the games, of course, but also about friendship, heroic playing (*Sandy Koufax: A Lefty's Legacy,* Jane Leavy), the sports economy (*Moneyball: The Art of Winning an Unfair Game,* Michael Lewis), and local history (*The Last Good Season: Brooklyn, the Dodgers, and Their Final Pennant Race Together,* Michael Shapiro). Sports also involve themes of memoir, gender, race, drugs, politics, health, youth, education, and crime. Every work we find here is about the game and the athlete, but about something else as well.

The nonfiction crime segment is relatively small among notable books, but it extends its tentacles toward other areas of the realm: works about economic and computer crime, corporate swindling and malfeasance, international terrorism, and the complexities of crimebusting organizations. All of these lead us toward conversations about cultures and values, justice and order, ethics and fairness. One seems to stand out among the notable books of 2002, Steve Hodel's noir-like *Black Dahlia Avenger: A Genius for Murder.* The blend—famous case, lurid details, parental secrecy, urban density, unexpected revelations, authentic detective work—reminds, as other examples might, that the truth in nonfiction is merely a version of the truth, and the crafting of it occurs in ways to inspire other thoughts and other possibilities. Even where crime is concerned, nonfiction addresses phenomena and experiences differently from the way fiction addresses them.

Nonfiction Themes

It is easy to see that categories of nonfiction are relatively boundless; they inform across the frameworks of knowledge. By necessity, strong works about politics and government are also substantive works of biography, history, memoir, and contemporary issues. Works about science may relate to all of these as well, as may works of military history. Nonfiction case studies of a particular thing or event can transcend all other genre categories, reaching everywhere for evidence. Consequently, nonfiction requires an emancipated sense of relevance and a wider sense of logic, with fewer isolating classifications, than fiction. Nonfiction works can inspire the part of imagination where the most profound and challenging explorations take place, and where traces of their implications remain when the reading is done.

Nonfiction works that describe lives and their outcomes may also be about moral choices, decisions of self-determination, or relationships to events and persons. Biography and memoir might easily be described through lenses of integrity, courage, philosophy, faith, ethics, and values. As we read these works, we are able to dwell within entire frames of life and behavior we cannot otherwise occupy.

Works of adventure, travel, combat, and sport move us to the edges of our own daily experiences, where we can envision the value of courage, risk taking, and championship. We encounter forms of testing in these narratives, where strength, endurance, strategy, and genius can be critical. Where humans are tried by conflict and cataclysm, as in tragedies and agonies of all kinds, the lessons to be learned may be remedial, healing, or sources of solace.

Narratives of change, transformation, and innovation or records of crime, medicine, and law also compose a literature of process and crisis, order and disorder, problem and solution. All depend on an articulation of thinking at the edges of change or amid the possibilities of chance. The literature of science might also demonstrate risk and hope as well as intelligence and insight.

Pragmatism, deliberation, and purpose may be addressed in works of history, politics, and government; through them we may come to understand how civilizations and cultures are formed and endure, and how leaders take and use power as circumstances permit. In all of these, the reader's task may be to go beyond the details—much as one does when reading fiction—to see the larger and more timeless contexts against which the narratives of actors and events unfold.

Nonfiction works reconstruct grounded, lived experiences— "grounded" because they emerge from process, conflict, practice, observation, and inquiry in a world where all of these things have specific consequences. They also draw readers by capturing the intimate details only deep inquiry can provide. They evoke feelings of empathy and adventure, excite our senses of logic and justice, and capture ideas drawn from human behaviors otherwise undocumented and lost. We value nonfiction for its immersions, its occasional densities, and for its expansions of our intellectual experiences. It is possible to learn from these extensions of mind and sensibility. The veracity and authenticity of nonfiction can touch our emotional, ethical, and logical centers. An active intelligence is nourished and practiced in such reading, because it makes fresh dimensions of experience visible, almost tangible. Our limits are continuously extended and our perceptions are revised. We read nonfiction to feed our desire to experience fresh truths.

Deep Dimensions of Nonfiction

It is possible to suggest that nonfiction addresses many more dimensions than the bare details of a situation, life, or event can suggest. Organized in small clusters, some recent nonfiction books can redefine both our expectations and our experiences of nonfiction; they are resonant and provocative examples. None of them is easy or unchallenging. While an individual book on this list might fit within several recognizable genres, we might more usefully come to identify such works not as "memoir" or "history," but as imaginatively constructed narratives, many kinds of crafted truths, that grasp us by the throat and keep us from imagining anything else. Neither a genre nor its variations matter; they are about something greater and more complex. Some are harrowing, some are pointed, some are instructive; none is perfunctory or thoughtless, and each reminds us of the continuing problems of identity and responsibility inherent in one life.

Deep Tellings

The writer engaged in deep telling is immersed in one event, a situation, condition, or community, to such an extent that the narration of information and experience unfolds in nearly microscopic detail. Such works are characterized by concentrated attention and a sense of comprehensive, authoritative treatment. The narrative essentially blankets the topic in a systematic way. See, for example, *The Noonday Demon,* Andrew Solomon; *The Perfect Storm,* Sebastian Junger; any work by John McPhee.

Inside Encounters

A form of participant observation, the insider narrative strives to present a member's view of a place or community. The writer gathers firsthand evidence and builds the narrative on willing communication with informants. Often the writer is present as an actor, recording events while actively participating in them. Such books carry the aura of investigative fieldwork. See, for example, *Salvation on Sand Mountain,* Dennis Covington; *Word Freak,* Stefan Fatsis; *The Spirit Catches You and You Fall Down,* by Anne Fadiman.

Rescued Histories

The intention of this kind of nonfiction is to restore an obscure part of the past through investigative methods in archives, news records, and personal interviews, when possible. The event may have been willfully covered to hide or deny evidence, or it may simply be neglected over time. Examples are similar to archaeological recovery. See, for example, *The Circus Fire,* Stewart O'Nan; *The Englishman's Daughter,* Ben MacIntyre; *The Devil in the White City,* by Erik Larson.

Lives in Contexts

Beyond biography, this kind of life-narrative is founded on the idea that every human span can be seen as an interpretation of actions, possibilities, ethics, and responsibilities. Such works draw their subjects as emblematic figures in the center of a shifting world. Such abstractions as courage and integrity are the critical lenses for observing, criticizing, and understanding the subject, striving to live up to both culture and destiny. See, for example, *Crazy Horse,* Larry McMurtry; *Explaining Hitler,* Ron Rosenbaum; *Theodore Rex,* Edmund Morris; *John Adams,* David McCullough.

Journeys and Places

Typically involving travel, unanticipated encounters, some dangers or risks, and evidences of past inhabitants, these narratives communicate a sense of the human place in a landscape. Within physical and geographic constraints, the writer strives to illuminate the biological, social, or cultural fabric of the setting, and the geography embodied in consciousness. Human beings need not be present. The writer often remains an outsider. See, for example, *On the Rez,* Ian Frazier; *Bad Land: An American Romance,* Jonathan Raban; *Reaching Keet Seel: Ruin's Echo and the Anasazi,* Reg Saner; *This Cold Heaven,* or *The Solace of Open Spaces,* Gretel Ehrlich.

Losses and Understandings

The history of humanity can be traced from conflict to conflict and loss to loss; wars define eras and the humans who live in them. Wars and their narratives also serve as critical markers of how cultures regard and define other people, how we remember our defeats and victories, and how we live with both. Dire events can become crucibles of conscience, and narratives of this kind help us to know what they mean. See, for example, *We Wish to Inform You That Tomorrow We Will Be Killed with Our Families,* Philip Gourevitch; *The Unfinished Bombing,* Edward Linenthal; *Neighbors,* Jan T. Gross; *War Is a Force That Gives Us Meaning,* Chris Hedges.

Growing-Through Narratives

The records of youth, narrated from within, dramatize what is not a growing *up,* but rather a growing *through.* We read about the force that pushes the subject from within, toward risk and individuality, against family, against the odds. We come to understand what it means to create a ruin of childhood and walk through its shards, to embrace small and large lies while keeping huge silences, and to harbor mistrust and fear as one hopes to be loved. We read and think, *Stop, take care, go forward, go on, go through.* See, for example, *Cherry,* Mary Karr; *The Blood Runs Like a River through My Dreams,* Nasdijj; *Autobiography of a Face*, Lucy Grealy.

There are many other deepened ways to categorize nonfiction than these. I think of *Complications,* by Atul Gawande, a superior exemplar of the doctor's narrative; *Ex Libris,* by Anne Fadiman, the best essays about reading one can find; *Manhattan 1945,* by Jan Morris, life in a place at a remarkable moment; *The Raptor and the Lamb: Predators and Prey in the Living World,* by Christopher McGowan, about the relationship between the devourer and the devoured.

These are among the many works beyond any adequate category: each book is always about something more.

Our Lives Are Nonfiction

The driven, engaged reader lives with many questions, unfinished inquiries, and moments of wonder about the world. The reader seeks the experiences of others and the narratives waiting to be told by others. Such readers are themselves grounded in a world where nonfiction makes a difference. They will read nonfiction to have mysteries explained, experiences recollected, questions answered, histories retold, and extraordinary experiences brought into the light of text. They will read to gather information, to make up, literally to construct their own minds. By pursuing the unfinished questions and unending curiosities of one life, a person makes sense of the personal conflict, the private observation, and the problematic crisis.

Our lives are nonfiction; we want them to hold the qualities we seek as we read: authenticity, confirmation, integrity, discipline, veracity, and insight.

To construct one life requires many stories. We are not surprised to find that even the relatively small and uneventful life, when it is told well, is part of a larger community of stories, a workplace, a family, a place on earth, with sky, weather, and a view. Nor are we astonished to find that the life of a reader entails more contexts than we might be able to count in a day and evokes more connections to other lives and experiences than we can imagine. Invisibly to ourselves, we compose a culture, construct an ethos, and live among curious others. In nonfiction the culture finds its memory, expresses its awe and fear, reconciles its surprises and anomalies, and articulates its problems so that they might become more visible and soluble.

Nonfiction stories, their protagonists, and their writers expand the reader's repertoire of rational knowledge and logical connection. They allow us to extract patterns of action and consequence; they permit us to transfer observations of these patterns from one situation to another. In this way, we might interpret the logical laws that construct a living world. Works of nonfiction construct imaginative, narrated versions of particular acts, lives, and situations. They are crafted truths that expand our understanding of the possible, shaped by both lived and understood experiences. Mihalyi Csikszentmihalyi writes, "Every piece of information we process gets evaluated for its bearing on the self." Information either creates disorder and response, he says, or it confirms our ideals and intentions, "thereby freeing up psychic energy" (Csikszentmihalyi 1990, 39). We carry so many unknowns with us that we might find no end to the possibilities of what nonfiction helps us to see in the living world, no end to the possibilities of response it evokes, and no end to the vigor and energy of thought it inspires.

Notes

1. The final phrase comes from Bruner (1973).

2. The notable books used for these observations appeared in the following places: *The New York Times Book Review,* December 8, 2002 ("Holiday Books"), pp. 10, 13, 34, 37–38, 66–70, 72, 74; *The New York Times Book Review,* June 1, 2003 ("Summer

Reading"), pp. 21–23, 25–26; "The Year in Books 2002," *Publishers Weekly,* November 4, 2002, pp. 28–37; and a summer nonfiction list appearing in *USA Today,* May 22, 2003, p. 8D, compiled by Ayesha Court.

3. See, for example, issues of the journal *Creative Nonfiction*, begun in 1993 and edited by Lee Gutkind at the University of Pittsburgh. See also Philip Gerard (1996) and Paul John Eakin (1999).

4. When grounded in research and inquiry, such works can inspire movements, and policy changes. Consider the effects of *Silent Spring,* Rachel Carson's report on pesticides, for example, or Michael Harrington's work about the American poor, *The Other America.*

References

Bruner, Jerome S. 1973. Going beyond the information given. In *Beyond the information given: Studies in the psychology of knowing*. Edited by Jerome Bruner, 218–38. New York: W.W. Norton.

Bruner, Jerome. 2002. *Making stories: Law, literature, life*. Cambridge, MA: Harvard University Press.

Csikszentmihalyi, Mihalyi. 1990. *Flow: The psychology of optimal experience*. New York: Harper and Row.

Eakin, Paul John, 1999. *How our lives become stories*. Ithaca, NY: Cornell University Press.

Gerard, Philip. 1996. *Creative nonfiction: Researching and crafting stories of real life*. Cincinnati, OH: Story Press.

Kidder, Tracy. 1999. *Home town*. New York: Random House.

Orlean, Susan. 2003. Lifelike. *The New Yorker* 79· 46–50.

Chapter 4

The Appeal of Nonfiction: A Tale of Many Tastes

Kenneth D. Shearer

It is nice to pick up a book and not be where you are at the moment.

—David Poe, aboard the U.S.S. *Abraham Lincoln* in the Persian Gulf, March 14, 2003 (Saint Louis 2003, 20)

Background

Like most American children, my first exposure to books was aural. The readers were most often three people: my sister, Joan; my Great Aunt Jenny; and my Aunt Helen. My sister, who is five years older than I, served as a role model; she motivated me, since it seemed likely that if she could read so well to me, in a few years I would also be able to read well to myself. My Great Aunt Jenny would read and reread to me as long as I wanted, and I wanted a lot of reading time. My Aunt Helen not only read very well, but she possessed a skill that no one else known to me had: she seemed to know all the stories and which ones of them would appeal most to me and my cousins. She was a public librarian, and, when I visited her, she took us to what then seemed to me an endless store of stories in her library in Marathon, New York. (At Aunt Helen's recent ninetieth birthday party, she reminded me that I proposed we get married so that she could read to me every day. Several obstacles undermined my plan, not least of them the views of my Uncle Gordon, who was then soldiering in WWII, on my marriage proposal.) Stories read to me captured my imagination and motivated me to want to read on my own. But the basic readers assigned in elementary school—texts that repeated a few words over and over to accustom students to them—created in my mind a major divide between what was read to me and what I could struggle to read on my own.

In the third grade, back in the 1940s in my school in Cedarhurst, Long Island, New York, with the pedestrian name of Public School No. 5, we read a textbook that, while stylistically banal, did catch my fancy. *If I Were Going* is the story of a nondescript, white-bread family who traveled first around the United States, visiting, if my memory serves, the ice-skating rink at Rockefeller Center in New York City and on to Boston and other places in New England, then down South, and on to the West through the Midwest. Later, they went on a transatlantic tour. What excited me by far the most was that they went to Egypt, where they rode on camels and saw pyramids. The family also made visits to a fishing village in England and a tulip farm in the Netherlands. At least that is the way I remember it now. The reading of this text led to many an afternoon looking at maps of both the United States and the world and imagining visiting various locales. I settled on an elaborate plan that included many national parks. But, when I tried to convince my mother and father that this would make a wonderful itinerary for our annual summer vacation trip, they were implacably opposed. They said something about insufficient money and the car not being up to such a workout. Happily, some of my travel aspirations materialized later in life, although the Egyptian pyramids were only briefly glimpsed through an airplane window once on a trip to Kuwait, and those pyramids still tug at me. Maybe next year.. . . I still love travel books and often wonder whether the appeal was initiated by reading *If I Were Going* in the third grade, or whether I liked that textbook because travel innately appeals to me. In any case, it literally opened up a world.

So here I am, recently retired from a long teaching career in the library and information science field, in my sixties, and still hopelessly interested in reading. And I have been asked to write on the appeal of nonfiction. Given the popularity of nonfiction, there is very little written on the subject of why people are drawn to it, while the appeal of fiction has received several serious treatments in the professional literature. To get a handle on the subject, I reflected on the differences between fiction and nonfiction, the nebulous notion of appeal, and the fact that some readers are usually attracted to fiction, some to nonfiction, whereas, like me, many others enjoy reading both. This exploration of the appeal factors of nonfiction includes autobiographical details because the appeal of anything must appeal to someone; to write as if that were not the case is to miss an essential ingredient in the understanding of the topic.

My reflections on these questions have led me to three conclusions: 1) nonfiction and fiction are not opposites; 2) the list of appeal factors of fiction identified in the readers' advisory literature overlaps the appeal factors of nonfiction but omits many factors of importance to readers of nonfiction; and 3) the appeal of informational works is most certainly not always utilitarian.

Fiction appealed to me first. Long before air-conditioning was a common amenity in homes, lying on a couch in our living room one hot summer day, I discovered the thrill of reading to myself and enjoying the experience the way earlier enjoyment of stories had depended on listening to more accomplished readers reading aloud to me. The book was Eric Knight's *Lassie Come Home*. We had a dog, part collie, named Lucky, which my father had saved from an abusive owner. I loved Lucky, and *Lassie Come Home* was grounded in how and why we love dogs, exploring that affection of owners and their pets in a dramatic series of scenes that took me far away from the uncomfortable heat of August, with its physical distress aggravated by the fact that my closest friend, Alan, was far away at camp. I learned that words can evoke very strong emotions; I feared for Lassie and suffered because she was in pain. The heat and my friend's absence never entered my mind while reading. Lassie's imaginary tribulations brought real tears to my eyes. And I wanted to repeat this experience of safe intensity. Reading was a magical form of transportation. Perhaps it was then that I learned that any engaging book is a travel book because reading takes us away for a while.

The first nonfiction book I remember reading was titled *Flying Saucers Are Real,* by a retired Air Force colonel, Donald Keyhoe, who was convinced that a phenomenon involving creatures from outer space was a genuine concern to the human race. It was fascinating to imagine the possibilities that such a development implied and rather scary fun to picture meeting up with extraterrestrials. Perhaps it is the juxtaposition of these early reading experiences that uniquely positioned me to notice that what is appealing about a novel can be its power to amplify our knowledge of everyday reality more fully, deepening my love of dogs, and that what is appealing about a work of nonfiction can be its power to stretch our imaginations, positing the situation of humanity in the presence of extraterrestrial intelligence. The longer I think about the two apparent opposites—fiction and nonfiction—the more it appears to me that there is a terrain of text ranging from a pure imaginary North Pole—call it "Wonderland"—in which nearly nothing is recognizable and where physical laws and mathematical basics cannot be relied on, all the way to a South Pole of verifiable fact—call it "the Lab"—whose assertions are tested by many devoted scientists over thousands of convincing replications. This textual landscape features many divergent degrees of exactitude, as well as a variety of kinds of truth and innumerable pleasing deceptions. I will name it Planet Bookscape.

Planet Bookscape:
The Fiction/Nonfiction Textual Terrain

The category of "nonfiction" is a catchall. It implicitly contains everything that is not fiction, not false. Is nonfiction unlike fiction because fiction is subjective, imagined, not of the real world? Is nonfiction uniformly objective, informative, and true? Librarians and best-seller lists, bookstore operators and common parlance have relied for a very long time on the distinction between fiction and nonfiction. It is common to speak of reading nonfiction as a serious, manly, and valuable undertaking, whereas reading fiction is a lightweight, emotional, and feminine sort of thing to do. Case closed? Or is it in need of more thoughtful attention? I vote for more thoughtful attention.

Let us explore the idea that fiction may not merely be the opposite of nonfiction, but rather that fantasy, realistic novels, accounts of ghosts and extraterrestrials, popular advice, metaphysics, religious beliefs, history, travel accounts, political and economic analyses, and scientific treatises are more akin to a textual terrain, with lots of ballooning space between two poles of pure imagination and scientifically verified facts. We begin the exploration by looking at disclaimers in novels—you know, the remarks that any resemblance between the characters in this book and real people is coincidental, even though we all know that the ability to create characters like the people we know is a hallmark of much good fiction. One example of this sort of disclaimer is made by Ian McEwan prior to the text of his novel, *Atonement*. He states that "this is a work of fiction. Names, characters, businesses, organizations, places, events and incidents are either the product of the author's imagination or are used fictitiously. And any resemblance to actual persons, living or dead, events or locales is entirely coincidental" (McEwan 2001, verso of title page). But the resemblance to real characters, places, events and incidents in *Atonement* is undeniably closer to reality than is the resemblance of those in *Alice in Wonderland*.

But, you may argue, in both cases that it is merely a question of degree of resemblance, both novels merely simulate reality to the degree convenient to their artistic purpose. Perhaps we can uncover a clue by noting

Truman Capote's nonfiction novel, *In Cold Blood*. In it, Capote shapes his account of a horrendous true crime as a novel but disciplines himself simultaneously to include only real names, characters, businesses, organizations, places, events, and incidents. He uses the techniques of journalists, biographers, historians, and behavioral scientists to test the veracity of his material, explaining in his acknowledgments, "All the material in this book not derived from my own observation is either taken from official records or is the result of interviews with the persons directly concerned, more often than not numerous interviews conducted over a considerable period of time" (Capote 1965).

Contrast Capote's statement with the statement in Irving Stone's novel, *The Origin: A Biographical Novel of Charles Darwin*. In Stone's acknowledgments, he gives lengthy thanks to the descendants of Charles Darwin for "permission to . . . use unpublished personal family materials . . . Charles Darwin's vast correspondence, both published and unpublished" (Stone 1980, 8). Stone has a bibliography at the end of his novel that includes material from books, articles, pamphlets, and newspapers. Although he has written a novel, Stone makes a rigorous effort to have every name, character, organization, place, event, and incident coincide with historical truth. He does imagine conversations and motivations, but nevertheless the difference between a Stone biographical novel and a nonfiction biography is hardly an unbridgeable chasm. They are both based on serious scholarship with aim of knowing a person's life better. (It reminds me that a professor, Ralph Robert Shaw, in my graduate education program at Rutgers University used to joke that Ranganathan's faceted Colon classification system had a whole lot of "leaky" facets.)

If the preceding examples merely seem to point to the odd quirk that some works of fiction have remarkably little fiction in them and that some works of fact are shaped like imaginative works, consider this entirely representative quote from Eric Berne's nonfiction best-seller, *What Do You Say after You Say Hello; The Psychology of Human Destiny* (Berne 1977, 213–15):

Little Pink Riding Hood was an orphan, and she used to sit in a clearing in the forest waiting for someone who needed help to pass by. Sometimes she would wander down the path in case anyone needed her in another part of the woods. She was very poor and could not offer very much, but whatever she had she shared freely.

After a couple of pages of Little Pink Riding Hood's tale, we learn that she "was still a cute kid and still liked to help people, but sometimes she thought the best thing to do would be to take an overdose of sleeping pills."

Now contrast Berne's nonfiction text with a typical passage from James Michener's fiction best-seller, *Caribbean* (Michener 1989, 403):

> The decades following the slave rebellion in Haiti saw vast improvement in the fortunes of blacks throughout the Caribbean. Great Britain abolished slavery everywhere in its empire in 1834, France by 1848. The United States engineered a cynical trick in 1863; President Lincoln abolished slavery in the middle of the Civil War, but only in the southern states, over which he had no control.

Large portions of Berne's nonfiction closely resemble fairy tales; large amounts of Michener's novel are accurate historical and geographical accounts. If we were to use excerpts from fiction and nonfiction and ask readers to identify which was which, it often would be impossible to sort them out correctly. In Peter Mayle's entertaining *A Year in Provence,* we could be forgiven for thinking that some of the amusing character sketches were from a novel. For instance, when algae attacked Mayle's swimming pool in his new home in the south of France, he badly needed help in removing it. Bernard had been promising to take care of the problem but did not show up as expected. Mayle gave up waiting for Bernard and was trying to scrub it off the sides of the pool when Bernard belatedly arrived and said that the strategy Mayle was using was all wrong, that it must be treated with a chemical product:

> We abandoned the green fur and went indoors for a drink, and Bernard explained why he hadn't been able to come earlier. He had been suffering from a toothache, but couldn't find a local dentist who was prepared to treat him, because of his strange affliction: He bites dentists. He can't stop himself. It is an incurable reflex. The moment he feels an exploratory finger in his mouth—tak!—he bites. He had so far bitten the only dentist in Bonnieux, and four dentists in Cavaillon, and had been obliged to go to Avignon, where he was unknown in dental circles. (Mayle 1990, 53)

When we close the covers of Mayle's book, we won't have learned how to remove algae from a swimming pool or much else of any practical informational value, but we will have been entertained by a charming story with a palpable feel for what it must feel like for a foreigner to live in Provence.

Now, please try this test. Identify the following quote as either fiction or nonfiction.

> Then he lights a cigarette, puts on a CD of Ukrainian folk music, and goes to get some ice at the same time that I head to the kitchen for a refill of wine. Away from Harvey, Archie and I have a chat about the brain. He tells me that when the two men were roommates, Harvey occasionally kept the brain out on the kitchen table, but only when he was working on it. "It was weird having it here at first. I mean it was hard to eat lunch with it around," concludes Archie in a loud voice.. . . "Like you're eating a ham sandwich and you're staring at this big piece of ham, but it just happens to be, you know, Einstein's Brain." (Paterniti 2000, 97)

The excerpt is from Michael Paterniti's *Driving Mr. Albert; A Trip across America with Einstein's Brain,* a fascinating true story that leaves a lot of fantasy and science fiction in the dust. Very unexpectedly, Dr. Thomas Harvey, a pathologist, decided on his own counsel to remove Albert Einstein's brain after his death on April 17, 1955, at Princeton Hospital, only to store it in his home refrigerator and take it out periodically for tests of dubious theories about the relationship of brain physiology and genius. The curious story narrates the fate of Einstein's brain, including among other unexpected developments, a surreal visit by Dr. Harvey and the author with the aged novelist, William S. Burroughs, the author of *Naked Lunch.* Few works of imagination can touch this nonfiction in terms of sheer, unexpected novelty.

What do you make of this quote?

> Prostrating myself mentally before my Guide, I cried, "How is it, O divine ideal of consummate loveliness, that I see thy inside, and yet cannot discern thy heart, thy lungs, thy arteries, thy liver?" "What you think you see, you see not," he replied; "it is not given to you, nor to any other Being from those in Flatland." (Abbot 1952, 80)

This excerpt comes from a classic by Edwin A. Abbot, *Flatland; a Romance of Many Dimensions.* Did you recognize it as a romance? It explores an imaginary world with its own social strata and customs, reminiscent of Swift's *Gulliver's Travels.* The book was recommended to me by Marion Humble, the director at the time at Peninsula Public Library in Lawrence, New York, and arguably the best readers' advisor it has ever been my pleasure to know. *Flatland* was classed in Peninsula Public Library in the Dewey 510s, mathematics. If you check the Library of Congress catalog today, you will see that it is classed there in mathematics, class QA. The edition I have in my collection is from publisher Dover's Books of Philosophy and Science.

Try one more test of your acumen for distinguishing between fiction and nonfiction.

Ten minutes past three. It was the last moment that the lake was only water, roaring with a force equivalent to that of Niagara River as it reaches Niagara Falls. Then it combined with every thing that lay in its path, hurling into the narrow valley, churning, flinging, and scouring a high wide path, now narrowing, now broadening, depending on the landscape it encounters, growing black, huge, monstrous, and fetid with debris....

It took almost an hour for the wave to reach Johnstown. (Cambor 2001, 242)

Did you recognize this as an account of the infamous Johnstown, Pennsylvania, Flood of 1889? Do you suspect it is the excerpted from David R. McCullough's extraordinary history, *The Johnstown Flood*? If so, you made an astute, if incorrect, guess. The quote is from Kathleen Cambor's novel *In Sunlight in a Beautiful Garden*, which is a perfect fictional companion to McCullough's nonfiction masterpiece.

The idea that "nonfiction" is not a single entity becomes even clearer if you recall that A's religion is B's myth and that C's valuable psychological insight is D's psychobabble. Marxist economics was classed as science in the former USSR's libraries, while in much of the rest of the world it was viewed as rot.

Theories are also a kind of fiction. Most people hope that these explanatory stories and idea structures will be applicable to some human use, but a reading of the longtime best-seller, *A Brief History of Time; From the Big Bang to Black Holes,* by the outstanding physicist Stephen W. Hawking, will convince the attentive reader that theories can be spun out one after another by Hawking as tales are spun by a fine storyteller. If Hawking finds a new fact that contradicts his most recent theory, he can always come up with a new one to deal with the revised nature of things. In no case does he confuse what he is doing with stating the Truth.

Even when mathematicians think that they are creating fantasy, they may prove to be wrong. The fact is that imaginary numbers—which you may recall are numbers using the square root of -1 and long written about by mathematicians as "imaginary" to indicate what they thought they were dealing with—turn out to have very real applications and that engineers find them useful when solving practical problems. And, of course, untold numbers of readers use the imaginary worlds created in novels to help them deal with real personal problems.

This theme could be developed indefinitely but the reader by now will realize that books do not form two entirely distinct classes, fiction and non-fiction; rather books form a terrain of individual works each created from different proportions of imagination and of fact, and they are shaped to serve a dizzying array of purposes. When a book first attracts our attention and turns out to continue to appeal to us as we read it, the happy coincidence is like a good meal or a satisfying conversation, a fine day or a stimulating vacation. Enjoying a book involves both the text that is written and also who the reader is at the time of reading it. Neither *Lassie Come Home* nor *Flying Saucers Are Real* would appeal to me now, much less *If I Were Going*. But all three served me very well at the right time.

What Is the Appeal of Books?

In Robert Burgin's ground-breaking treatment of readers' advisory service and nonfiction, he sets forth a completely convincing argument that nonfiction shares with fiction the appeal factors that have been set forth in the library and information science literature, including Characterization, Pacing, Story Line, Setting, and Use of Language. Through the use of multiple examples, Burgin shows that each of these appeal factors is found in such books as *Angela's Ashes, The Perfect Storm, A Year in Provence,* and *It's Not about the Bike.* He quotes from reviewers to show conclusively that they recognize these factors in nonfiction books (Burgin 2001).

During the course of his discussion, Burgin distinguishes between recreational nonfiction and research-related or job-related nonfiction, with the apparent assumption that all reading of fiction is undertaken for recreational purposes. Many students who are assigned to read novels would find this an arguable assumption. (I remember trying to trudge through James Joyce's *Finnegan's Wake* and finding it very hard work, as was William Faulkner's *The Fable*. Neither attempt on my part had anything to do with a school, research, or job requirement but rather reflected my curiosity to explore authors who were highly regarded by noted critics.) It seems to me that the reading of much nonfiction does not belong in categories characterized as primarily recreational, on one hand, or research or job related, on the other. And I want to explore this idea further.

Biography and autobiography are, ipso facto, about the development of character. It is very difficult to find a more compellingly readable story than Richard Wright's *Black Boy,* his wrenching and beautiful tale of how he developed and nurtured his brilliant mind in a totally hostile environment. (Especially moving to librarians is the way in which Wright, in a segregated South of long ago, enlisted the help of a white man who was himself the object of bias. The white man allowed Wright the use of his public library card, a treasure denied to African Americans, to obtain access to books that Wright desperately wanted to read, under the guise that he was merely a simple-minded gofer for the white man. Ironically, the white man had no intellectual life and was ignorant of the books that were so appealing to Richard Wright.)

Biography is not the only branch of nonfiction that trades in appeal factors identified for fiction. The idea that a history is a story is embedded in its very name, "hi(story)." At the beginning of former Librarian of Congress Daniel J. Boorstin's *The Discoverers; A History of Man's Search to Know His World and Himself,* he writes "A Personal Note to the Reader," which includes the following account of what his book is about:

The obstacles to discovery—the illusions of knowledge—are also part of our story. Only against the forgotten backdrop of received common sense and myths of their time can we begin to sense the courage, the rashness, the heroic and imaginative thrusts of the great discoverers. They had to battle against current "facts" and dogmas of the learned. I have tried to recapture those illusions—about the earth, the continents and the seas before Columbus and Balboa, Magellan and Captain Cook, about the heavens before Copernicus and Galileo and Kepler, about the human body before Paracelsus and Versalius and Harvey. (Boorstin 1983, xv)

Boorstin tells a story of the people who have shaped the views that educated people now hold of time, the earth and seas, nature, and society, our very sense of what is true and what is false. He works his magic by staging these discoverers as they come to recognize that incorrect ideas, once generally and deeply believed to be truths by everyone including themselves, were faulty. *The Discoverers,* which holds such an appeal for many people, appeals, in part, according to its blurb, because "In this book the long human quest for what man does not yet know becomes a mystery story played on an ever-changing stage." As a reader of many mystery stories, I can attest that this is claim has merit and offers an insight into the book's appeal, but something crucial is missing. It seems to me that Boorstin's history is more aptly characterized as a Mystery story than as a mystery story, more an exploration of the unraveling of the mysteries of science than a "who done it."

Other nonfiction also deals with Mysteries. The best-selling book of all time is said to be the Bible; the Koran is also phenomenally widely read and studied over great parts of the earth. The key writings that underpin major religious belief systems clearly appeal to something in vast numbers of readers over long periods of time. Sacred texts answer questions about how to live a good life, how and why to be moral and ethical, the meaning of life, where the universe comes from, and the nature of death, among other basic issues of deep concern to people. They posit scientifically unverifiable answers to widely shared human questions and offer meanings. They, and myriad related religious works, form a set of rules to conduct life and help adherents to stick with them. (Fiction usually does not do this kind of thing, although it can help in understanding emotions and providing a sense of self and how to conduct one's relationships with others.)

Another category of nonfiction that enjoys great popularity but seems to appeal to readers for reasons that are basically different from fiction, is how-to and advice. These books attempt to offer ways to cope better with, for want of a more precise distinction, manipulating the outer world (how to become a millionaire or to get higher SAT scores or to cook Italian cuisine) and handling the world of the inner life (how to find abiding love or to understand your teenager or to gain positive thinking or inner strength). An early example of the advice category is Machiavelli's *The Prince,* which curious and fascinating book includes chapters on "How Provinces Are to Be Governed" and "How Princedoms Should Be Measured" and which was written in the sixteenth century to help Lorenzo de' Medici, the Florentine ruler and statesman, to consolidate and increase his political power. Parallels to Machiavelli's book are found today in best-selling business and political titles.

The expectation of the reader of a how to book is that such a book may make a difference in what the reader is able to do after reading it that was not doable before. The reader hopes for a practical, positive difference in the experience of life. I read a book, *Eat, Think and Be Slender,* that helped me one summer when I was nineteen and very overweight to lose fifty pounds in ten weeks. Another summer, at age thirty-three, three books aided me to stop smoking two packs of cigarettes a day. (Especially helpful during the worst times of temptation to abandon the struggle to stop smoking were pictures of the diseased lungs of people who had died from emphysema. These pictures gave me the grit to avoid smoking that "just one" cigarette that would have broken my will.) Those how-to books are among the most beneficial ones I have ever read, although devoid of any appeal factor for fiction and not gracefully written. Were they "true"? That is not remotely relevant, because they did the job for me and that was the entire point. Would they work for everyone or even have worked for me at other times in my life? No. But having access to them when they would work was invaluable to my health and I remain in their debt.

Once again I draw a conclusion without further elaboration: although Burgin is absolutely correct that the appeal factors of fiction are applicable to much nonfiction, the factors already identified do not exhaust the list of factors in nonfiction that appeal widely to readers. In addition to informational and advice books, there are books that deal with the Mysteries, meanings, beliefs, and other matters.

Appeal Factors on Planet Bookscape

Since we have only recently discovered the Planet Bookscape, let us orient ourselves to some of the main features of this former Terra Incognita. Because it is yet to be explored and mapped, only some of its features are described here. We have already seen that it has two magnetic poles, Wonderland and the Lab. These poles are sources of attraction on the planet. Near the Wonderland pole we find places visited by Alice and Gulliver; there is an institution of learning called Hogwarts and a horrifying Inferno, which was depicted in excruciating detail by Dante. In the same hemisphere, flying saucers are real and séances are successful. Alchemy and necromancy flourish; the Loch Ness monster and Frankenstein's monster roam freely. Politicians usually live in this part of the planet and frequently orate to all who will listen. Moving closer to the Equator, we come upon realistic fiction, and right on the Equator itself there is an island occupied by Robinson Crusoe, an imaginary character, engaged in entirely utilitarian activity. On the opposite pole, we find physicists and chemists testing assumptions and verifying facts. There we find mathematics textbooks and grammars, reference works, and gardening primers. Critics live close to the Lab. They challenge anyone who cannot document assertions. At various latitudes of the Lab hemisphere are found territories with autobiographies, advice, interpretation, and belief. As we approach the Lab pole, style counts for less; at the Wonderland pole, style is nearly everything.

To gain a deeper understanding of how books appeal to readers on the Planet Bookscape, it is important to note that the appeal of substance and the appeal of style are mixed confusingly together in the list of Character, Story Line, Pacing, Setting, and Language: (1) *what* the book treats (Character, Story Line, and Setting) has a different nature than (2) *how* the author treats it (Pacing and Language). That distinction is fundamental. When I read books to help me stop smoking, stylistic elements such as Pacing and Language, were of no concern. On the other hand, when I read *The Prince,* I enjoyed it in large part because of Machiavelli's remarkable conciseness, point of view, and style; I had no interest in ruling a republic, much less one in sixteenth-century Italy, and I loathe his brand of advice; it pollutes humanity's hopes for civility. In any case, my curiosity about the meaning of Machiavellian uses of power had been aroused, and only reading his book could fully satisfy my curiosity.

Subjects that appeal in books, with examples of popular nonfiction books that exemplify them, are as follows:

- Character (Dave Pelzer's *A Child Called "It": One Child's Courage to Survive*)

- Story Line (Daniel J. Boorstin's *The Discoverers; A History of Man's Search to Know His World and Himself*)

- Setting (Jonathan Raban's *Passage to Juneau; A Sea and Its Meaning*)

- Advice (John Gray's *Men Are from Mars, Women Are from Venus: A Practical Guide to Improving Communications and Getting What You Want in Relationships*)

- Scientific Nature of Things (Carl Sagan's *Cosmos*)

- Belief (Dalai Lama and Howard C. Cutler's *The Art of Happiness*)

- Human Behavior (Barbara Ehrenreich's *Nickel and Dimed*)

- Interpretation (Thomas Friedman's *The Lexus and the Olive Tree*)

- Beauty (Thad Carhart's *The Piano Shop on the Left Bank; Discovering a Forgotten Passion in a Paris Atelier*)

- Theory (Thor Heyerdahl's *Kon-Tiki*)

Stylistic factors that appeal in books include the following:

- Pacing (David G. McCullough's *The Johnstown Flood*)

- Skilled Use of Language (Tracy Kidder's *House*)

- Humor (Frank B. Gilbreth and Ernestine Gilbreth Carey's *Cheaper by the Dozen*)

- Illustration, through examples, problems, tables, pictures, and so on (Edward R. Tufte's *Envisioning Information*)

- Emotional Appeal (Helene Hanff's *84 Charring Street Road*)

- Invocation of Curiosity (Michael Paterniti's *Driving Mr. Albert*)

- Readability (All of the Above)

These subjects and stylistic factors may not exhaust all the sources of appeal of books for readers, but they do provide a much fuller picture of the complex ways that authors appeal to readers on Planet Bookscape. In every case, examples of both fiction and nonfiction books that exhibit these appeal factors may be produced. In fact, most books that meet with a large audience exhibit multiple appeal factors. Some factors, such as theory and the scientific nature of things, are more likely to be associated with the appeal of nonfiction. (But, when searching through the list of appeal factors with respect to the novels of Ayn Rand, *The Fountainhead* and *Atlas Shrugged,* I conclude that Rand's novels, proselytizing as they do for unfettered capitalism, appeal to many readers on the basis of Theory.) The Skilled Use of Language is more likely to be associated with the appeal of fiction, but works among my all time favorites, Henry David Thoreau's *Walden; or Life in the Woods* and Tracy Kidder's *House,* among innumerable works of nonfiction, are greatly enhanced because of their authors' Skilled Use of Language. (In Kidder's case, the structure of the book and the crafting of the sentences beautifully reflect the care used by the architect and builders of the house.) Humor is the factor that appealed so much to Burgin in his discussion of Bill Bryson's *Notes form a Small Island,* but it is equally welcomed by most readers of fiction.

Authors who appeal to a wide readership recognize what makes readers read. C. W. Ceram, in his classic account of archaeology, *Gods, Graves and Scholars; the Story of Archaeology*, exemplifies his sure sense of what makes readers tick, writing in his foreword:

> Archaeology, I found, comprehended all manner of excitement and achievement. Adventure is coupled with bookish toil. Romantic excursions go hand in hand with scholarly self-discipline and moderation. Explorations among the ruins of the remote past have carried curious men all over the face of the earth. Yet this whole stirring history, I discovered, was buried in technical publications that, however great their informative value, were never written to be read. I also learned that not more than three or four attempts have ever been made to bring this dramatic story to light. Yet in truth no science is more adventurous than archaeology, if adventure is thought of as a mixture of thought and deed. (Ceram 1952, v)

C. W. Ceram introduced me to a lifelong interest in Mayan civilization. It was the reason that I visited the splendid architectural and artistic triumphs of pre-Columbian Mexico at Chichen Itza, the single most exciting travel experience of my life. His book, which I read more than thirty years before the trip, still resonated—not in particulars, but in the feeling of what an awesome thrill it must have been to come upon these marvels in the jungles of the Yucatan. In the early morning, before the crowds arrive, you can still imagine some of what it must have been like for John Lloyd Stephens and James Catherwood to uncover these magnificent ruins.

You may recall that the first book that I read with excitement was *Lassie Come Home.* It took my mind away from the distractions of the heat of August and the fact that my close friend, Alan, was away at camp. Alan remains a very close friend and was the best man at my wedding. Even though he became a publisher and I became a professor and even though we settled in different parts of the country, we have always stayed in touch. We see more of each other now that we are both retired. Alan is one of the few people who have told me that they read only nonfiction. I e-mailed him recently and asked why. He said in reply, "My greatest satisfaction in reading comes when I feel that I have learned something new. That's why I am reluctant to read fiction. Call me crazy. If a book happens to be written in a lively and engaging way, so much the better, but for me the main attraction has to be that I am learning things of significance to my understanding of the world around me. For occasional light reading, there is always the *New Yorker*." If we look at the list of appeal factors, it is clear that Alan places a very high value on the Scientific Nature of Things. He is also fond of other informative categories, including Story Line, in the form of history, and Character, in the form of biography. Note that Alan favors informational nonfiction not so much for what Burgin calls meeting "specific information needs" (Burgin 2001, 213) but rather because, Alan, like many nonfiction readers, follows a more generalized reading pattern: book after book after book, constantly learning new things, neither job-related nor school-related, but preferring to use discretionary time to learn more. Of course, an author's "lively and engaging" way of writing makes his experience more attractive.

A book that I recently loved reading is Thad Carhart's *The Piano Shop on the Left Bank; Discovering a Forgotten Passion in a Paris Atelier*. It exhibits a majority of the appeal factors that we have identified. Carhart tells a story of an American in Paris who leaves his corporate job and takes up writing in a serious way. He writes warmly of meeting an enterprising craftsman, a philosophical Frenchman, who refurbishes used pianos and who, during the course of the book, becomes his good friend. Carhart's love of music, pianos, and life, as well as his feeling for the serendipitous magical moments in life, are all skillfully made palpable in one of my favorite books in the past decade. I especially relished his discussion of the different piano teachers he had studied with, partly because I am taking piano lessons and partly because I have taught most of my professional life. The student's point of view and relationship to the teacher intrigue me.

My enthusiasm while reading *The Piano Shop on the Left Bank* spurred my wife, Ann, who usually prefers fiction, to ask me to give it to her when I finished reading. She, too, became completely enamored. I questioned her about what appealed so much to her about it. Ann said, with a smile on her face in recollection of the reading experience, "What appealed was the wonderful integration of the author's personal story and friendship with Luc with his reflections on French manners and customs, and the history of the piano and more broadly music-making in general. It is all so beautifully written!"

Well, I had around that time been looking for a small token gift to give Alan for having us to his home recently and had wondered whether Carhart's book would strike the right note. Alan does love classical music, and that gave me hope that it would please him. I gained confidence that it would make a suitable present because Ann also loved it, even though she and I often diverge on books we prefer. It seemed more likely that Alan would like it too, since it appealed over a spectrum of tastes.

When Alan finished reading it, he e-mailed me saying, "By the way, I finished the book on the piano; it was so very enjoyable. I hoped it would go on and on; each chapter was a delight. I know I learned a lot about pianos, pianists, and how to listen to piano music." In a later message, he added, "I just heard a plug for Fazioli pianos on WQXR, and thanks to that nice book, I know what they are." Alan resides in the Lab hemisphere of Planet Bookscape; although she takes vacations, Ann's permanent residence is in the Wonderland hemisphere of Planet Bookscape. A wanderer, I have been known to winter near the Lab and then, gratefully, summer near Wonderland.

Just as I am certain of the fact that Ann, Alan, and I all enjoyed *The Piano Shop on the Left Bank,* I am also sure that our reading experiences were different. The factors that appealed to me in that book are not exactly the same ones that appealed to Ann or Alan. It is as if we stood on the same mountain and one luxuriated in the beautiful day, one studied the splendid geology, and one enjoyed the magnificent view.

And that is the moral of this tale.

References

Abbot, Edwin A. 1952. *Flatland: A romance of many dimensions.* New York: Dover.

Berne, Eric. 1977. *What do you say after you say hello: The psychology of human destiny.* New York: Grove Press.

Burgin, Robert. 2001. Readers' advisory and nonfiction. In *The readers' advisor's companion.* Edited by Kenneth D. Shearer and Robert Burgin, 213–27. Englewood, CO: Libraries Unlimited.

Cambor, Kathleen. 2001. *In sunlight in a beautiful garden.* New York: Farrar, Straus and Giroux.

Capote, Truman. 1965. *In cold blood.* New York: Random House.

Ceram, C. W. 1952. *Gods, graves and scholars: The story of archaeology.* New York: Knopf.

Mayle, Peter. 1990. *A year in Provence.* New York: Knopf.

McEwan, Ian. 2001. *Atonement.* New York: Nan Talese/Doubleday.

Michener, James. 1989. *Caribbean.* New York: Random House.

Paterniti, Michael. 2000. *Driving Mr. Albert: A trip across America with Einstein's brain.* New York: Dial Press.

Saint Louis, Catherine. 2003. What they were thinking. *New York Times Magazine* (March 30, 2003): 20.

Stone, Irving. 1980. *The origin: A biographical novel of Charles Darwin.* New York: Doubleday.

Chapter 5

Hearing and Seeing: The Case for Audiovisual Materials

Michael Vollmar-Grone

Film and television, newspapers, books and radio together have an influence over individuals that was unimagined a hundred years ago. This power confers great responsibility on all who work in the media . . . [as well as] each of us who, as individuals, listen and read and watch.

Bstan dzin rgya mtsho, Dalai Lama XIV 1999, 210

Introduction

Witnessing an event has a power beyond measure, as historically evidenced by the quotation attributed to Confucius, "One seeing is worth one thousand tellings" (modernized to "A picture is worth a thousand words") . Although there is power in the printed word, the "You Are There" experience differs greatly from reading a writer's interpretation. Granted, there are filters in the recording process, such as the videographer's choice of angles, lenses, or focal points, but seeing and hearing an event entrenches the viewer firmly within the experience.

The current generation has always had access to cable television and immediate satellite transmissions. The preceding generation grew up with broadcast television and live coverage, and an earlier generation was amazed by the instantaneous nature of radio transmissions.

Imagine their feelings when the voice of the president of the United States was heard simultaneously throughout the country. President Warren Gamaliel Harding addressed the nation periodically after taking office in 1921. Coverage of the 1920 election was the first broadcast, although only to the Pittsburgh community on station KDKA and in Michigan over the Detroit News' amateur station 8MK. But the new president used the new media effectively. In fact, on November 5, 1921, Harding was heard on every continent when his speech inaugurated the use of a new high-power RCA transmitter (Moore 1992).

All prior generations experienced mass communications on a severely time-delayed basis and as seen primarily through the eyes of writers, not subject to the personal interpretation available through recorded moving visual images and sounds. Then, breaking news did not reach the majority of the population for weeks or even months. For instance, the Battle of New Orleans continued for two weeks after the War of 1812 had ended. How many deaths and injuries could have been averted if only they had known?

Fast-forward to today and the recent generations, who have grown up immersed in mass media that capture man's triumphs and tragedies, follies, and foibles, watching history as it happens and watching the events surrounding it unfold, able to be endlessly played and replayed. Randy Pitman (2001) reports on a customer who once requested a copy of Dr. Martin Luther King Jr.'s historic "I Have a Dream" speech. When presented with the text, the customer rejected the printed version as he wanted primary source material, which is an audio or video recording of the speech as it was presented.

Besides the power to capture history, audio and video media can bring to life those creative works that by their very nature are intended to be seen or heard rather than read. *Beowulf,* acknowledged as the oldest narrative in any modern European tongue, was carried for generations only through oral tradition. Shakespeare wrote on the page for the stage, but his beautiful works are far more accessible when performed by those who can interpret the vernacular.

A Few Caveats

Preferring to keep this a positive meditation, the *non*'s will be abolished for the duration of the chapter. Since the librarian's ubiquitous term "nonprint material" can be literally defined as anything that is not printed (say, a rock or a petunia or Aunt Shirley's bouncing baby boy Bob), the term "audiovisual material" will be used instead. Similarly, since "nonfiction" is anything that is not fiction, that term, too, will be considered a misnomer, and instead, the term "informational materials" will be substituted. For the purposes of this examination, then, the term "nonfiction nonprint item" will be abandoned for "informational audiovisual materials."

So let the journey using "informational audiovisual materials" begin. Along this path, a better mind frame for librarians will be to view themselves as guides, or docents, rather than Bawana Dons busting the trail to information retrieval. That is the challenge of the readers' advisor, or in this case the audiovisual advisor, to show the delights of the trail on a pleasant saunter rather than blindly forging ever onward toward a defined destination of acquired information. The tourists will be exposed to myriad diversions with able librarians assisting their explorations.

But before this journey of discovery commences, a few steps back into the history of libraries will give an appreciation for the path underfoot and those trails hidden throughout the jungle.

Historical Use of Informational Audiovisual Materials

The history of audiovisual materials in public libraries has a long but supportive role. Evidence of the use of audiovisual materials can be traced back nearly one hundred years, when early films were shown in library auditoriums. Some progressive librarians embraced the format. Patrick Williams, in his book *The American Public Library and the Problem of Purpose,* excerpts American Library Association president Hiller C. Wellman's 1915 conference speech:

Photographs and prints of all kinds, music rolls, scores, lantern slides, phonograph records . . . stereoscopes, radiopticons, and lanterns...are often supplied. Concert giving by libraries with victrolas is becoming not unusual; and now we are introducing moving picture shows. (Williams 1988, 32)

Over the years, public libraries adopted new formats as they became ubiquitous rather than as emerging technologies and then discarded those formats as they fell from popular use. The past two decades have witnessed the removal of Beta videotapes and vinyl recordings while the new alphabet soup of formats, including CDs and DVDs, has been added and touted as the new panacea for storage and retrieval. However, futurists are predicting within a few short years the demise of the disc technology and the transfer to chip technology. PCMCIA cards (similar to those used in laptops) will replace the discs as chip technology increases its storage and rate transfer capacity.

One thing is certain: formats will continue to change. What does not change is the basic desire for information. So the issue ought not be specific formats; rather, the issue is what format delivers information most effectively for a particular person and need. Librarians bring their expertise, motivation, and support to achieve excellence in the delivery of service and materials. The mission remains the same while specific formats are merely tools.

Reasons Audiovisual Materials Are Not Fully Utilized

Too often, librarians do not refer customers to audiovisual materials for three specific reasons:

1. Unfamiliarity with formats

2. The lack of reference sources for informational audiovisual materials

3. The difficulty of accessing information in linear formats such as tape

Unfamiliarity with Formats

Unfamiliarity with formats includes little or no exposure before, during, or after library school. Library schools continue to virtually ignore the audiovisual formats. There has also been criticism expressed regarding library schools not being known for their expertise in training future librarians in book advisory services. Combining the two difficulties makes for dismal prospects for training in audiovisual advisory services. Public libraries tend to be the bastions of print centricity where items not read are looked on as the out-of-favor stepchild, good for the hard work of attracting the masses as dangling carrots rather than for their own powers of information transmission.

Lack of Reference Sources

The lack of reference sources for audiovisual materials is a problem identified by Randy Pitman (2001). Fortunately, Pitman is helping fill the video niche with his magazine, *Video Librarian,* and its companion Web site (URL: http://www.videolibrarian.com/ [Accessed July 18, 2003]), while Robin F. Whitten offers audiobook news and reviews with the *AudioFile Magazine* and Web site (URL: http://www.audiofilemagazine. com/ [Accessed July 18, 2003]). Still, the industry standards devote little space to the audiovisual spectrum, although some information can be gleaned by regular reading.

Pitman recommends using other libraries' catalogs that are hopefully "fully cataloged and—optimally—searchable by subject keyword and format simultaneously" (Pitman 2001, 235). Additionally, libraries such as those at the University of California at Berkeley and Indiana University feature some outstanding Web pages devoted to AV materials. Gary Handman maintains the UCB Media Resources Center pages (http://www.lib.berkeley.edu/MRC/ [Accessed July 18, 2003]) and is the moderator of VideoLib listserv (http://www.lib.berkeley.edu/VideoLib/ [Accessed July 18, 2003]), a very active list with highly knowledgeable members.

A list of recommended resources is included at the end of this chapter.

Difficulty of Accessing Information in Linear Formats

Information can be difficult to isolate in tape format. Fortunately, disk and digital technologies, such as compact disc and DVD, provide nearly instant access to portions of a work. That overcomes this limitation, if the material is well produced. Songs, speeches, and specific scenes can be quickly and easily found.

So why should anyone care whether people use audio/visual formats?

Media Literacy

The development of curricula in media and visual literacy will not only sharpen people's ability to decipher their world, but it will also contribute to a broadening of the public sphere. Literacy is never just

> about reading; it is also about writing. Just as early campaigns for universal print literacy were concerned with democratizing the tools of public expression, the written word, upcoming struggles for media literacy must strive to empower people with contemporary implements of public discourse: video, graphic arts, photography, interactive digital media. (Ewen 1996, 413)

Educators involved with media literacy have calculated that by the time a person has finished high school, she or he will have spent about 11,000 hours in school, watched 15,000 hours of television, and listened to about 10,500 hours of popular music. Additionally, people communicate through reading and writing only about 15 percent of the time. Therefore, it logically follows that people ought to be informed consumers and knowledgeable transmitters of audio and visual information.

Gary Ferrington defines the concepts involved ("What Is Media Literacy?" URL: http://interact.uoregon.edu/MediaLit/mlr/readings/articles/whatisml.html [Accessed May 11, 2003]) as follows:

> A media literate person is not only an informed consumer of information, but is also one who is able to communicate using pencil, paper, computer, camera, and audio and video recorder. Being able to communicate in a variety of media should be as natural as it once was to communicate with words alone. The concept of traditional literacy has expanded to include not only text, but pictures and sounds.

Media literacy as an area of educational practice began with the film, television, and visual communications movement in the 1970s, during which educators recognized that audiovisual media employed unique visual and aural language frameworks to encoded information. The ability to read the subtext of a motion picture, television program, advertisement, or photograph, for example, became important components in an expanding definition of literacy.

Ernest L Boyer, president of the Carnegie Foundation for the Advancement of Teaching, advocated media education in the 1980s ("Media Literacy Quotes." URL: http://www.med.sc.edu:1081/Media_Lit_Quotes.html [Accessed July 30, 2003]).

> It is no longer enough simply to read and write. Students must also become literate in the understanding of visual images. Our children must learn how to spot a stereotype, isolate a social cliché, and distinguish facts from propaganda, analysis from banter, and important news from coverage.

According to Robert Kubey, "Literacy is the ability to access, analyze, evaluate and communicate messages in a variety of forms" (Kubey 1996, 166). He defines "access" as the ability to locate, organize, and retain information; "analyze" as the ability to make use of categories, concepts, and ideas; and "evaluate" as requiring a prior knowledge to interpret work, reach logical conclusions, and appreciate the aesthetic qualities of work. Communication occurs through writing and speaking, among other forms. In addition, these skills are currently broader because of the development of additional forms of media.

But Kubey believes several factors hinder the use of video, specifically in education. Television's ubiquitous presence in American homes reinforces its status as an entertainer rather than an information provider. He also argues that many teachers believe that the visual arts are unnecessary, perhaps even redundant, and distracting from core curricular elements related to reading and language arts.

However, many educators agree that people learn using varying degrees of seeing, hearing, and touching. The Bradford College Web site, among others, provides general information about learning styles ("Action Learning for Lifelong Professional Development." URL: http://www.bilk.ac.uk/college/research/allpd/TMP1001493393.htm#accelerated [Accessed July 31, 2003]). The KiteCD education resource Web site offers additional information concerning learning styles ("Learning Styles." URL: http://members.aol.com/KiteCD2/artcl_learnstyl.htm [Accessed July 31, 2003]). These educational resource sites indicate that the three broad categories of learning styles are auditory, visual, and tactile/kinesthetic. Most people tend to be visual learners. Visual learning occurs through reading, viewing pictures and slides, looking at graphs and charts, and other methods involving the sense of sight. By contrast, auditory learners understand best when they hear new things. Listening to the tape of a famous speech; singing songs about a subject; and choral reading are some of their preferred methods. Finally, a person who is a tactile/kinesthetic learner relies on body movement or touching to help assimilate information. Clapping out rhythms, creating a model, and feeling actual artifacts are a few methods such individuals use to learn.

Each individual has her or his own favored method of learning and will favor that method when confronted with anything new. But people can learn using any and all methods. Many educators believe that using all three learning styles to teach a subject is the most effective way to help people learn.

Because each person is most successful when material is presented in her or his own favored style, it is important for anyone giving instructions to use the student's style. But it is also important for individuals to be able to learn and conceptualize ideas presented in a style that is different from their favored one. By presenting new information in methods from all three learning styles, an instructor provides the student with the information in the student's most successful method of learning. In addition, the teacher gives the student the opportunity to experience the same information in a new way. This assists the person in expanding his or her learning strategies to become more successful lifelong learners.

Thus, by offering audiovisual materials and printed materials, librarians are more fully able to meet all people's needs.

Goals and Techniques of the Readers', Viewers', and Listeners' Advisor

For this discussion, and ideally all of the time, the term "readers' advisor" also refers to those who perform viewers' advisory and listeners' advisory services. The goals are the same, as are most of the techniques. Basically, advisors are helping people find what interests them, fulfilling the definition of "What's a good book, a good video, or a good audiobook?"

Ultimately, the goal is to match the customer with the materials that fulfill his or her needs or wants. This is accomplished essentially in conversation with the customer, trying to determine what the needs or wants may be. There may not be right and wrong answers. Subjective judgments are often necessary. For instance, although Bill Bryson's humorous *A Walk in the Woods* has subject headings such as "Natural History, Appalachian Trail" and "Appalachian Trail, Description and Travel," it may not be appropriate, and certainly will not be particularly helpful, for someone who simply wants a factual backpacking travel guide to the Appalachian Trail.

The standard opening question for those specializing in audio and video materials remains, "Please tell me about a video or audiobook that you enjoyed." That simple inquiry can open conversations that may reveal memorable experiences. Sometimes articulation triggers realization and understanding and so helps both the librarian and the customer.

General Guidelines for Working with Readers, Listeners, and Viewers

With that end in mind, it is easy to understand why an advisor functions more as a consultant rather than as an information provider. In this role, an advisor is able to establish an open and welcoming climate. When people feel comfortable, they reveal more, which helps to elicit information concerning their reading, viewing, and listening interests. Using open-ended questions further reveals their leisure pursuits. While hearing what the customer is saying, active listening skills are of crucial importance. By paraphrasing the customer's answers, the advisor can know the right path is being pursued.

The level of enthusiasm brought by the advisor cannot be understated. Being excited about the materials and processes helps reinforce their importance to the customer and so validates the quest. But with that enthusiasm comes the danger of value judgments, which, if in opposition to the customer, will surely close the discussion. So it is of paramount importance that advisors do not guide the discussion in the direction of personal interests and values in trying to find those materials that fit the customer's interests and values.

So how are materials of interest found? By being format literate, advisors may more closely match customers' wants and do so with a better choice of materials. Advisors can look for works on a particular topic or works by specific writers, producers, directors, or even by narrators. Genres may be searched. Movies are often grouped into broad categories such as documentary, how-to, and travel. Audiobooks, too, reflect their literary genres such as biography, history and self-help. Links may be sought between people or works to additional works that a customer finds entertaining.

Advisors help people understand what they are seeking. Sometimes people do not know why they enjoyed a particular work. By using open-ended questions, advisors can discover how a work may be of interest. For instance, the question "What did you like about Michael Moore's documentary *Roger and Me*?" might reveal the specific appealing characteristics such as the dogged pursuit of "fat cat" industrialists, the comical overstatements, or the quirky characters. This conversation may also disclose whether the serious subject of gun control seen through Moore's particular blend of humor and outrage in *Bowling for Columbine* might be of interest.

Does the previously mentioned Bryson audiobook appeals to the interests of hikers, travelers, and armchair tourists? Is it a compelling story line? Are the characters interesting? If so, then the listener may also enjoy his Australian excursion, *In a Sunburned Country,* which Bryson reads. But if the compelling factors were William Roberts's narration or the uniquely American setting of *A Walk in the Woods,* then the second title would not fulfill those expectations. But once those factors are identified, the customer is on the road to discovering other works for reasons she or he may not have previously been able to articulate. In short, by determining what aspect of a work excited the customer, the advisor can find similar works.

Knowledge Areas

Advisors need to be familiar with the current culture. At one time, only highbrow literature, the classics, were considered worth reading. Traditionally, public libraries embraced high culture rather than middle or low culture. Fortunately in today's society, there is room for all, especially in those institutions that find value in serving the public tastes and sensibilities.

Staying current with new releases helps identify emerging trends including new series, promising authors, insightful documentarians, and versatile narrators, among others. Trade publications such as *Library Journal* and specialty magazines such as *AudioFile* and *Video Librarian* are valuable resources. Vendor brochures are sure to highlight popular and emerging materials.

Additionally, materials at varying levels can be enjoyed. Just because an item is identified as Young Adult should not preclude its use by adults. Even within the so-called adult materials, there is a variety of difficulty levels. While some titles may be better suited for relaxation, others challenge our minds and experiences. A breezy travelogue may well be a better choice for a long drive where concentration is better reserved for the road and surroundings. An involved and intricate world history is undoubtedly better reserved for listening in the safety and more tranquil setting of home.

Other Format Considerations

Experiences can be more powerful when seen or heard than when read on the printed page. All can be accessed by anyone. The only limiting factor is the depth of understanding of an experience. Literacy is not necessary. That has both positive and negative aspects. Sexuality, violence, and profanity can have greater impact on the senses when viewed or heard rather than read. Hearing and seeing Dr. Martin Luther King deliver his "I Have a Dream" speech can stir physical and emotional reactions.

Only books are books. The relationship experienced between a person and a work is discernibly different in different formats. Movies are rarely the verbatim book. Emphasis may be placed on different elements and aspects that translate better in that format. Errol Morris's filmed version of Stephen Hawking's *A Brief History of Time* effectively utilizes moving imagery and sound to tell the story that static illustrations cannot. An audiobook narrator brings the extra dimension of interpretation and performance not present in just the reader-writer-editor relationship of printed books.

Audiobooks are often available in both abridged and unabridged versions. It has been reported anecdotally that some unabridged fans vehemently defend and insist on only the whole and complete book. Abridgement fans tend to enjoy listening to a greater number of titles or getting to the core of the information more quickly. Presently, it is not uncommon for an author to approve the abridgement of his or her original work.

Conclusions

A librarian's role may be crucial in helping people use their precious leisure hours as respites in this hustle and bustle world. For some, the library can be an oasis in the dessert, a calm port from the threatening storm.

Clearly, three aspects are fundamental to our mission: how the customer is treated, how selection suggestions are made, and how the advisor uses his or her knowledge of materials and people.

All people ought to be treated with respect for individual tastes, interests, and abilities. One format or form of literature ought not be indiscriminately chosen over another. Talking about personal listening and viewing experiences will encourage others to do so.

Suggestions ought to be made according to the understanding of the customer's interests and desires. Encouraging people to share their experience with previous materials often enlightens future choices and provides insights into their preferences to help find additional materials. What can block finding new materials are assumptions about factors such as age, gender, race, ethnicity, and marital status. For instance, it is commonly held that men traditionally have preferred informational titles to works of fiction and that men are typically more visual by nature. By extension, the conclusion that videos are a natural fit for men's informational and format preferences might be reached. But the assumption ought not be universally applied. To do so would not serve the individual.

Format is a part of the search for materials. The printed page better conveys information about some topics, whereas others may be better suited to audio or visual formats. Another consideration is which format works best for the individual, whether he or she is an auditory, visual, or tactile/kinesthetic learner. Some prefer reading, others learn better through audiobooks, while others may gain more from videos.

Finally, how the advisor's knowledge is used to connect materials and people is critical. While having an intimate knowledge of every book, movie, and audiobook in the library and beyond is impossible, the advisor ought to have a sense of genres, topics, and formats as well as the tools to find what is available.

Each search by the customer is an individual search. Although a specific person may be intellectually able to devour any item presented, sometimes the desire is for relaxation rather than intellectual stimulation and challenge.

Despite what some Luddites may say, formats are not inherently bad. Listening or viewing can be as important, and in some situations more important, than reading or producing products. Videos are seen by some as a waste of time, time taken from productive activities. Others may view any entertainment as wasteful. Still others may conclude that anyone simply listening or viewing something is not engaged in profitable activity and is therefore idle and potentially worthless.

People ought to be free to use leisure time as their time, time that is gone forever once it is past. Americans are constitutionally entitled to "life, liberty, and the pursuit of happiness." Additionally, courts have found that Americans have the right to ask for and receive information from their public libraries.

In 1960, Charles Brightbill wrote in *The Challenge of Leisure:*

The future will belong not only to the educated man, but to the man who is educated to use leisure wisely. (Brightbill 1960, 14)

Irrespective of antiquated gender notions, that future is today. The mission of librarians everywhere ought to be helping anyone find library resources that will aid in their pursuit of knowledge, information, and enjoyment.

Recommended Resources

The Internet Movie Database (URL: http://us.imdb.com [Accessed July 18, 2003])
    The description of available video resources begins with this acknowledged treasure of a Web site, the Internet Movie Database. It is a wealth of free information about theatrical and documentary movies, television programs, and the people who created them. A caveat must be noted. Much of the information was furnished through online submissions. Although accuracy cannot be guaranteed, the site is a powerful tool.

    Searches can be conducted in a variety of methods including title, cast/crew, character, and plot outline. For instance, searching for documentarian Errol Morris finds his contributions listed separately under actor, director, writer, editor, producer, and even miscellaneous crew. Links to professional reviews are available for many of the titles.

The Video Librarian (URL: http://videolibrarian.com/ [Accessed July 18, 2003])

    Randy Pittman offers *Video Librarian* online as well as in a print version. Each month, the Web site offers a few free reviews. But paying subscription charges opens a whole world of wonders. "Video Librarian Plus!" features the printed version of *Video Librarian* magazine plus online access to more than 12,000 full text video reviews searchable by title, description, date, and star rating. Also included are a calendar of upcoming video releases, a searchable database of one thousand distributors, and expanded newsbriefs.

The University of California at Berkeley Media Resources Center (URL: http://www.lib.berkeley.edu/MRC [Accessed July 18, 2003])

    Features some very useful Web pages including "Video Reference Tools and Selection Aids: A Highly Selective List." Gary Handman, who is the moderator of the VideoLib listserv, maintains the pages. Another helpful page offers "The Great Desert Island" list of informational titles that was garnered from the collective suggestions of the VideoLib listserv participants. The listserv also features a searchable archive. To subscribe, send an e-mail message to http://www.lib.berkeley.edu/mailman/listinfo/videolib. In the message area, type the word SUBSCRIBE followed by your name. The subject area can remain blank. For more information, contact Gary Handman at ghandman@library.berkeley.edu.

Another highly useful Web site is the Indiana University Bloomington Libraries' Media Services Collection (URL: http://www.indiana.edu/~libsalc/film/www-resources.html. [Accessed September 9, 2003]). It is full of information and links to electronic journals and databases, film reviews, purchasing sources, film history, and film festivals.

Other Resources

    Critical reviews for both audio and video materials can be found in industry publications such as *Library Journal, School Library Journal,* and *Booklist.* Consumer-oriented reviews may be found in magazines such as *Billboard, Entertainment Weekly, Premiere,* and *Variety,* as well as newspapers. Local critics may be more tuned to the tastes of local customers than national columnists but are less likely to feature documentary or informational titles.

    AudioFile Magazine and its Web site (URL: http://www.audiofilemagazine.com/ [Accessed July 18, 2003]) are considered by some to be first and foremost among resources for audiobooks. The site features hundreds of free reviews and news about audiobooks. The subscription service, AudioFile PLUS, includes access to an archive of more than 12,500 audiobook reviews, six issues of the printed magazine, and the annual sourcebook, the "Audiobook Reference Guide." The archive can be searched by title, author, narrator, subject, ISBN, or keyword. The magazine confers the Earphone Award for the best audiobooks each month.

Publisher's Weekly, in print and Web site, offers best-seller lists and reviews of informational and fiction audiobooks (URL: http://publishersweekly.reviewsnews.com/ [Accessed July 18, 2003]).

A notable audiobook publisher is Recorded Books (URL: http://www.recordedbooks.com [Accessed July 18, 2003]). Unabridged recordings are the specialty.

The online media sellers also have very useful databases often complete with illustrations. Two of the larger are Amazon (URL: http://www.amazon.com/ [Accessed July 18, 2003]) and Barnes and Noble (URL: http://www.barnesandnoble.com/ [Accessed July 18, 2003]).

Library vendors offer Web sites packed with information. Ingram is at URL: http://www.ingrambookgroup.com/ (Accessed July 31, 2003) and Baker and Taylor at URL: http://www.btol.com/ (Access July 31, 2003).

References

Bradford College. Action learning for lifelong professional development. URL: http://www.bilk.ac.uk/college/research/allpd/TMP1001493393.htm#accelerated (Accessed July 31, 2003)

Brightbill, Charles K. 1960. *The challenge of leisure.* Englewood Cliffs, NJ: Prentice Hall.

Bstan dzin rgya mtsho, Dalai Lama XIV. 1999. *Ancient wisdom, modern world: Ethics for a new millennium.* London: Little, Brown.

Ferrington, Gary. What is media literacy? URL: http://interact. uoregon.edu/MediaLit/mlr/readings/articles/whatisml.html (Accessed May 11, 2003).

Ewen, Stuart. 1996. *PR: A social history of spin.* New York: Basic Books.

KiteCD. Learning styles. URL: http://members.aol.com/KiteCD2/artcl_learnstyl.htm (Accessed July 31, 2003).

Kubey, Robert. 1996. *Media literacy in the information age: Current perspectives.* New York: Transaction Press.

Moore, Don. 1992. The 1924 radio election. URL: http://www.swl.net/patepluma/genbroad/elec1924.html (Accessed August 11, 2003).

Pitman, Randy. 2001. Viewers' advisory: Handling audiovisual advisory questions. In *The readers' advisor's companion.* Edited by Kenneth D. Shearer and Robert Burgin, 229–36. Englewood, CO: Libraries Unlimited.

Williams, Patrick. 1988. *The American public library and the problem of purpose.* Westport, CT: Greenwood Publishing Group.

Part III

Nonfiction Readers

Introduction

Readers' advisory is, of course, ultimately concerned with providing a service to readers, and so the third part of this book focuses on nonfiction readers and what motivates them.

In Chapter 6, Catherine Ross examines interviews with almost two hundred adults who read for pleasure to determine the ways in which fiction and nonfiction readers are different and the ways in which they are similar. Ross finds that many of the individuals read both fiction and nonfiction for pleasure, that interest in a subject may breach the distinction between fiction and nonfiction, or that story is important for many nonfiction readers. She also finds interesting diffcrences; for example, individuals who read only nonfiction have a strong desire to read about what is "real" or to increase their knowledge, desires that (for them) can't be satisfied by fiction. Ross's findings are not only fascinating in their own right, but they support such key concepts for readers' advisory services as the importance of the interview, nonfiction appeal factors, and nonfiction genres.

Duncan Smith, creator of the readers' advisory tool Novelist, examines four nonfiction readers in depth in Chapter 7: a Pulitzer Prize–winning journalist; the current head of Duke's Graduate Program in Literature; an entrepreneur as he becomes a pilot; and a young graduate student coming to grip with the 1960s. Through these examples, Smith looks at the rich variety of ways in which stories (in this case, true stories) engage readers, the ways in which nonfiction readers (like fiction readers) can be renewed, transported, and fascinated.

The focus of Chapter 8 is nonfiction and young readers. Crystal Faris argues that nonfiction satisfies the curiosity of children and supports the brain development that takes place during the preteen years in particular. She also notes the importance of nonfiction reading for boys and suggests ways in which youth services librarians can promote nonfiction by reading nonfiction, staying current, knowing how to evaluate nonfiction titles, and marketing nonfiction. Her list of awards for nonfiction children's books will be particularly helpful to those working with children and teens.

Marcia Kochel devotes Chapter 9 to an examination of readers' advisory for nonfiction in the school library media center. Kochel, the co-editor of *Gotcha! Nonfiction Booktalks to Get Kids Excited about Reading* and *Gotcha Again! More Nonfiction Booktalks*, shows how nonfiction is often ignored by teachers, librarians, and even the publishing industry. She then argues that nonfiction is important for children, that there are many high-quality nonfiction titles for children, that children read nonfiction for pleasure, and that nonfiction reading increases student achievement. Kochel then lists ways in which school media librarians can promote nonfiction through collection development, booktalks, collaboration with teachers, and displays.

In Chapter 10, Alma Dawson and Connie Van Fleet look at providing nonfiction readers' advisory services to multicultural audiences. They note the popularity of nonfiction titles among people of color, pointing out that half of the *Quarterly Black Review*'s one hundred essential books for African Americans are nonfiction. They urge librarians to provide equitable advisory services through mission statements that include support for the needs of a diverse clientele and collection development policies that take into consideration the needs of diverse audiences. Dawson and Van Fleet then examine several threads in multicultural nonfiction, including social histories that emphasize the achievements of a particular culture, personal histories, and guidance or self-help titles. In each case, the authors show how multicultural nonfiction helps cultures understand themselves and understand one another.

The chapters in Part III of the book, like those in the previous parts, highlight the theme of expansion of readers' advisory services. Here, we expand our user base to include those who read, view, or listen to nonfiction and we begin to understand their particular needs. At the same time, the traditional readers' advisory methods—the reader's advisory interview, our knowledge of sources, or understanding of why people read or view or listen for pleasure—can help us meet those needs.

Chapter 6

Reading Nonfiction for Pleasure: What Motivates Readers?

Catherine Ross

A collection of articles such as this one on readers' advisory and non-fiction depends on a prior assumption that reading nonfiction is somehow different from reading fiction and therefore deserving of its own separate treatment. Of course, we know that *libraries* treat nonfiction differently from fiction, separating it physically from fiction on the shelves, subdividing it by topic, providing far more detailed cataloguing, and so forth. But what about readers? Do they distinguish between fiction and nonfiction? Do they experience the two kinds of reading very differently, for example, by turning to fiction when they want a pleasurable experience but choosing nonfiction when they want to find out facts about the real world? Are there special qualities about the nonfiction reading experience that attract readers? What is known about nonfiction readers' experiences with books that can be applied in the readers' advisory transaction? To find the answer to this question of the readers' experience, I have for some been engaged in a study of avid readers who read for pleasure. I have a transcribed set of 194 intensive, open-ended interviews with adult readers, undertaken as part of a larger study on reading for pleasure.

I interviewed 25 of the readers, and the other 169 readers were interviewed by graduate students enrolled in successive offerings of my course on Genres of Fiction and Reading in the Masters Program of Library and Information Science at the University of Western Ontario. As a course assignment, each student was asked to interview the keenest reader she or he could find. That is to say, the interviewed subjects were not randomly chosen but were deliberately selected as individuals who read a lot and read by choice. This study has been described elsewhere (Ross 1999). Briefly it can be said that the people chosen to be interviewed resembled the population of heavy readers in general in being more likely to be female, youngish, and well-educated: 65 percent were female and 35 percent were male. Interviewees ranged in age from 16 to 80, distributed as follows: age 16–20, 3.6 percent; age 21–30, 44.8 percent; age 31–40, 18 percent; age 41–50, 14 percent; age 51–60, 11.3 percent; age 60–80, 8.2 percent. The level of education was generally high, although the study included some readers, especially older readers, who had received little formal education.

One of the questions that interviewers asked was, "What would it be like for you if for one reason or another you *couldn't* read?" To be considered an appropriate subject for this study on avid readers, an interviewee couldn't say calmly, "Oh, well, I guess I would have to play cards more often or take up knitting." And in fact they didn't say that. A typical reaction was, "I can't imagine it." One person said, "I wouldn't be me. I wouldn't be the person I am if I didn't read or wasn't able to read.... It frightens me, so I don't even want to consider it as an option." When encouraged to say more about life without reading, interviewees said that life would be "empty," "boring," "an intellectual wasteland," "a prison"; not to be able to read would be "very terrible," "very upsetting," "awful," "catastrophic"; "it would be like not being able to see color." One person said, "My panic is to be in the house without anything to read. That makes me just absolutely, totally panic stricken. I can't live without reading. Blindness probably scares me more than anything."

The analysis presented in this paper focuses on what interviewees said about reading nonfiction for pleasure. Interviewees were not prompted with a specific question about nonfiction but rather were asked open-ended questions about their reading in general, such as the following:

How do you choose a book to read for pleasure?

Are there types of books that you do *not* enjoy and would not choose?

What are you currently reading?

Has there ever been a book that has made a big difference to your life in one way or another?

In discussing particular choices they made and books that they had enjoyed and found meaningful, many readers choose to talk about nonfiction. Of the themes that emerged from an analysis of the readers' talk about nonfiction, some are predictable, others more surprising.

1. Many readers read BOTH fiction and nonfiction for pleasure.

Some readers said that they *never* read nonfiction (too boring, too much like school or like their work-related reading) and some said that they read *only* nonfiction (fiction wasn't real enough). But a great many readers read both. They often have several books on the go and choose which one to read at any given time depending on their mood and the time available. Charles (age twenty-three, program coordinator) said that "for my purest of pleasure reading, I'm still reading science fiction and fantasy . . . but I am reading more nonfiction than I have in the past—politically oriented books. Books about current leaders, books about current issues, and most recently books focusing on social issues. . . . I'm finding that gaining that type of knowledge [about current issues] through books is pleasurable and enjoyable and fulfilling."

The distinction between reading nonfiction for information and reading fiction for pleasure was not supported in the readers' talk about their reading experience. Beryl (age forty-four, librarian) reported that she finds such distinctions "very hard to make": "I get a great deal of pleasure out of reading to inform myself, and yet I wouldn't say that's reading for amusement. Reading has a kind of connotation of escape for me anyway. I can't make the distinction at all. I think some of the most 'escapist' stuff ends up boring me because it doesn't involve me enough." Jane (age twenty-two, student) who "just like[s] to know things," said she browses in reference works with no particular topic in mind, just for enjoyment: "I like to go through reference sections and browse the dictionaries and other reference books. I like to find out things." Many nonfiction readers found the same satisfaction of good storytelling in biography, history, and travel books that novel readers found in novels. Marsha (age twenty-six, student) said she "always thought biographies were going to be factual, boring dull stuff, but I realized you can read them like a book, like a fiction book. They're a story."

2. An interest in a particular subject can trump the distinction between fiction and nonfiction.

Bookstore managers know this, and, for example, often put war fiction together in the same area as nonfiction treatments of war. Many readers said that they would become interested in some topic and then read everything they could on it. Andrew (age twenty-eight, graduate student) reported, "I'm just coming to the end of a period when I've been reading everything I could get on King Arthur—*The Once and Future King,* the Mary Stewart four volumes on Merlin and King Arthur, and *The Mists of Avalon,* which is very good. I had a real interest in the Celtic period in Britain from reading these things, and that led me to reading a little bit about the history of Celtic Britain. So it can jerk either way. The history can lead me into reading about Arthur, and then Arthur leads me back into the history."

Popular fictional genres that appeal to large groups of readers can be twinned with nonfiction that satisfies the same appeal. Hence fans of detective fiction may be interested in true crime; readers of Westerns may be attracted to historic accounts of the opening of the West and the frontier; horror readers may be attracted to nonfictional accounts of the occult. Goneril (age forty-three, sales/service representative) said, "I still like a good mystery and a little bit of horror. . . . The genre that I really liked for a while—I was hooked on—was the true stories, nonfiction. It's the murderer who kidnaps somebody and keeps them in a box—I guess I'm fascinated by the fact that are there really monsters out there, people that do that." Laurie (age thirty-four, student) said that she "loved *The Exorcist.* I read that about four times. I read nonfiction as well about the occult and truer stories about hauntings or demonic possessions."

3. Exclusive nonfiction readers say they want to read about things that are "real."

Some readers, especially young male readers, said that they wanted their reading to contribute to their total store of important knowledge and for that reason they avoided fiction. Judy (age fifty-one, homemaker) reported that she preferred nonfiction because, "I like the truth in my life." Neil (age twenty-six, chemical technician) recalled that when he was a child, he read science books on space and astronomy because "reading was a means to an end. I read for knowledge. I really liked knowing things." If he was going to do all the work of reading, there needed to be a payoff in terms of a significant addition to his store of knowledge: "To me a popular novel is just a harder-working version of TV. If I want to get enjoyment out of a popular novel, I can just watch TV and get the same enjoyment. . . . I enjoy getting something out of reading. I think that's what it is. I can never understand the people that say, 'Yeah, I read the book, but I can't remember it.' " Jeremy (age twenty, student) said that he reads nonfiction and avoids fiction because "it's fiction; I mean it's someone else's imagination. Like I have my own imagination, so I see no reason to read something that someone has thought up, if it's not factual. . . I just can't get into fiction—just the fact that this author may have thought this up. I just can't get into fiction. If it's not factual or reality, then I tend to tune out." Neil and Jeremy evidently think of nonfiction and fiction in hierarchical terms, with nonfiction, reality, and productive learning at the top of the reading ladder.

There were a number of other readers who, although not so dismissive of fiction as Neil and Jeremy, nevertheless strongly responded to the sense of "real life" that they got from nonfiction. Esther (age thirty-two, elementary teacher) reported that she reads historical fiction "along the *Shogun* line" and nonfiction books such as *The Ten Thousand Day War* about Vietnam or *The Forgotten Soldier* about the German soldiers of World War II or *A Man Called Intrepid* about Allied intelligence operations in World War II. She enjoyed these books because they contained "a lot of information," but she wouldn't read a mystery or fantasy book or western because "it doesn't add to what I know." Clarence (age sixty, self-employed) is primarily a reader of history and biography and pursued a series of interests: books about living in Alaska; books on American presidents; books on the American Civil War; Pierre Berton's books, *The National Dream* and *Klondike,* on the building of Canada's national railway and the Klondike gold rush respectively. For Clarence, a strong element in his enjoyment of these books is that "people existed that did those things" and so he enjoys learning about "real life history"—"you can know that they are real and that they actually happened."

4. Some readers reported that nonfiction was easier than fiction to read when you were likely to be interrupted.

Novels require the reader to enter a world and live there for a time, getting to know the characters and remembering their relationships to each other and the challenges they face. For this reason, readers said that you have to read fiction "in a long block of time," but many kinds of nonfiction could be picked up and put down. Rene (age thirty-two, physician) said that now that she is looking after small children, her reading is "so interrupted—I mean you can't concentrate on anything because you're having to stop every page or two. Now I find that I'm more likely to read a nonfiction thing that I'm reading bits of." Derek (age twenty-seven, student) said that he finds it "easier to read nonfiction than to read fiction." He has read a lot of nonfiction including "whole tons of stuff on Malaysia," a lot of books on Eastern religions, Paul Theroux's travel books, "a lot of books having to do with animals when I was working at the zoo" . . . "Fiction really depends on my mood, but nonfiction doesn't as much."

While readers value the prolonged experience of uninterrupted reading when they are immersed in the world of the book, they also value books such as letters, memoirs, cookbooks, and encyclopedias that can be dipped into and read a bit at a time, as magazines are read. Marsha said, "I'm reading *The Selected Journals of Lucy Maud Montgomery* and a book about the

Jesuits that I just started. These are the kinds of books that I'll read a little bit at a time over a year or something. I don't try and finish them right away." Trevor (age twenty-three, student) said that he had read many times William Shirer's *The Rise and Fall of the Third Reich* because it is "the sort of book that you could dip into at any place and just start reading, which is something I really like about books. Just pick it up, open to a random page, and start reading." Patricia (age forty-eight, teacher) said, "Currently I have very little time for leisure reading, but I read constantly. . . . I am quite a compulsive reader in that I will read anything. . . . If I ever have an idle moment, I usually have a magazine or something. I have two or three books on the go right now that I just kind of pick away at whenever I have an odd moment. One is a book by Faith Popcorn called *Clicking* about future trends in terms of marketing opportunities."

Readers who say they like nonfiction because they can read it a bit at a time were usually referring to those nonfiction books that are made up of smaller self-contained units, such as letters or cookbooks. In contrast, point 13 later in the chapter describes another kind of nonfiction that resembles novels in that they tell a story with a connected beginning, middle, and end that propels the reader through the book.

5. Some readers feel they "should" read nonfiction to increase their knowledge.

Perhaps it was because they were being interviewed about their reading and became self-conscious, but a number of readers said that they felt they "should" expand their reading tastes and read more nonfiction. But enjoyment is still key. They won't read it unless they enjoy it. Adam (age twenty-four, librarian) said that he read to expand his mind, but this self-betterment is a happy by-product of an activity that is pleasurable: "It's not like I sit down and go, 'Oh, I'm going to better my mind by reading this.' But that's the result. I think that when you devote a lot of time to reading anything, you're presented with a number of new ideas you'd never thought of before and those ideas help you in your life—in handling all kinds of human situations."

Guilt alone is not a sufficient inducement. Marsha (age twenty-seven, physiotherapist) confessed, "I really should try to read history books. . . I should try to read a wider variety of books to expand my knowledge. . . . But I feel that my reading is for pleasure and therefore I really don't get involved in areas that don't particularly appeal to me. For instance, I can't sit down and read a book on government policies in different countries, or how to get the most from your money. . . . I read for pleasure, not really to learn something, and so I read books that give me pleasure."

Similarly Anita (age twenty-five, student) said, "My latest thing is that I've decided that all I read is fiction, and I really only read fiction. So I started just in the past two years trying to read nonfiction stuff. My father and my oldest sister are both scientists and they read a lot of stuff like *The Dancing Wu Li Masters*. . . . It describes the history of recent physics, getting into the philosophical aspects. . . . I just kind of had this feeling of inadequacy that I wasn't reading the right things. . . I really think that I have to start reading something about history, and I really feel I should start reading nonfiction; you know, something historical because I feel there's a gap in my knowledge. But I can't read unless I enjoy it. I really can't force myself to read a book, no matter how much I think, 'I really should read this because it's good for me.' If I'm not enjoying it, I just can't do it."

6. Readers distinguish between two types of reading: reading for pleasure and reading to take something away.

Sally (age forty, library assistant), who admitted that her nonfiction reading is "almost none," said, "I feel a bit guilty about that. I have a hard time getting meanings out of nonfiction. It doesn't seem to speak to me. I just don't deal with it very well. If there comes a point in my life where I have to know something—my grass is dying—well, I'll go and get a book on grass and I'll read what is absolutely essential for the moment. . . . But I don't consider that recreational reading." That is, some reading is like prospecting, where the reader is looking for some nugget to take away, and the faster the nugget can be found and the book closed, the better. This type of reading can be contrasted with what Sally refers to as "recreational reading," where the experience of reading itself is the goal.

In her book, *The Reader, the Text, the Poem* (1978), Louise Rosenblatt, distinguishes between these two kinds of reading, calling the former "efferent reading" and the latter "aesthetic reading." She argues that readers bring to their reading not only prior knowledge but also particular dispositions about how they read texts. Readers can choose to see the text as primarily "referential," in which case they take an efferent stance (from the Latin *effere* to carry away). Efferent readers read to find some particular information or fact that they can transfer from the reading situation and use in their everyday lives. Or readers can choose to see the text as primarily "poetic," in which case they take an aesthetic stance. In aesthetic reading, the important thing is not the message that can be extracted but the reader's lived-through and immediate experience of encountering the text. Ivor (age twenty-six, graduate student) makes a similar distinction when he contrasts voluntary reading with required reading: "I give more attention to things that I don't have to read—that I've chosen to read. I think it's because in novels or in history I'm really looking for a sort of wholeness—I want to get everything out of them. But reading for a job or for school, basically what you're looking for is what you can use."

7. The stance taken by the reader is not determined by the text.

Sally doesn't consider a book on grass to be recreational reading, but the same book that one person reads "efferently" could be recreational reading for someone else. Library classification depends on the assumption that certain basic differences inhere in the texts themselves and that these differences map on to how people actually use the books. Hence we distinguish between books intended to be read straight through, such as novels and biographies, and books intended to be consulted, such as encyclopedias, manuals, and atlases.

However, many readers described how, especially in childhood, they read encyclopedias and other reference books for pleasure. Larry (age twenty-four, student) reported that he "can sit down and be thoroughly entertained reading an atlas or a dictionary." Maurice (age fifty-seven, professional engineer) recalled that when he was eight or nine, he "got involved in reading for information" and read a twenty-volume home encyclopedia for children called *The New Book of Knowledge:* "I used to read that like a novel, from cover to cover. I would start at Pig and read everything in the P's. . . . And I used to read chemistry books like novels. I'd pick them up and read from page one to the end. . . . Everything I read was brand new information." Similarly Robert (age fifty-seven, professor of English) said that the most important book for him growing up was *The World Book:* "I lived in that encyclopedia . . . It's absolutely critical in the development of my reading. I'd look up something under P and I'd read it and then keep reading one thing after another. . . . An encyclopedia is another form of the epic, of course; it's how you think of all knowledge in relation to a total containing form." Stephen (age forty-eight, professor of English) recalled his elementary school experience in a one-room school, where he was free to read from *The New Book of Knowledge* when he had finished his assignments: "I think I went through every one of those twenty volumes. It had a lot of pictures, and I read the captions under the pictures and a fair number of the articles. I would take a volume that I hadn't gone through recently, and go through it again. First page to last page. The things I remember about it were largely about history and geography. It had marvelous maps and a lot of things about European royalty and Napoleonic Wars and so on."

When readers take the "aesthetic" stance to a nonfiction book, they are more likely to report taking pleasure in its literary qualities and resources of language. Edward (age fifty-four, military historian) declared, "history in itself is a literary form, a fine literary form . . . and I read history as literature . . . I recently reread R. H. Tawney's *Religion and the Rise of Capitalism,* which was one of the really important books I read at University and one of the ones that really formed my thinking and my outlook towards life. I read one page and suddenly realized that I was reading a master—I had forgotten how great his mastery of the language was. Words take on new meaning when they are put into the right framework. Sentences, almost a paragraph long, and you don't lose the thread for one moment with that entire sentence. It becomes a little work of art on its own. That is the sort of thing that now in reading gives me the greatest kind of pleasure."

During any given reading or from one encounter with a book to the next, a reader may shift back and forth between an efferent stance and an aesthetic stance. Clive (age fifty, airline pilot) contrasted two experiences with the same book: he recently consulted a book on canoeing for "fact-finding," but earlier he had read the same book for the experience of pleasurable reading. The main factor determining the reading experience is the activity and purposes of the reader: "If I want information, I tend to go to books. I'm thinking of buying a canoe, so I've had a couple of books out [from the library] on this subject by Bill Mason. Except I don't class that as reading; that's just finding out stuff. . . . I don't really regard that as reading, because it's fact-finding. With the Bill Mason, the first time I got *The Path of the Paddle,* I read it through, just because the subject interests me. But the other day when I went through it, I'm going through finding out facts about canoes, etc., so it's a different type of experience."

8. Readers read nonfiction to follow up on their interests in and engagement with the world.

For decades, reading studies (Cole and Cole 1979; Madden 1979) have repeatedly found that "heavy readers" not only read more books than light readers and nonreaders but also do more of almost everything else, including traveling, attending sports events and concerts, visiting museums, and participating in community organizations and politics. For many, reading is a way of being engaged with the world. These readers like to know about things and they read to find out. Jane (age twenty-two, student) said, "I like to go through reference sections and browse the dictionaries and other reference books. I like to find out things. I still don't know to hot wire a car, but other things I've been curious about I have found out about. Something will occur to me and I will start off learning about it. . . . I just like to know these things." Grace (age twenty-seven, student) said that she went through a stage of reading a lot of art books because "I guess it's just the awareness thing again—to know about them. . . . I don't think it a prestige thing. I just really want to know about them."

9. For some readers, a passion for a single topic is the impetus for reading.

Some readers have a passion for a particular topic—horses, planes, ancient Egypt, the American Civil War, the Shackleton expedition to the Antarctic, and so on—and will read everything on this topic they can get their hands on. Larry (age twenty-four, cell biologist) "never found fiction to be very satisfying," but reads a lot of nonfiction, especially on eighteenth-century American history: "That includes all aspects of eighteenth-century American history—sociology, architecture, gardening, landscaping, art, politics, just about every aspect of eighteenth-century history—biographies and diaries." In pursuing their intense interest, these readers are willing to read any format, including histories, biographies, letters, encyclopedias, screenplays, and fictional treatments, so long as the beloved subject matter is the focus. In childhood, the topic of interest, especially for boys, is often dinosaurs or space or volcanoes. Mark (age forty-two, music educator and composer) recalled "going through the dinosaur stage. Every kid loves dinosaurs, so you read books on that. Just about everything that I ever became curious about, I would just go to the library to find stuff out about it."

Especially for novice readers, a strong interest in a topic can play a key role in motivating the reader to persevere to the point where they have built up the volume of reading experience needed to be confident readers. In *Children Talk about Books*, Donald Fry (1985) describes Clayton, a struggling beginning reader in his second year in junior school whose special topic is farming. Clayton selects information books on tractors and farm animals and makes up stories that all begin, "One day I was going to the farm." When he does eventually become engaged with fiction, the book that interests him is *Watership Down,* which adds to his specialist store of information about rabbits and the countryside.

10. Sometimes readers don't want to do something; they just want to read about it.

Books about cooking, gardening, crafts, and travel have a double appeal. Someone who plans to cook something, plant something, make something, or travel somewhere may want to read about it first. Denise (age fifty-eight, law clerk) says, "I am one of these people who loves gardening books. I am working my way through a book on ferns which some people would find deadly boring, but I find it very interesting because I can relate to something that I plan to plant." This sounds like efferent reading, where Denise will take away some information about ferns that will help her plant ferns in her garden. But many readers are like Virginia (age sixty-five, library volunteer) who says, "I will read a gardening book not so much for the information, but for the ambience of the garden." A number of readers explicitly distinguished between the pleasure of doing an activity and the pleasure of reading about it. Larry (age twenty-four, cell biologist) reported, "I don't have to be using a cookbook to enjoy it. I can sit down and read a cookbook and enjoy it." Rita (age fifty-five, homemaker) was even more emphatic: "Somebody did introduce me to Paul Theroux's travel stuff. It was somebody who had been a train buff and they said [to read] *The Great Railway Bazaar* and then of course *Riding the Red Rooster* . . . I did go out and get his *The Old Patagonia Express*. And, my God, that was a wonderful book! And then I got his others, and it was really like being on a train journey. Now, for me, I'm not crazy about train journeys. Getting there has never been half the fun, as far as I'm concerned. So I enjoyed reading it because I didn't have to do any of this dreadful stuff like sitting in this train for ninety-nine hours. But it was still wonderful to read."

11. Part of the joy of reading is serendipitous discovery.

We tend to think of nonfiction as a place to find answers to questions we already have. Hence interviewees said that nonfiction was important for getting specific information on a known topic. Topics specifically mentioned included parenting, health, birth control, fitness and nutrition, self-help, pet care, cooking, interior decorating, gardening, crafts, travel, sports, remodeling a van, choosing a consumer product, and using computer software. In these cases, the helpful book was specifically designed to address the particular questions that were motivating the reader. Mark (age forty-two, music educator and composer) refers to this kind of reading as "hunting" and contrasts it with "fishing," where you don't have a known topic in mind. This latter type of book becomes a vehicle of discovery: "When I go to a library . . . a lot of times it's like wading into that river and going fishing. You don't know what's going to happen when you get there. Libraries are still a magical place for me. About a year and a half ago, I came across a book, just totally haphazardly, called *Hanta Yo*. It is about a thousand pages long and it is written by a woman, an American woman, named Ruth Beebe Hill and this was her life's work. She spent twenty years of her life studying the Sioux and writing a book: a fictional account of the Lakota Sioux Indians between about 1790 to 1830. She was getting ready to think about publishing when she ran into a seventy-eight-year-old Sioux grandfather who was looking for his counterpart on the opposite side to write such a book. Only he wanted it to be translated into the Sioux first, because in the Sioux language there are no comparable words for English concepts such as 'because' or 'guilt' or 'weed.' . . . So, in order to make this English language book feel right and not use any words that were not part of the Lakota language, they translated it into the Lakota Sioux and then back into English again. . .

"And it is those kinds of things that are like the special fish that you catch. If I'd gone hunting, I don't know that I would have found that book but by going fishing and just casting out in different places I could inadvertently come across it. So that's the entertainment side of the library for my, the fun part of reading for pleasure—just seeing what you can come up with. And there's a lot of things that you throw back, you just pick that up; it looks good, it looks promising, you read four pages and no . . . oh no."

12. Readers read biographies in areas related to their interests or their own lives.

When readers say they enjoy history or biography or some other category of nonfiction, they don't mean that just any book in that category will do. They enjoy biographies or memoirs, but only about the category of person they are interested in—sports heroes or members of the Royal Family or scientists or writers or political leaders. Many readers say that they have become interested in finding out about the lives of artists, writers, and musicians whose work they enjoy. Joan (age thirty-one, elementary school teacher) said, "I start with authors and then read their biographies. When Barbara Pym died, I waited for books to come out about her." Dorothy (age thirty, freelance writer) said, "I read biographies; I read letters. I like to read about artists and writers. May Sarton's journals, I really love. I like memoirs. I don't read science as a rule. I'll pick a book if it's about or by someone whose work I'm interested in. For example, right now I'm reading the letters of T. S. Eliot. I just picked it up—it was among the new books in the nonfiction section at the local branch of the library." Pam (age twenty-three, student) said that she is currently reading an autobiography of the English composer Sir Michael Tippitt, an interest that is "driven by my interest in music. I also have been reading lots of technical books on playing the violin and all that sort of thing because I've been wanting to improve my technique." Aline (age twenty-two, student), said, "I also read nonfiction. Biographies. I like to see what happened behind the public persona. Katharine Hepburn for example—I would like to read her biography. Trudeau's memoirs. But I wouldn't sit down and read Neil Armstrong, first astronaut on the moon, because his life doesn't appeal to me."

Biography readers, like novel readers, often say that they enjoyed particular books because "they were secretly about me." The connection between the textual life and the reader's life may be that the biographical subject embodies the reader's wish-fulfillment dream of the possible. Joy (age twenty-seven, student) said, "I really like to read biographies and autobiographies—especially of old movie stars like Ava Gardner and Betty Grable and those types of people. I like to read about royalty, members of royalty. I have all kinds of stuff on Princess Diana, but before she came into the picture I read stuff about Elizabeth and Margaret and Queen Alexandra. I always like to read about women, because I'm a woman and I can identify with them. I just don't find men's lives as interesting. It always seems the women had like, you know, lovers—and just so many things going on. I guess you can kind of pretend. Like, 'I'd love to have a life like this.' Or you could, for a little while, pretend that that is your life."

Biographies in particular are often read as blueprints and models for living. Janice Radway (1987, 275–76) has described how the editors of the Book-of-the-Month club select literary fiction that they think will be useful to people "searching for suggestions, models, and directions about how to live. . . . Thus the editors demanded always that [chosen titles] permit readers to map the insights gained from the experience of reading onto the terrain of their own lives." Sebastian (age twenty-two, recording engineer) said that his reading *Personal Power* by the "motivational guy" Tony Robbins influenced the way he read "because Tony Robbins emphasizes that you can learn how to achieve things by emulating other people who have succeeded. Since I've read that, I've tried to read more biographies or autobiographies. And I've also thought more about what I want to do with my life." Similarly Clarence (age sixty, self-employed) prefers "real-life history and biographies of people" because, he said, "I can see that a person can actually accomplish something and do something in their life of which I feel I haven't accomplished. And yet, if I read these books, I can see where these people have come in a lot of cases from very little means and yet they have been able to accomplish something." Where Sebastian and Clarence seek exemplary models of successful accomplishment, Joan (age thirty-one, elementary school teacher) is looking for models for coping with the ordinary tribulations of life. Joan reads diaries, memoirs, and biographies of family life because she wants to know "how people spend their time and get through life": "It's probably because I'm looking for security. I'm honestly interested in how people react under different conditions— how they get through life and face their problems. In fiction you understand that things are tough for people, but they seem to be solved so easily— things tend to work out. It doesn't work that way in real life. Maybe that's why I seem to like reading about families, written from a woman's point of view."

Stories of special lives can invite the reader to dream of possibilities beyond the everyday. Virginia (age sixty-five, library volunteer) reported that as a child she was "inspired to be a dancer" and "read a book called *Swish of the Curtain,* about a family of orphans that somehow managed to get into the theatre. I thought this was wonderful. If only I was an orphan and I could go and dance."

13. Story is a key element in the appeal of
many nonfiction books.

Nonfiction writers have learned from the fiction writers how to tell a good story, develop characters, set a scene, and create suspense. Journalists have always referred to what they write as "stories." And sometimes it's hard to tell fiction from nonfiction. Australian author Thomas Keneally's Booker Prize–winning *Schindler's Ark* was published as fiction in Great Britain and as nonfiction in North America under the title *Schindler's List*. The key for many readers is the presence of narrative—the story. This element is apparent in one of the most enduring genres of nonfiction, the survival (or not) of characters who take on extreme challenges such as sailing solo around the world or climbing, as in Jon Krakauer's *Into Thin Air*, to the top of Everest. Debbie (age twenty-nine, copy editor) said she had recently read a lot of "biographies and autobiographies about survival—'I crashed in the Arctic and survived for three months'—about people who had fought odds and survived."

Implications for the Readers' Advisory Transaction

These findings suggest nonfiction represents a substantial share of the pleasure reading of avid readers. Because this population is far more likely than average to be library users, their experiences and preferences can be used as a starting point for thinking about how to improve readers' advisory service in the nonfiction area. This research has some implications for practice.

1. Conduct a readers' advisory interview. The interview is the key to being able to make appropriate suggestions (Ross, Nilsen, and Dewdney 2002). If the reader says he or she is looking for a biography, remember that readers can be very selective about the types of biographies they enjoy. It is important to ask an additional question, "Can you tell me about a biography book that you've read and enjoyed?" or "What kinds of lives are you interested in reading about?" If the reader says that she want a history book, ask her to tell you about the kind of history book she is in the mood for. It may turn out she wants historical fiction or a regency romance.

2. Help readers cope with the problem of what Sharon Baker (1986) calls "overload" by creating displays focused on topics of known interest such as the following: survival stories, King Arthur, biographies of successful people, health and fitness, travel, cookbooks, investments. Create hybrids of both fiction and nonfiction that have the same elements of appeal, for example, true

crime and mystery stories with a forensic slant such as Patricia Cornwell and Kathy Reichs. Feature particular writers in a display that includes books written *by* the writer and books *about* the writer, such as biographies, memoirs and letters, and, in some cases (e.g., Michael Cunningham's *The Hours*, which includes Virginia Woolf as a character), other people's novels. Include a variety of formats, such as documentaries on video or movie soundtracks on CD.

3. Think about nonfiction books in terms of appeal factors, which Saricks and Brown (1997) have identified as pacing, characterization, story line, and frame. In the case of biography, the appeal may be character or it may be plot or story line. Many biographies tell a gripping story of an heroic struggle against the odds to achieve a dream or simply to survive. Use reviews and book blurbs to help you identify the appeal factors, looking for distinguishing terms like "fast-paced" or "characters that you care deeply about" or "the inside story of X" or "quirky humor."

4. Become aware of nonfiction genres in the same way that you learn about the differences between science fiction, fantasy, mystery, and romance in order to advise readers about fiction. Just as the mystery genre is subdivided into cozies, police procedurals, hardboiled, and so on, so travel books or cookbooks or nature books are categories with many subcategories. Some people want to read about idyllic getaway spots in romantic settings, and others are intrigued by those "Journeys to Hell" (Burgin 2001) such as *A Perfect Storm* and *Into Thin Air*.

5. Be aware of the nonfiction counterparts of popular genres of fiction: mystery/true crime, horror/occult, westerns/historical accounts of the Old West, action-adventure/survival stories, war stories/history and biography centered on warfare.

References

Baker, Sharon L. 1986. Overload, browsers and selections. *Library and Information Science Research* 8: 315–29.

Burgin, Robert. 2001. Readers' advisory and nonfiction. In *The readers' advisor's companion*. Edited by Kenneth D. Shearer and Robert Burgin, 213–27. Englewood, CO: Libraries Unlimited.

Cole, John Y., and Carol S. Gold. 1979. *Reading in America, 1978*. Washington, DC: Library of Congress.

Fry, Donald. 1985. *Children talk about books: Seeing themselves as readers*. Milton Keynes, UK, and Philadelphia, PA: Open University Press.

Madden, Michael. 1979. *Lifestyles of library users and nonusers*. Occasional Papers No. 137. Urbana-Champaign: University of Illinois Graduate School of Library Science.

Radway, Janice A. 1989. The Book-of-the-Month Club and the general reader. In *Reading in America: Literature and social history*. Edited by Cathy N. Davidson, 259–84. Baltimore, MD, and London: Johns Hopkins University Press.

Rosenblatt, Louise. 1978. *The reader, the text, the poem: The transactional theory of the literary work*. Carbondale: Southern Illinois Press.

Ross, Catherine Sheldrick. 1999. Finding without seeking: The information encounter in the context of reading for pleasure. *Information Processing and Management* 35: 783–99.

Ross, Catherine Sheldrick, Kirsti Nilsen, and Patricia Dewdney. 2002. *Conducting the reference interview*. New York: Neal-Schuman.

Saricks, Joyce G., and Nancy Brown. 1997. *Readers' advisory service in the public library*. Chicago: American Library Association.

Chapter 7

True Stories: Portraits of Four Nonfiction Readers

Duncan Smith

If you have ever told a tall tale, read a story, or provided an explanation to a group of small children, you have probably been assailed with volleys of "Did it really happen like that?" or "Is this true or just make believe?" If you've never had this experience, you can see what it is like by watching the Long Expected Party scene in the movie version of *The Fellowship of the Ring*. In that scene, Bilbo Baggins tells about his run-in with some trolls. While he tells his tale, the camera focuses on the faces of a group of hobbit children. In those wide eyes and open mouths, you see the power of story at work—transporting each and everyone of them to a cold, damp forest floor where they lay in sacks listening to three trolls argue about how best to cook them (Tolkien 1982, 35–41). The scene is even more powerful when you realize that in the world of the film, Bilbo is not making this up. He is reporting a particularly ticklish moment from his own personal history. Bilbo is telling his eager listeners something that really happened.

Whether you are of the school that says that hobbits are really small versions of ourselves or not, we (like those young hobbits) can be transported by story. Some us want stories like Tolkien's *The Lord of the Rings*. Others want to read about things that are closer to the world we call real. Regardless of which story you chose (and some chose both), that choice is intimately connected to who you are and how you want to experience the world. Freud tells us we are never done with the core primitive struggles that daily wrestle in our minds. The Oedipal complex that dominates our lives between the ages of five to seven may recede into the background as we go to school, go to college, launch careers, and marry, but it stays with us lurking in the background of our overscheduled lives. If Freud is not to your taste, Wordsworth is working the same material in his "Ode: Intimations of Immortality from Recollections of Early Childhood" when he pens "The child is father of the man."

This chapter explores the ways that a particular class of story calls to its readers. We are going to be following a Pulitzer Prize–winning journalist through the South, learn why the current head of Duke's Graduate Program in Literature lived at the Book-of-the-Month Club, watch my business partner become a pilot, and finally follow a young graduate student as he goes from the classroom to the White House. These personal journeys will show the relationships that exist between the lives of readers and the stories that call to them. These relationships are not casual, and in the case of the four readers explored here, the stories just happen to be true.

The Late Great Unpleasantness:
Tony Horowitz and the Civil War

At the heart of Tony Horowitz's evocatively titled *Confederates in the Attic: Dispatches from the Unfinished Civil War* (Horowitz 1999) is "six foot tall, rail thin" Robert Lee Hodge. Hodge is a "living historian" (aka Civil War reenactor), one of a growing number of men and women who spend weekends and vacations recreating the battles of the War between the States. There is much more to these individuals' quests for authenticity than twelve-mile forced marches to Gettysburg with a live chicken thrown over each person's shoulder and sleeping on the ground hugging your squad mates to keep warm (a maneuver called "spooning," which was designed to counter thin uniforms and lack of fires). These historical interpreters (another term preferred to the distasteful "R" word) spend days pouring over original Civil War photographs at the National Archives, can tell you the thread count of a Virginia cavalry officer's uniform circa 1863, and have a dietary regime that would be the envy of any New York runway model. (The ideal weight for a living historian portraying a Confederate soldier is in the neighborhood of 135 pounds—a figure derived from studying pension records.)

Reading Horowitz's book, we learn that Hodge is a guru for serious hard-core reenactors. Through Hodge, Horowitz lets us participate in his initiation into this group of Civil War enthusiasts. Hodge, however, is only a foot soldier in *Confederates in the Attic*. This book isn't just about the odd way a Pulitzer Prize–winning journalist spends his free time. It isn't just about driving through the South meeting eccentrics either, even though we meet plenty—the Sons of Confederate Veterans in Salisbury, North Carolina; the historian Shelby Foote in his Memphis home; and Soren Dresch, owner of the Ruffin Flag company in Georgia, which manufactures and sells Confederate flags and memorabilia. This book is really about Tony Horowitz's personal odyssey, a journey he undertakes to discover the source of his lifelong fascination not only with the War of Northern Aggression but with Confederates. Because, you see, there are Confederates in the Horowitz family attic.

Although no white-bearded, gray-clad relatives sit upstairs in the Horowitz family's Connecticut homestead muttering about what we could have done at Gettysburg and shouldn't have done at Appomattox, Tony knows that they are there. They are there because he put them there. One of the manifestations of young Tony's obsession with the Civil War is that as a third-grader he painted a mural depicting scenes from the Civil War on his attic bedroom walls. His goal was to illustrate the entire conflict, but unfortunately he ran out of wall in 1863, leaving his early masterpiece unfinished. The soldiers in his mural were not wearing the Union blue you would expect from a young Connecticut Yankee. The soldiers on Tony's walls were Albert Sidney Johnson, General Pickett, and his soldiers—Confederates all.

Like most of the fascinations of young boys, Tony's interest in the Civil War wanes as he grows older. Johnston and Pickett are covered up with posters of Jimi Hendrix and the starship *Enterprise* going where no man has gone before. His interest in the Civil War is not extinguished. It just lies dormant until a chance encounter with Robert Lee Hodge renews it. The thirty-something author of *Confederates in the Attic* is different from our nine-year-old muralist. The author of *Confederates in the Attic* feels closer to the African Americans enslaved in the South than to their masters. His Jewish ancestors knew something about slavery and about fighting for freedom, and as an adult, he is more interested in racial equality and justice than in the glory of the South's Lost Cause.

Not everyone in Horowitz's book feels the need to don period costumes and march barefoot through the Shenandoah. Many of the folks in *Confederates in the Attic* are content to read about the war, engage in "what if" conversations with anyone who will listen, and maybe occasionally attend a meeting on the topic.

The story of Mike Hawkins is typical. He is the color sergeant of the Rowan County (North Carolina) Sons of Confederate Veterans. Horowitz meets Hawkins at the organization's Lee/Jackson Birthday Party, where members' knowledge of the Civil War is tested with questions such as, "How many horses did Nathan Bedford Forest have shot out from under him?" (The correct answer, by the way, is twenty-nine; Horowitz 1999, 25) When the author visits him in his house trailer, Hawkins paints the following picture of his life: "At work I mix dyes and put them in a machine. I'm thirty-six and I've spent almost half my life in Dye House No. 1. I make eight dollars and sixty-one cents an hour which is okay, 'cept everyone says the plant will close and go to China" (Horowitz 1999, 30). Mike's house trailer contains a bedroom filled with second-hand books on the Civil War. Mike describes what his reading means to him as he flips through a book of Civil War photographs: "When I'm reading, I feel like I'm there, not here. And when I finish I feel content. Like I've been away for a while" (Horowitz 1999, 30). Hawkins is particularly well read on the battle of Sharpsburg. The reason for his special interest in this battle is that his great-great grandfather lost a leg at Sharpsburg.

Horowitz's fascination with the Civil War is also steeped in family tradition. While Charleston, South Carolina, "until the early nineteenth century had the largest Jewish population in the country, with a quarter of all American Jews living in South Carolina" (Horowitz 1999, 62), there were no Horowitzes in the South Carolina 1st marching beneath the Stars and Bars. Tony's ancestors did not immigrate to the United States until 1882 when his great grandfather left Czarist Russia to avoid the draft. Soon after Poppa Isaac Moses arrived in lower East Side Manhattan, he bought a book of Civil War sketches. Moses shared this book with all his children and grandchildren, including the future muralist. He also passed down his enthusiasm for the War to Tony's father. At one point, Horowitz's mother tells the following story about an early date with his father:

> She had once visited a few battlefields while being courted by my father forty years before. "His idea of fun on a mid-summer afternoon was going to Bull Run," she said. "It was hot as hell and I wasn't a bit interested. I thought it was weird." (Horowitz 1999, 381)

So Tony comes by his interest in the Civil War honestly, having it visited upon him by his father and his father's father. As we read his book, we suspect that he actually had little choice in the matter. An obsession with the Civil War was bound to be passed down to him as surely as his family's hair and eye color. Tony, however, does not passively accept his family's Civil War gene. He aggressively explores it. Through his writing we experience his struggles to reconcile his feelings and connection to this important part of our nation's past. He speculates that part of Pop Isaac's interest in Bull Run, Shiloh, Gettysburg, and Appomattox was an attempt not only to understand something about his new country's recent history but an attempt to become more "American." While Pop Isaac didn't actually fight in the war (or any war), his reading and studying about the war to make it part of himself would be something that would seem natural to a young, Jewish man steeped in the rabbinical tradition. It is also possible to see the roots of Tony's fascination not only with the war but with Confederates. Like the modern day Confederates in his book, his family has lost its ancestral home having emigrated from Russia. Even though Tony's family settled in the north, his religious tradition (with its own history of being surrounded by nations of superior force as well as being conquered, exiled, and dispersed) resonates more with the Confederate States of America than with the reconstructed United States.

Another ancestral state of the Horowitz family (Israel) was also once a divided kingdom. At one point, the homeland of the Jews was divided into Israel in the north and Judah in the south. Like the Confederacy, the southern kingdom was eventually conquered and absorbed into the northern one to make a united Israel.

All of the people featured in *Confederates in the Attic* are looking back to a past that is viewed as richer and more purposeful than the world in which they live. Both Robert Lee Hodge and Mike Hawkins are attempting to bring the experience of this lost glorious time back into their lives. Hodges does this by trying to physically relive the experience of those times. Hawkins recovers this lost richness through reading.

In her book, *Necessary Losses,* Judith Viorst engagingly explores the issue of loss in our lives. She writes that part of being human "is confronting all that we never will have and never will be" (Viorst 1986, 16). She goes on to say that central to understanding our lives is understanding how we deal with loss. She agrees with Freud "that our past, with all of its clamorous wishes and terrors and passions, inhabits our present and his belief in the enormous power of our unconscious—of that region outside of our awareness—to shape the events of our life" (Viorst 1986, 17). Our deep connections to Freud's unconscious and our pasts not only shape our lives but, as we have seen with Mike Hawkins and Tony Horowitz, our interests as well.

Janice Radway's Feeling for Books

Janice Radway, the author of *Reading the Romance: Women, Patriarchy, and Popular Literature* (Radway 1991) and *A Feeling for Books: The Book-of-the-Month Club: Literary Taste, and Middle-Brow Desire* (Radway 1997) is also engaged in a civil war of sorts. When Radway began writing *Reading the Romance,* she taught in the American Civilization Department at the University of Pennsylvania. She is now the chair of the Graduate Program in Literature at Duke University. Given her career in academia, you would expect her to be more interested in Jane Austen than in Nora Roberts, in J. D. Salinger than in Harper Lee, but that is not the case. Radway is more interested in readers than authors. Her area of research focuses on how the American general reader recognizes a good book and how the reading experience fits into their lives.

Reconstruction

In *Reading the Romance,* Radway studies a group of romance readers who patronize a romance bookstore in a small Midwestern town. Reading her book, we see into the lives of women who daily drift between the roles and demands of being a mother, a wife, and a worker, women who are always on call and responsible for meeting the demands of others—except when they are reading. These women are readers who choose to read primarily (if not exclusively) those paperback love stories that account for almost 55 percent of all popular paperback titles in the United States. We are also told about reading behaviors that will amaze some and shock others. For example, when these women encounter a book by a new or previously unread author, they always read the ending first.

Radway uncovers a treasure trove of attitudes and behaviors and identifies the ways reading enriches the lives of the women she interviews and lives with. Her book is filled with revelations and insights from the daily lives of these women. She is able to reveal these intimate details from the lives of Dot and her readers because she has dwelt among them. Radway didn't do the research for her book by sitting in her well-appointed faculty office doing close reading and an exegesis of Kathleen Woodiwiss's *The Flame and the Flower.* Instead, she actually lived with these women, moving in with Dot (the romance bookstore owner) for one week during one of her visits to Smithton, going to work with her, eating at her table. Radway has looked into the faces of the women who completed her surveys. She has heard sighs over later afternoon cups of coffee at the end of a hard day at work and the beginning of getting dinner ready. Radway has seen the knowing smiles and assured nods as readers talk about how Heather, the heroine of *The Flame and the Flower,* transforms her kidnapper into her lifetime lover because we knew she both could and would.

Radway is an ethnographer. Think of her as a literary Margaret Mead, as someone who is not content to merely study the artifacts of her area of scholarship (i.e., books). She wants to see how these objects animate the lives of readers; she wants to discover the reading rituals that elevate the checkout woman at the Food Lion to the high-priestess of her life or transform the greeter at Wal-Mart into an heiress. She is a "living literature interpreter," more kin to Robert Lee Hodge than her tweed-and-cashmere-clad colleagues who are counting commas and deconstructing Pynchon.

Having mapped the undiscovered country of the romance reader, our literary anthropologist turns her attention to another often-derided collection of books—those titles selected by the Book-of-the-Month Club. Armed with a grant from the Guggenheim Foundation, Radway spends several months sitting in editorial committee meetings at the club's New York offices, reading the reader reports that are the backbone of the club's selection process, and interviewing the club's editors and founders. While *A Feeling for Books* does look at Harper Lee's *To Kill a Mockingbird,* Leon Uris's *Exodus,* Irving Stone's *The Agony and the Ecstasy,* Richard Wright's *Native Son,* C. W. Ceram's *Gods, Graves, and Scholars,* and Bruce Catton's *Stillness at Appomattox*, Radway digs underneath the books themselves in an attempt to unearth the thinking behind the selection of this group of titles and their commercial success, a success that has led many academics to view the club's titles as inferior to the ones they teach and the Book-of-the-Month Club as the literary equivalent of Championship Wrestling or NASCAR.

It is hard to know what our anthropologist expected to find as she sat through the Book-of-the-Month Club selection committee meetings and sorted through the reader reports written by each of the present and past members of that committee, reports that outlined each editor's thinking about whether the assigned title was suitable for inclusion in the club. One thing she didn't expect was for her research to move out of the realm of the scholarly. Radway was not prepared for her research to get personal, but it does.

To look at the Book-of-the-Month Club editors, as described by Radway, you would think that they were faculty members at prestigious Northeastern colleges. They could pass for faculty members at Penn or Drew or Vassar or for Radway's colleagues at Duke. Many share Radway's educational and socioeconomic background and like her are no doubt current in literary theory. When they talk about books, however, they don't speak of technical sophistication or academic rigor. Instead of embracing these traits, hallowed in the Ivory Tower, the club's editors used their presence as reason enough to eliminate a title from consideration. Selection committee members tended to talk about how a book would be read. They discussed the type of reading experience that a book would provide instead of its content and execution. As she listens, Radway begins to hear echoes of something, echoes of someone slumbering in her distant past. What is awakened is the remembrance of the way she used to read before she was wrapped in years of literature courses.

A Feeling for Books has three sections. The first is "an ethnographic account of the editorial practices employed by the in-house editors at the club during the years 1985–1988" (Radway 1997, 14). The second section of the book concerns how America's change to a consumer society created a need for the Book-of-the-Month Club and how the club not only responded to but contributed to this change. The final portion of the book is an autobiographical account of Radway's relationship with the Book-of-the-Month Club and how some of its titles shaped her life.

When Radway first goes to New York to begin her fieldwork with the club, its editors and their selection process, she describes her relationship with the Book-of-the-Month Club as one of indifference. She joined the club as a graduate student to get a copy of the Concise Oxford English Dictionary. Radway's history with the club, however, is deeper than her utilitarian use of it as a vehicle for cheaply obtaining a treasure trove of information on the English language. Her true relationship to this middlebrow institution emerges as she digs through the club's archives and the books that the club had chosen to offer its members. As she looks through these titles by authors like Thor Heyerdahl, Herman Wouk, C. W. Ceram, and Bruce Canton, she is surprised not only by the number of titles that she recognizes but by the number that she has actually read.

Many of the titles that she remembers reading come from a specific period in her life. Unlike her friends, who spent their freshmen year in high school attending classes, trying out for cheerleading and cheering at Friday night football games, Radway spent hers at home shrouded in plaster. In September of her freshman year, Radway underwent surgery for scoliosis. The Bergen County, New Jersey, teenager spent an entire year at home in a body cast. During that year, Mr. Shymansky, her high school librarian, would stop by with boxes of books. These books formed the basis of Radway's day:

> deserted by my friends, who had swirled off as a group to the new high school at 7:45, I opened book after book.... For me, reading was a lifeline, what [the novelist Richard] Powers calls "narrative therapy" and "the cure of interlocking dreams." Fear and loneliness grafted me to those books and made them routes to new worlds. For me, as for the past judges and present day editors at the Book-of-the-Month Club, those books rendered me "earless, eyeless, motionless for hours," they left me feeling "swept away." Ultimately they left me

> with a passion for deep reading and enriched too . . . by the idea that in the future I was to "rush great-heartedly upon experience."
> (Radway 1997, 306)

Radway had always supposed that the boxes of books her high school librarian brought her were from the newly built high school library. What she realizes as she browses through old catalogs in the club's Manhattan offices is that the titles that swept her away and readied her to embrace experience were Book-of-the-Month Club selections.

In part because of this insight, Radway devotes the final third of her book to her experiences of rereading a selection of these titles that were her companions on those autumn and winter days of 1963 and 1964. She is no longer reading as an eager adolescent but as a seasoned and experienced scholar. The contemporary Radway is schooled in gender studies, the politics of culture, and literary exegesis. As she rereads these books, she is shocked at how blind she was to the overt and implied racism, imperialism, and chauvinism contained in these titles. During her rereading, however, she also remembers and embraces her younger self, a self for whom reading was a passionate, thrilling, and transfiguring experience instead of a performance designed to demonstrate one's knowledge of a critical superstructure built around authors who are dead, white, and male.

One of the titles that she rereads is C. W. Ceram's *Gods, Graves and Scholars*. Published in 1954, Ceram's book takes the general reader deep into the arcane world or archaeology. As he takes us through the ruins at Pompeii, the jungles of the Yucatan, and the deserts of the Valley of the Kings, Ceram dramatizes and humanizes both the expeditions and male scientists who direct them. He praises the rigor and painstaking drudgery of unearthing the ancient world's buried treasures including King Tut's tomb. Radway also points out that the author deftly connects these geographically and temporally distant worlds to our own. While the contemporary Radway is critical of Ceram's overt statements about Western man's superiority to the Australian aborigine and the fact that all of Ceram's heroes are male, she also acknowledges that this book had a profound effect on her when she read it in 1963. She tells us that "for months afterward, I told anyone who asked that I wanted to be an archaeologist when I grew up" (Radway 1997, 331).

As we know, Radway did not grow up to be an archaeologist. Instead, she grew up to be a skilled researcher whose area of expertise is reading and its role in the lives of everyday people. Her methods, however, are much closer to Lord Carnarvon and Howard Carter, the liberators of King Tutankhamen from his tomb, than to her literature colleagues. After all, how many English professors ever did fieldwork? She is also on a mission that echoes Ceram's desire to rescue archaeology from the dusty archives of academia; she is seeking to rescue books and reading from the airless classrooms of university English departments, where reading has been professionalized. The result not only enriches our understanding of what many us read and how we read; we also participate in Radway's recovery of her earlier reading self and witness the return of her feeling for books.

Distinctions

When Radway is writing about the "culture of the middlebrow" and exploring her discomfort in the high-culture realm of academia, she is employing a hierarchy that divides us into groups based on the books we read, the films we attend, and whether we watch television at all. Herbert Gans is just one of the researchers who has put forth a system for classifying ourselves by taste. Writing in the 1970s, he divides the United States into five taste cultures: high, upper-middle, lower-middle, low, and quasi folk-low (Gans 1974). These divisions are just one example of the many ways we try to classify people, behaviors, and the things that populate our world. If you have ever asked anyone what sign they are or exchanged your Myers-Briggs type with colleagues, you are using classification systems that are more familiar to us than the taste cultures outlined by Gans and explored by Radway.

Geoffrey C. Bowker and Susan Leigh Star explore this urge to group like things together in their book *Sorting Things Out: Classification and Its Consequences* (Bowker and Star 2002). They discuss the centrality of these grouping behaviors in our lives and assert that "to classify is human." Bowker and Star trace the renaissance of formal classification schemes to the seventeenth century, when increased travel and burgeoning scientific discoveries led to a need for a system to organize all of the new information that was flowing across the globe (or at least across Europe). The Enlightenment not only led to these new discoveries, it provided a mind-set that was ideally suited to the creation of classification systems. That mind-set was the belief that everything had a place and that we were smart enough to put it there.

Bowker and Star examine classification frameworks as diverse as the International Classification of Diseases, the classification system used by South Africa's Apartheid government to group its citizens by race, and the Nursing Intervention Classification, a method for defining the work of nurses by task. They also give a passing nod to a classification system that we are all familiar with: the Dewey Decimal System.

Dewey's system was designed to organize human knowledge by providing a topical arrangement for that knowledge as it was represented in *library materials* (read: *books*). It is the one that most library users in the United States navigate with varying degrees of success. It is typical of the classification systems explored in *Sorting Things Out,* and it suffers from the same challenges of the systems named in Bowker and Star. One of these challenges is that the longer a specific classification is around and the more widely it is adopted, the greater the likelihood that its theoretical underpinnings, its trade-offs, and its exclusions will become invisible to its users.

In the case of the Dewey Decimal System, especially in public libraries, a whole class of materials has been cast out of the system even though Dewey made a place for it. If you walk into a public library, you will see a significant part of the collection arranged by Dewey number. If you roam around, however, you will discover a well-used portion of the collection off to the side and arranged by either author's last name or by genre. Whether this is based on the library's high-culture distaste for middle and low-brow fiction or a response to readers' demands for a separate grouping of these materials is beyond the scope of this article. This separation of fiction from nonfiction is just one example of how a classification system has been adapted to meet the requirements of the institution's staff, its users, or both.

The rationale behind the separation of fiction and nonfiction is interesting in part because it raises the specter of the user. Dewey's system was designed to classify containers of knowledge by their contents, not by the individuals for whom these materials were being collected. His system is also silent about the intended use of these materials. In Melvil Dewey's library, the books are arranged neatly in rows of shelves, and books on a similar topic are grouped together. But you will look in vain in the gray and green volumes of the twenty-second edition of the Dewey Decimal Classification and Relative Index for any heading that coordinates topic with users and users with the intended uses of the books in Melvil's collection.

Here is how this omission might result in a library user being cast adrift in a public library. It is not unusual for job hunters to come to the library to find books on writing a resume. Such enterprising individuals would probably be directed to the 650.142 section, where they would find books like *101 Best Resumes for Grads* (Black and Betrus 2003).

What Dewey's heading doesn't take into account is that the genre of resume books has subgenres just like mysteries. Mysteries can be divided into many subcategories, with police procedurals and legal thrillers being just two examples of popular ones. The right book for our enterprising reader (whom we have classified as job hunter) depends both on the user's situation and the intended use of the book. If the reader is only seeking an example of a resume, then books such as *101 Best Resumes for Grads,* which give models of resumes by occupation or job title, might be just the ticket. If the user is applying for a job in a different industry, however, he or she might need a title that uses a workbook approach to help the job hunter quantify his or her skills and choose between resume formats (chronological versus functional, for example). In that case, a book like *Resume Magic: Trade Secrets of a Professional Resume Writer* by Susan Whitcomb (2003) may be a better choice. If our reader is not only looking for a job but interested in changing careers, then a book such as *What Color Is Your Parachute?: A Practical Manual for Job-Hunters and Career Changers* (Bolles 2001), which actually discourages a resume-based approach to job hunting, might be the best choice. But the Bolles title would probably be nearby in the 650.14 section, under the Dewey heading "Success in obtaining jobs and promotions," instead of with the resume books.

A skillful librarian would help our job hunter negotiate not only the Dewey Decimal System but the books contained in 650.142 and the 650.14 sections and would inform the job hunter that the library also has books on preparing for a job interview, thereby getting the reader ready for the next phase of landing that ideal job. This example also points to another hidden assumption of Dewey's system.

Created and refined at the turn of the next to the last century (1800s to 1900s), Dewey's system reflects the utilitarian attitudes that dominated that time period. Libraries existed to support learning and self-improvement. Their collections contained classic works and the titles relating to the academic interests of the day. They were cathedrals of learning where users worshipped the twin gods of purposeful study and cultural enrichment. This is the time when librarians were referred to as "apostles of culture" and libraries were the "people's university."

While libraries during Dewey's day contained fiction, these materials were collected only because of their popularity; their use was actively discouraged. A significant part of the charter meeting of the American Library Association in 1876, which Dewey attended, was devoted to the "fiction problem." The nature of that problem was how Dewey and his colleagues could get readers to stop reading frivolous and mind-numbing novels and begin reading all of the great and high-minded works of nonfiction that Dewey and his colleagues had at great effort and expense meticulously collected and cataloged.

Dewey's shadow does not only fall over the books in the library's collection. It also looms large over the ways in which librarians think about responding to user requests for information. The same utilitarian orientation that gave us the Dewey Decimal System also biases us toward valuing books that have a practical purpose. By contrast, Rebecca Clay, in an article written for the American Psychological Association, points out that not all of our mental activities are purposeful and focused (Clay 2001). Clay discusses the work of Rachel and Stephen Kaplan, psychologists who are interested in creating "restorative environments." They base part of their work on a distinction that William James, a contemporary of our Dewey, makes about attention. James talks about two types of attention: directed and fascination. When we think about books and how they are used, we tend to think about nonfiction when readers have task-focused questions:

getting a job, building a deck, writing a paper. These tasks require directed attention. We also tend to think about fiction titles when we think about fascination.

These distinctions, however, are false. Many of the readers in Radway's *Reading the Romance* talked about how much they learned about history from reading historical romances. Learning is frequently a reason given by fiction readers when they discuss why they read fiction, and learning is something that we tend to associate with focused or directed attention. Conversely, Mike Hawkins's description of his nonfiction reading about the Battle of Sharpsburg ("When I'm reading, I feel like I'm there, not here. And when I finish I feel content. Like I've been away for a while" [Horowitz 1999, 30]) could have come out of the mouth of many a fiction reader.

Library-based information services are modeled on Belkin's premise of anomalous states of knowledge (Belkin 1982), which theorizes that individuals have gaps in what they know about the world. The drive to reduce or eliminate these anomalous states leads people to ask questions and to seek the answers to those questions, sometimes in the books and resources in libraries. Readers, however, not only possess anomalous states of knowledge. They possess (or are possessed by) anomalous states of experience. These anomalous states of experience also drive readers to seek satisfaction. Sometimes, without a specific task or outcome in mind, they come to the library and browse shelves of books arranged by Dewey number looking not for information or knowledge, but for experience.

Roger Rohweder:
In Pursuit of One Hundred Years of Flight

On a warm, sunny October afternoon about two months before the centennial celebration of the Wright brothers' first sustained, powered flight in a heavier-than-air craft, two hundred people are milling around the Sanford (North Carolina) Regional Airport, attending the Wings of Carolina open house. At the show, people can look at life-size replicas of World War I fighters like a Sopwith Camel and the Fokker fighter made famous by the Red Baron, peer inside a life flight chopper, and see the Hammer brothers' ultralight that has won them the national title two years in a row. Attendees can also buy a ride in a helicopter or enter a drawing for a free skydiving lesson. Representatives from the Federal Aviation Administration and the Air National Guard stand around literature-stacked folding tables ready to talk with anyone who pauses to glance at their brochures.

These literature-laden tables are in the club's new hangar, which is one of the reasons for the event. Roger Rohweder, my business partner and flying club president, is beaming as he runs behind another set of tables laden with hot dogs, cheeseburgers, soft drinks, chips, and T-shirts. Today is a personal triumph for him and not only because the new hangar is finally finished and because attendance at the open house is greater than expected. A major contributor to his sunny disposition is the fact that the sun is indeed shining and the called-for afternoon rain showers are nowhere in sight. Looking up, attendees see a crystal clear blue sky, which is the perfect backdrop for the two airplanes (one bright red and the other bright yellow) that are bringing the day to a close with "loop the loops" and barrel rolls.

If you listen to these private pilots talk, you can hear a language that sounds almost like English. The word *slippery* is used to describe the *White Lightning,* a small, sleek plane that is very, very fast. None of these individuals would describe this perfect afternoon as sunny and warm. It would be *clear with unlimited visibility, temperature 60 degrees, and winds at 5 knots from 190 degrees.* Pilots live in a world all their own. Like us, they measure their lives in hours; but they only count the ones spent in the air.

Like Horowitz and his fascination with Confederates, Roger didn't have a choice when it came to flying. Although no Rohweders were present at Kitty Hawk on the cold and windy December day in 1903 when the Wrights made history, Ralph Rohweder, Roger's father, got his pilot license at the age of seventeen in 1934, only thirty years after the Wright's first flight and only seven years after Lindbergh's solo flight across the Atlantic. An early childhood memory of Roger's is his father landing a plane on their small ice-bound lake in Lake Villa, Illinois. His father spent his life flying and trying to make a living around planes. Ralph Rohweder even flew across the Atlantic with famed aviator Max Conrad in a plane not much larger than the *Spirit of St. Louis.* Many of Roger's brothers and sisters took ground school, and he and his pilot brother are in constant communication, with the main topics being airplanes and flying.

Roger fits the profile for being a pilot. He has intense focus and drive and is not risk averse. Like many other pilots, he has owned motorcycles, and, in addition to being a pilot, Roger is a certified scuba diver. He also left a secure position at Oracle, the premier technology company where he was working on video-on-demand software, to start a small company with two other guys, a company whose only product for about ten years was a little database called NoveList. This was a career move that most of his Oracle colleagues just could not understand.

Roger is also an excellent example of how a reader navigates through nonfiction, giving us an example of someone who uses this class of materials to resolve anomalous states of both knowledge and experience.

To become a pilot, one goes through ground school. This involves attending classes and studying textbooks such as Jeppesen Sanderson's (1996) *Aviation Fundamentals.* Like any other textbook, *Aviation Fundamentals* it is divided into chapters and contains illustrations and checklists to ensure that students understand the keys concepts presented in the specific units. Through the textbook and class lectures, student pilots learn about the concepts of lift, airport traffic patterns, and the effects of weather on airplane performance.

After ground school, a student actually spends time flying with an instructor and eventually solo. Prior to getting a license and becoming an official pilot, one has to take and pass a written licensing exam. Many would-be pilots get ready for this exam by using test-prep books. Like many other test-preparation titles, these books are based on previous tests and give sample questions to let students assess whether they are ready for the real exam through questions such as this one:

With calm wind conditions, which flight operation would require the most power? A. A right-hovering turn, B. A left-hovering turn, C. Hovering out of ground effect. (Correct answer: B) (Aviation Supplies and Academics, Inc., 1997)

Both of these types of books are used to complete specific tasks and resolve anomalous states of knowledge. Roger successfully completed this test and got his license on January 26, 1999. He flies as often as his family, work, and weather will allow, but he knows that even in a perfect world, he will never have enough hours in the air. There will always be flights that got delayed and eventually cancelled trips that will never be made.

But when he can't physically be in the air, Roger can psychically be there through books, especially those that describe the pilot's flying experience, like one of Roger's favorite pilot narratives, *Zero Three Bravo* (Gosnell 1993).

Zero-Three-Bravo is Mariana Gosnell's single-engine Luscombe Silvaire, and her book details her three-month solo flight across America. Unlike Lindbergh, who needed the most straightforward route across the Atlantic, Gosnell meanders around the United States, lingering at small-town airports and visiting with the people who inhabit them. On her flight, Gosnell meets folks like Al Morris, who was a pilot in World War I and now lives in a house next to a runway. She also introduces us to all of the folks behind the scenes, like airplane mechanics and the operators of small-town America's many airports. Gosnell also provides plenty of detail about the her close calls in the air, with enough graphic detail that pilot and novelist Clyde Edgerton says, "If you have ever dreamed of flying a little airplane, this book will get you as close to that experience as any book can."

When Roger got his pilot license in 1999, he was licensed to fly under visual flight rules (VFR). In other words, he was allowed to fly when weather conditions permitted and could not legally fly in weather with low-visibility or fly through clouds. Like many pilots, he found these rules restrictive and began to pursue an instrument rating, which would expand the conditions under which he could fly. Getting an instrument rating involved more ground school, more practice time with a flight instructor, and passing another exam. It also involved spending time in a flight simulator that simulated a variety of flight conditions in which instruments were required, like the experience of landing a plane in adverse weather conditions. These simulations enable pilots seeking an instrument rating to experience instrument flying without actually endangering themselves, an instructor, or a plane. The time spent in a simulator both helps test a student's knowledge of instrument flying and gives them the experience of flying under these conditions. These simulations approximate the experience of flying in a way that is vaguely reminiscent of our living historians simulating the experience of the Civil War.

It is doubtful that the demands of family, work, and life in general will allow Roger to spend three months flying solo around the United States. For him, this represents an anomalous state of experience. Gosnell gives him the means of resolving this anomalous state through her book, and by reading it, Roger gets to log all of those hours in the air—if not in his official log-book, at least in his easy chair.

David Carr: Turning Point, 1968

The Dow began 1968 hovering at 905. In January, the United States suffered a major setback in Vietnam when the Tet Offensive demonstrated that the Viet Cong could strike at will anywhere in South Vietnam. Twenty-two-year-old David Carr was looking forward to completing his masters in teaching at Columbia as Eugene McCarthy began his run for the White House and Lyndon Johnson announced that he would not seek reelection.

When he discusses 1968, Carr describes himself as someone who "grew up in northern New Jersey, in a very white town" and who "went to a very white school without a lot of social differentiation" (Carr 2003a). The main differentiator in his town was not race but religion. Talking about his hometown's demographics, Carr says, "You were either a Catholic or a Protestant or more specifically, you were either Catholic or Presbyterian" (Carr 2003b, 201).

In 1968, Carr's career goal was to be an English teacher and open the world of Literature (capital *L*) to honors students. Before beginning graduate school, Carr spent some time in Virginia, where he saw firsthand how common prejudice and racial discrimination were in that part of the country. During his time in Virginia, he also heard Dr. Martin Luther King Jr. speak on these topics, the first of two occasions when Carr would hear Dr. King speak in person. His experiences in Virginia showed Carr that the world was more complex than the one in which he grew up and somewhat messier than the one portrayed by national television networks in the 1950s and 1960s.

In 1968, Carr began keeping a list of the books he was reading, something that is not surprising for a graduate student preparing to teach high school English. His list contained many of the titles you would expect: *Lord of the Flies, Death of a Salesman, This Side of Paradise, Pale Fire,* and *Lady Chatterley's Lover.* The list also contains some titles you wouldn't expect, titles such as Eldridge Cleaver's *Soul on Ice* and *The Autobiography of Malcolm X,* books voicing the black experience and venting the pent-up rage that many African Americans were feeling.

In addition to reading Cleaver and Malcolm X, Carr also took a course in African American literature and read authors such as Richard Wright and James Baldwin and titles such as *Brown Girl, Brownstones* by Paule Marshall. Carr describes his reading during this period as a vehicle to "fill in some gaps in my reading and my experience. I realized that the narrowness of my upbringing was entirely inappropriate for the culture of the times" (Carr 2003a). Carr was reading Cleaver, Malcolm, and Wright not necessarily to gain information about the black experience but to access the experiences of African Americans through their writing. He talks of these books and his reading of them as a way for him "to feel and understand empathetically" the lives of people who were different from him. His reading allows him to contextualize a wide array of behaviors and ideas and language that he could otherwise never have assimilated or explained to himself and others.

In the spring of 1968, students seize the president's office at Columbia as on-campus demonstrations against the war escalate. Carr comes up out of the subway at 116th Street, finds the university's gate closed, and realizes that "this is a different world than the one I had entered, a world that was different from the one that existed when I got on the subway that morning." (Carr 2003a). On April 4, David turns twenty-three, and at 6:01 P.M., Martin Luther King is assassinated in Memphis.

Riots erupted in more than 125 cities all over the country, and entire sections of Detroit, Washington, Chicago, and Philadelphia are looted and burned. As the news about Dr. King's death becomes known and violence begins to break our across the country, Robert Kennedy faces an African American audience in Indianapolis. While his advisors urge him not to honor his speaking engagement, Kennedy delivers a brief speech in which he quotes his favorite poet (Aeschylus) and invokes the culture of ancient Greece as he urges everyone across America to dedicate themselves to taming the savageness of man and to making gentle the life of this world.

Later that year, Carr goes to interview for a teaching position in Princeton, New Jersey, and finds the school closed because its office had been fire-bombed the day before. He eventually secures a high school faculty position in the Princeton school system in part because of his knowledge of African American literature.

Waiting for the new school year to begin, Carr takes a job working with mostly African American children in a Head Start center. His day involves making sure the children are fed and getting their snacks, but he also engages them in educational experiences designed to prepare them for entering the public school system. He is listening to a portable radio in the center when he learns that while making his victory speech after winning the 1968 Democratic primary in California, Robert Kennedy is assassinated.

Confronted with all of this, Carr begins to ask himself the question that is familiar to all of us in the post–September 11 world: How do I think about this? What do I feel? "I was not an activist. I did not drop any kind of drugs. I didn't smoke anything. I didn't hike around Europe with a backpack. I became a teacher" (Carr 2003a).

Carr instinctively turns to reading to find out how to "think about this." Thirty years later, sitting in his office at the University of North Carolina at Chapel Hill, he can articulate how reading helped him "think about this." Carr views reading "as a subliminal life, our way of carrying out a dialogue and processing things through an imagination that is not here and now but is here and now" (Carr 2003a). In essence, reading is our way of experiencing and assimilating knowledge and experience that are beyond the microcosm of the lives we are living.

Through his reading, Carr finds his way to think about things. His model for thinking about the changed world of the sixties is Malcolm X. "Malcolm's autobiography was among the most significant books I ever read. It was a book that I later used when I was teaching adult education, because Malcolm is constantly shifting identities and learning and embracing the future, embracing a new identity. He can admit that he was wrong; he can revise the way he thought about his life and the way he thought about other lives. It's a model for adult development apart from its brilliance in interpreting the African American experience" (Carr 2003a).

Carr continues, "In the *Autobiography,* I found a record of human transformations that I had never seen before. My own childhood was not so far away that I could see the differences between living as I had, and the life that Malcolm Little had lived. As he changed his names—Malcolm Little to Detroit Red to a prison number to Malcolm X to El-Hajj Malik El-Shabazz (and then to Saint Malcolm)—he demonstrated the resilience of his gifts. It is this quality of an evolving life that has been most important in the three and a half decades since I read the book" (Carr 2003a).

It was during spring break at the University of North Carolina when I videotaped Dr. Carr about 1968. New leaves were beginning to appear at the ends of stiff, barren branches, and the oaks were finally letting go of the dead, brown leaves that they had clung to through a very harsh winter. Sitting in his faculty office, talking about Malcolm X and Cleaver's *Soul on Ice,* the holder of an outstanding teacher award from the University of North Carolina wonders if he made the right choice when he became a teacher. He compares his becoming a teacher to imagining what it would have been like for Cleaver to become a policeman. "It was like embracing the source of all my agony and identifying myself with the institution that had constructed me. I came to see that schools as institutions were really terrible places. In part, because I saw what they did to minority kids, but I also saw what they did to majority kids as well" (Carr 2003a). Carr is talking about schools that were not facing up to a changing society, institutions that ignored the turmoil going on around them and produced students who were "all schooled up" instead of students excited about learning and equipped to do it.

Books again come to Carr's rescue as he reads John Holt, Herbert Kohl, George Dennison's *The Lives of Children,* Ivan Illich's *Deschooling Society,* and a host of others committed to educational reform. As he reads these books, he realizes that (like the title of a particularly popular book on educational reform) teaching *can* be a subversive activity. So Carr does in fact become an activist but one who works from inside the system instead of one who marches around it waving banners and yelling at policemen.

"So many spirits and ideas and worlds got burned up by the events of the sixties and seventies." One of these was Cleaver, who Carr feels let politics get in the way of his writing. "I don't mean that his political writing wasn't good writing. What I mean is that there was an essayist there who had a sensibility that got burned up" (Carr 2003a). Carr is also sensitive to the loss of Cleaver as an essayist because it is his chosen form.

One of the essays contained in Carr's (2003b) book *The Promise of Cultural Institutions* is a speech that he gave at the White House Colloquium on Libraries, Museums, and Life-Long Learning in October 2002. Titled "Each Life," this essay opens with Carr inviting his audience to visualize that "As morning spreads across the nation we can imagine the opening of about 40,000 doors and gates to public and academic libraries, museums, history centers and sites, gardens, arboreta, zoos and aquaria" (Carr 2002). Along with his White House audience, his essay also asks us to "imagine the people of those American places entering and beginning to search for something they require" (Carr 2002). He goes on in his essay to say that everyone entering these institutions this morning is carrying questions or desires that may have begun in their family or in school, questions encountered and desires awakened through reading books or through conservations with friends, colleagues, and sometimes strangers. For Carr, the hope of the country and the hope for all of us is that we live in a world where we are free to seek, to search for the knowledge and experiences we need to "make something more of ourselves" (Carr 2002). He is offering us the model that worked for him and for Malcolm X, a life that is based on "the everyday habits of curiosity" (Carr 2002).

"It is never satisfied, the mind, never."[1]

Lily Tomlin does a parody of a certain type of television commercial that begins "I am not an actress. I am a housewife just like yourself." A nervous Tomlin keeps looking down and away from the camera, unable to look directly at it the way a professional actress would. Tomlin's character wants us to try "Grrrr," a detergent that gobbles up stains like a thousand tiny little piranha fish. Our minds are also like piranha fish; they gobble up not only information and knowledge, they gobble up experience, too.

When readers ask us for help in finding a "good" book to read, they are inviting us to assist them in addressing a question that truly matters, a question whose answer is going to make a difference in their lives. Whether these readers are seeking the latest award-winning novel, the latest best-seller (which may or may not be shelved in the fiction section), or a story about real people, living in real places and doing real things, they are looking for more than just another author or title. They are asking us to help them connect the books we are suggesting to their lives. Whether we suggest books that we ourselves have read or choose to introduce readers to resources that will lead them to discover new titles on their own, we need to recognize that responding to this call for assistance means understanding not only books but readers and how they use books to both understand their world and expand their experience of it. Providing excellent service to our readers means understanding that their requests for reading guidance do not occur in a vacuum. Like each of the readers examined in this chapter, every reader is engaged in an ongoing process of deepening his or her understanding and experience. This journey is a universal one, and for many of us, how far and how deep we go on this quest is the measure of our lives.

In his book *The Hero with a Thousand Faces,* Joseph Campbell (1973) argues that certain motifs are common to the human experience regardless of race, nationality, geography, or time. One such motif is the hero on a journey. A key element of this motif is that the hero responds to a call to adventure, a call that takes him out of the everyday into a world that is connected to the universal. Each culture has its own archetypal hero, but Campbell argues that all heroes share a common pattern of call, trial, growth, and return.

Likewise, each of the readers in this chapter is an individual, but each represents something about all readers. Each of the readers in this chapter is driven by an innate need to expand his or her experience of the world by drawing on the experiences of others through their written words and their stories. Horowitz hears echoes of himself in Robert Lee Hodge's hard-core approach to reenactment. Radway renews her ability to read not only with her mind but her heart. Roger Rohweder sits in cockpits of planes he has never seen and flies to places he has never been. David Carr melds with Malcolm X and knows what it is like to change when you find yourself in a world that is no longer the one you thought you knew.

Like these four archetypal readers, all readers have found themselves at one time or another renewed, transported, and fascinated not only by tales of imaginary kingdoms peopled with "little people" but by stories that are true.

Note

1. Stevens 1974, 247.

References

Aviation Supplies and Academics, Inc. 1997. *Private pilot test prep.* New-castle, WA: Aviation Supplies and Academics.

Belkin, N. J. 1982. ASK for information retrieval: part 1. Background and theory. *Journal of Documentation* 38: 61–71.

Black, Jay A., and Michael Betrus. 2003. *101 best resumes for grads.* New York: McGraw-Hill.

Bolles, Richard Nelson. 2001. *What color is your parachute?: A practical manual for job-hunters and career changers.* Berkeley, CA: Ten Speed Press.

Bowker, Geoffrey C., and Susan Leigh Star. 2002. *Sorting things out: Classification and its consequences.* Cambridge, MA: MIT Press.

Campbell, Joseph. 1973. *The hero with a thousand faces.* Princeton, NJ: Princeton University Press.

Carr, David. 2002. Each life: Cultural institutions and civic engagement. The White House Colloquium on Libraries, Museums, and Lifelong Learning. URL: http://www.imls.gov/conference/namls2002/carr.htm (Accessed December 11, 2003).

Carr, David. 2003a. Interview by Duncan Smith, 13 March.

Carr, David. 2003b. *The promise of cultural institutions.* Walnut Creek, CA: Altamira Press.

Clay, Rebecca A. 2001. Green is good for you. *Monitor on Psychology* 32: 40–42.

Gans, Herbert J. 1974. *Popular culture and high culture: An analysis and evaluation of taste.* New York: Basic Books.

Gosnell, Mariana. 1993. *Zero three bravo: Solo across America in a small plane.* (New York: Touchstone.

Horowitz, Tony. 1999. *Confederates in the attic: Dispatches from the unfinished Civil War.* New York: Vintage Departures.

Radway, Janice A. 1991. *Reading the romance: Women, patriarchy, and popular literature.* Chapel Hill: University of North Carolina Press.

Radway, Janice A. 1997. *A feeling for books: The Book-of-the-Month Club, literary taste, and middle-class desire.* Chapel Hill: University of North Carolina Press.

Sanderson, Jeppesen. 1996. *Aviation fundamentals.* Englewood, CO: Jeppesen Sanderson, Inc.

Stevens, Wallace. 1974. The well-dressed man with a beard. *The collected poems of Wallace Stevens.* New York: Alfred A Knopf.

Tolkien, J.R.R. 1982. *The hobbit or there and back again.* Rev. ed. New York: Ballantine Books.

Viorst, Judith. 1986. *Necessary losses: The loves, illusions, dependencies, and impossible expectations that all of us have to give up in order to grow.* New York: Free Press.

Whitcomb, Susan Britton. 2003. *Resume magic: Trade secrets of a professional resume writer.* Indianapolis, IN: JIST.

Chapter 8

Nonfiction and Young Readers

Crystal Faris

As a newly minted MLS and practicing children's librarian, I attended a workshop with Dr. Beverly Kobrin, a recognized proponent of encouraging children to read nonfiction. She had boundless enthusiasm, jumping around the utilitarian library meeting room and turning it into a place of discovery and fascination. She put a pencil through a plastic bag of water over my head, and I was sold on informational books for children.

My new fervor was not matched by my colleagues, however, and I soon understood that most youth services librarians preferred reading and recommending fiction. The committees composing booklists for children ignored suggestions of nonfiction. The committees organizing Mock Newbery and Mock Caldecott discussions located fiction titles that were "musts" for the list and left no room for nonfiction. These local committees reflected national committees as well, with children's nonfiction receiving fewer awards and fewer recommendations than its more popular relation—children's fiction.

Why Nonfiction?

The same things that fascinated me about Dr. Kobrin's pencil-through-the-plastic-bag trick also fascinate young people. When she put the pencil in the bag, why did water not leak out around the pencil? My fingers itched to try the experiment myself. Would I get the same result? Would it work with all types of plastic bags? Did the same principle that sealed the bag around the pencil work in other ways as well?

Curiosity

Children and adolescents are curious. They want to understand the world around them, to know what is true, to acquire information, and to make connections between what they already know and new information. Nonfiction reading satisfies those desires. More than satisfaction, nonfiction brings pleasure to young readers.

Brain Development

Much research has been done on brain development, particularly in infants. We know that through the first several months of life, the human brain grows at a rapid and dramatic pace, producing millions of brain cells. Watching infants grow and learn is an amazing thing. They seem to absorb new information easily and gain new skills rapidly. A toddler's favorite word, following "No," is "Why?"

Brain development does not stop after infancy, however. In fact, we know now that a second stage of development—almost as intense as the first—occurs during preteen years. Dr. Jay Giedd of the National Institute of Mental Health discussed this second wave of development on the PBS program *Frontline*. He spoke of the knowledge that rapid brain development occurred in the womb and during the first eighteen months of life. Then he continued, "But it was only when we started following the same children by scanning their brains at two-year intervals that we detected a second wave of overproduction" ("Frontline: Inside the Teenage Brain." URL: http://www.pbs.org/wgbh/pages/frontline/shows/teenbrain/etc/synopsis.html [Accessed September 9, 2003]). This second wave occurs roughly between the ages of ten and thirteen and is quickly followed by a process in which the brain prunes and organizes its neural pathways. "In many ways, it's the most tumultuous time of brain development since coming out of the womb," says Dr. Giedd ("Frontline: Inside the Teenage Brain." URL: http://www.pbs.org/wgbh/pages/frontline/shows/teenbrain/etc/synopsis. html [Accessed September 9, 2003]).

Logic would then tell us that informational books are important for all children as their brains develop, but these factual books may be even more important to ten- to thirteen-year-olds. Preteens return to that favorite word of their toddler years, "Why?" When the brains of preteens grow, there is no better time to provide interesting and enjoyable informational books.

Boys and Reading

Michael W. Smith and Jeffrey D. Whelan published their research on boys and education/reading in the appropriately titled *Reading Don't Fix No Chevys* (Smith and Whelan 2002). The boys in their study needed to have clear goals when reading. They read for information, to find out what happens, to fix or make something. The boys felt that much of the literature they used in school did not meet these goals and were too vague for them to have a clear sense of why they were reading. Assigned reading did not give them a good sense of whether they were achieving what they were supposed to achieve.

According to Smith and Whelan (2002), research also shows that boys do not comprehend narrative fiction as well as girls, that boys have much less interest in leisure reading than girls, that boys are more inclined to read informational texts, and that boys like to read about hobbies, sports, and things they do or want to do. By the time they are in middle school, most boys label themselves as nonreaders. These same boys, however, when pressed, will reveal that they read magazines, newspapers, comic books, graphic novels, and informational materials. In short, they enjoy reading what most schools do not assign and what most libraries do not market to children and adolescents—nonfiction.

Libraries need to build "guy-friendly" collections, according to Patrick Jones and Dawn Cartwright Fiorelli (2003). One of the most "guy-friendly" collections that we can offer is one strong in areas of interest to boys—particularly nonfiction. Then we must let the boys know that the nonfiction areas are as valid as the fiction area. Jones and Fiorelli (2003) include in their article nonfiction areas of interest to guys in Dewey order:

000–299	World Records / Computers / Bigfoot / UFOs / Unexplained / Monsters / Parapsychology / Mythology
300–399	Scary Stories / Urban Legends / True Crime / Forensics / Military / Study Guides
500–599	Dinosaurs / Snakes / Sharks / Wolves / Outer Space / Reptiles / Natural Disasters / Math Riddles
600–699	Anything with Wheels (bikes, cars, trucks, etc.) / Sex / Electronics

700–799	Almost any Sport (professional and participatory) / Game System Codes / Magic / Drawing / Comics / Optical Illusions / Hip Hop / Rock Music / Cartoons / Star Wars / Special Effects / Puns
800–899	Jokes / Poetry / Story Collections / How to Write Poetry / Riddles
900–999	Wars / Biographies of Athletes, Musicians, Actors, Explorers

Jones and Fiorelli (2003) enforce the need for "guy-friendly" collections with the appalling statistic that one in thirty-two people in the United States is "currently in jail, in prison, on probation, on parole, or has been one of those things. The majority of these people are male. The majority of the male prison population has limited education; many are high school dropouts. The limits of education are almost always revealed in reading problems. If we want young men to have their hands clutching a graduation diploma rather than the bars of a cell, then it is time to start overcoming the obstacle course we've set up in . . . libraries in order to ensure that guys read" (Jones and Fiorelli 2003).

Reality Reading

Reality is fascinating. We all love a story, but tell us the story is true and we enjoy it even more. Witness the recent phenomenon of reality television. Some of the most popular shows on television do not involve actors delivering scripts created for them by professional writers but regular people put in bizarre situations, usually in the hopes of meeting the right person or winning an amazing amount of money.

"Reality TV has nothing on reality reading," states Mary Arnold, Regional Teen Services Manager of the Cuyahoga, Ohio County Library, in material she presented at the American Library Association 2003 Annual Conference (Arnold 2003). She proceeds to list the following qualities of "reality reading" for young people:

- Narratives with the power and drive of story
- Targets a variety of developing personal interests
- Supports visual learning styles
- Appealing formats, less daunting for reluctant readers
- Stimulates patterns of lifelong curiosity and inquiry
- Connects with developmental needs

- Popular with readers fascinated with facts

- Targets those who read to do

Narrative nonfiction reads like fiction but with the added bonus of being true. Jennifer Armstrong's *Shipwreck at the Bottom of the World* tells the "extraordinary true story of Shackleton and the Endurance." The author informs the reader at the book's beginning that every crew member survived this astonishing experience of being shipwrecked while trying to reach the South Pole. However, the author's vivid narrative usually has the reader convinced that someone could die at any moment.

Personal interest leads young readers to discover new information from nonfiction. Following the release of the Disney movie *Finding Nemo,* nonfiction picture books about ocean life were in demand at most local public libraries. The movie's ironic gag with Bruce the Shark's attempts to give up eating fish is all the more humorous to a young child who has just enjoyed a book about the species such as Seymour Simon's *Shark.* In *Shark,* the reader is treated to an up-close photo of row upon row of teeth in the open mouth of a sand tiger shark.

An abundance of illustrated nonfiction pleases the visual learning styles of young readers. Artist Steve Jenkins creates stunning and informative cut-paper collage picture books for all ages. His book, *The Top of the World,* takes the reader on a climb of Mount Everest.

Illustrations, photographs, editorial cartoons, and sidebars explaining the terms or the addition of fascinating tidbits of information combine in much nonfiction for young readers to present an appealing format, attractive to reluctant readers. Karen Blumenthal's *Six Days in October* grippingly recounts the 1929 stock market crash in such an appealing format that adolescents come away not only understanding the crash but the stock market in general.

Lifelong curiosity and possible future related careers may develop from reading excellent nonfiction as a child. Young children often request books about firefighters or astronauts or cowboys. Older children seek books about celebrities or other famous people. *Action Jackson,* by Jan Greenberg and Sandra Jordan with illustrations by Robert Andrew Parker, introduces Jackson Pollock to young readers in beautiful clear prose. Could that be the beginning for an artist or a lover of art? Jim Murphy's *An American Plague* tells the "true and terrifying story of the yellow fever epidemic of 1793." Could that be the beginning of a lifelong interest in medicine or disease research?

Nonfiction books often provide comfort and information and challenge through the developmental stages and life changes that children and adolescents experience. Parents often request books for children dealing with moving through stages such as beginning school or suffering from the loss of a loved one. Adolescents deal with the changes in their bodies and in their relationships to parents. They begin to gather information and turn it into knowledge relevant to their personal lives. They desire to affect change not only in themselves but in the world. Peter Nelson's *Left for Dead* recalls the fascinating story of sixth-grader Hunter Scott and his history fair project on the sinking of the U.S.S. *Indianapolis* at the end of WWII. The navy covered up this incident, and the ship's captain received an unfair court-martial. Hunter Scott's work led to setting the record straight.

A fascination with facts abounds in young people as well as adults. Trivia board games continue to sell, and trivia game shows continue to draw an audience. A barnesandnoble.com reader review of *Oh, Yuck!: The Encyclopedia of Everything Nasty* by Joy Masoff, raved about her daughter's reading of the book: "My 9-year-old daughter actually turned off the video game so she could bone-up on gross trivia. At breakfast this morning she says, 'Hey Mom, guess what: Vampire Bats pee while they suck blood from their prey so they will be light enough to fly away.'"

Finally, many adolescents read to accomplish something. Books about video game systems provide tips about reaching the next level of a game or about creating your own characters. Science projects in books offer fun experiments to attempt. Sports books challenge athletes to improve. In fact, the June 2003 issue of *Golf Digest* included an article titled "How to Get Junior Reading This Summer" and reviewed several books on golf for young readers.

The Youth Services Librarian's Role

What then is the role of a youth services librarian in nurturing the curiosity of children and teens? How can you encourage these library users to discover information and pleasure in reading nonfiction? The following are six areas in which to focus your thoughts and to sharpen your nonfiction reader's advisory skills.

1. Read Nonfiction

Good youth services librarians read children's and young adult books. Most youth services librarians read fiction children's and young adult books. Youth services librarians tend to be "fiction-centric." If you prefer fiction, be deliberate about adding nonfiction to your "Must Read" list. I believe that even the most "fiction-centric" youth services librarian will be amazed at the stunning visuals in many recent nonfiction books as well as the unusual perspectives and complex subjects that make for fascinating reading. These quality books are winning the nonfiction awards. Add these award winners to your readers' advisory lists. In addition, Kathleen

Baxter's "NonFiction BookTalker" column in *School Library Journal* provides excellent sure-to-be popular nonfiction titles for your reading pleasure.

2. Stay Current

Read reviews of nonfiction books for children and teens as well as fiction— not just the reviews in the subject areas where additions need to be made to the collection for homework support. Listen to your young patrons and note any changing areas of popular interest. Pay attention to movie releases so you can display nonfiction books in related subject areas. Maintain contact with curriculum libraries in your school district(s) to know the subject areas that will be taught and that may inspire a student's curiosity. Weed, weed, weed outdated nonfiction titles. Nothing hurts a student more than to use wrong information from a library book in a report. Nothing takes away library credibility faster than a nonfiction pleasure reader finding only old-fashioned information books in the stacks.

3. Build a Core List

When reading nonfiction, keep a list of those titles that would be winners with children and adolescents. Just as you store a core list of mystery authors in you readers' advisory brain, store a core list of nonfiction authors. As a result, nonfiction titles will come to mind when the child in front of you must do a book report and appears to view it as the most awful task possible. Surprise him or her with a few trivia facts from a great nonfiction read as well as titles from your favorite fiction reads. Young people enjoy having a choice, and you may be surprised at how often they will choose the nonfiction you recommend. You may be surprised at how easy and fun it is to sell a nonfiction read.

4. Evaluate Titles

Critique the children's and young adult nonfiction that you read. In developing and maintaining a browseable nonfiction collection as well as a homework-supporting nonfiction collection, be critical. Evaluation criteria for children's and young adult informational books include the following:

- Is it accurate?
- Is the author qualified?
- Is the information current?
- Are there any stereotyping or sweeping generalizations?

- Are the illustrations used effectively?
- Is the reader encouraged to think?
- Is the writing style appropriate and stimulating?
- Does the format and organization aid in understanding the information?
- If there is an index, is it useful?
- If there is other back matter, does it advance the information?

5. Visit Stacks

When you walk into your children's or young adult area, what do you see? If it is similar to most public library children's rooms, you see plenty of room to browse picture books, face out displays of fiction books, displays of fiction titles, and bulletin boards or flyers highlighting story programs full of picture book fiction titles. You may also see nonfiction stacks so crowded with homework-related materials that browsing for nonfiction pleasure reads is not encouraged. If your young adult area is similar to those in most public libraries, you see shelves lined with fiction, new books on display, maybe some self-help and teen issue books, and possibly a few graphic novels. Think seriously about how to make the stacks more browser-friendly and how to add nonfiction pleasure reading to displays. While you are in the stacks, find children or teens and offer suggestions for great reads. Let them know that you can recommend a good nonfiction books as easily as a fiction title.

6. Market Information

Make the stacks inviting to browsers. Place books face out in nonfiction stacks. Create an easy nonfiction area near the picture books for the very young and curious. Add nonfiction to displays; for example, place informational books on the Gold Rush with the historical fiction or factual books about the ocean with those recommended summertime "beach reads." Offer nonfiction-only displays to subtly remind children and adolescents that reading nonfiction is as valuable as reading fiction. Insert nonfiction titles to subject and grade-level recommended booklists and develop nonfiction-only printed booklists. Celebrate the Siebert Award as well as the Newbery and Caldecott. Incorporate nonfiction into baby, toddler, and preschool story hours. Hold parent-and-son book discussion groups using nonfiction books. Integrate nonfiction into formal booktalks.

Conclusion

From the beginning of library services to children and teens, the librarian's goal has been to offer the right book to the right child or teen at the right time. Often the right book is nonfiction. Nonfiction satisfies a young person's curiosity. Nonfiction stimulates brain development. Nonfiction may inspire a reluctant reader to give a book a try. Reality is fascinating, and through nonfiction reader's advisory, youth services librarians have the opportunity to inspire children and teens to gain knowledge.

Awards for Nonfiction Children's Books

Fascinating nonfiction books for children and teens are named as award recipients each year. Listed here are several awards given primarily to informational books published for young people. These awards highlight the best in nonfiction books. Your knowledge of these awards will provide you with a broad base for your nonfiction reader's advisory.

ALSC/Robert F. Sibert Informational Book Award

The ALSC/Robert F. Sibert Informational Book Award is given by the Association for Library Service to Children, a division of the American Library Association. According to the ALSC Web site, this award "is intended to honor the author whose work of nonfiction has made a significant contribution to the field of children's literature" ("ALSC/Robert F. Sibert Informational Book Award." URL: http://www.ala.org/Content/NavigationMenu/ALSC/Awards_and_Scholarships1/Literary_and_Related_Awards/Sibert_Medal/Sibert_Medal.htm [Accessed September 9, 2003]). Each year, a committee selects one book for children up to and including the age of fourteen to win the award. Honor books are usually named as well. The first award was named in January 2001 and recognized books published in the calendar year 2000. Medal winners have included *Sir Walter Raleigh and the Quest for El Dorado* by Marc Aronson; *Black Potatoes: The Story of the Great Irish Famine, 1845–1850* by Susan Campbell Bartoletti; and *The Life and Death of Adolf Hitler* by James Cross Giblin.

Orbis Pictus Award

The National Council of Teachers of English (NCTE) established an annual award for promoting and recognizing excellence in the writing of nonfiction for children, with the first award recipients named in 1990. According to the NCTE Orbis Pictus Web site, the name "commemorates the work of Johannes Amos Comenius, *Orbis Pictus—The World in Pictures* (1657), considered to be the first book actually planned for children" (The National Council of Teachers of English. "NCTE Orbis Pictus Nonfiction Award." URL: http://www.ncte.org/about/awards/sect/elem/106877.htm [Accessed September 9, 2003]). This award is presented each November to one title. Up to five Honor Books and additional Recommended Titles may be named. Previous recipients include *When Marian Sang: The True Recital of Marian Anderson: The Voice of a Century* by Pam Muñoz Ryan and illustrated by Brian Selznick; *Black Potatoes: The Story of the Great Irish Famine, 1845–1850* by Susan Campbell Bartoletti; *Hurry Freedom: African Americans in Gold Rush California* by Jerry Stanley; and *Through My Eyes* by Ruby Bridges.

The International Reading Association (IRA) Children's Book Awards

IRA Children's Book Awards are given for an author's first or second published book directed toward a children's or young adult audience (preschool to age seventeen). Currently, awards are given for fiction and nonfiction in each of three categories: primary, intermediate, and young adult. Nonfiction has been a part of the awards since 1995. Previous nonfiction winners include *The Pot That Juan Built* by Nancy Andrews-Goebel; *If the World Were a Village: A Book about the World's People* by David J. Smith; *Headin' for Better Times: The Arts of the Great Depression* by Duane Damon; *Aero and Officer Mike* by Joan Plummer Russell; *Pearl Harbor Warriors* by Dorinda Makanaonalani Nicholson and Larry Nicholson; and *Meltdown: A Race against Nuclear Disaster at Three Mile Island* by Wilborn Hampton.

Washington Post—Children's Book Guild Nonfiction Award

First given in 1977, this annual award honors an author "whose total work has contributed significantly to the quality of nonfiction for children." ("*Washington Post*—Children's Book Guild Nonfiction Award." URL: http://www.childrensbookguild.org/awardnonfiction.htm [Accessed September 9, 2003]). The award is announced each March at the business meeting of the Children' Book Guild. Every youth services librarian should be aware of the names of these authors as they consistently produce fascinating and accurate nonfiction for children on a variety of subjects. Past winners include Steve Jenkins, George Ancona, Jim Murphy, Diane Stanley, Laurence Pringle, Jean Craighead George, and Rhoda Blumberg.

The Flora Stieglitz Straus Award

Established in 1994, the award is presented annually for a distinguished work of nonfiction that fulfills humanitarian ideals and serves as an inspiration to young people. The Children's Book Committee at Bank Street College of Education names the recipients. Previous award recipients include *No More! Stories and Songs of Slave Resistance* by Doreen Rappaport; *Carver: A Life in Poems* by Marilyn Nelson; *Ida B. Wells: Mother of the Civil Rights Movement* by Dennis Brindell Fradin and Judith Bloom Fradin; and *Iqbal Masih and the Crusaders against Child Slavery* by Susan Kuklin.

Notable Social Studies Books for Young People

Each year the National Council for the Social Studies (NCSS) in cooperation with the Children's Book Council (CBC) selects outstanding books in the field of social studies for children in kindergarten to eighth grade. The annual bibliography has been created since 1972 and includes both nonfiction and fiction. According to the NCSS Web site, "The selection committee looks for books that emphasize human relations, represent a diversity of groups and are sensitive to a broad range of cultural experiences, present an original theme or a fresh slant on a traditional topic, are easily readable and of high literary quality, and have a pleasing format and, when appropriate, illustrations that enrich the text" (National Council for the Social Studies. "Notable Social Studies Books for Young People." URL: http://www.socialstudies.org/resources/notable [Accessed September 9, 2003]).

Outstanding Science Trade Books for Students K–12

The National Science Teachers Association (NSTA) selects outstanding children's science trade books each year in cooperation with the Children's Book Council (CBC). They have produced this bibliographic project each year since 1973. From 1973 through 2001, the books selected were primarily targeted at grades K through 8. Beginning in 2002, the list was expanded to include high school as well.

References

ALSC/Robert F. Sibert Informational Book Award. URL: http://www. ala.org/Content/NavigationMenu/ALSC/Awards_and_Scholarships1/ Literary_and_Related_Awards/Sibert_Medal/Sibert_Medal.htm (Accessed September 9, 2003).

Arnold, Mary. *Reality reading: Nonfiction for young adults*. URL: http://www.ala.org/Content/NavigationMenu/YALSA/News_and_ Events/BooktalkingArnold.pdf (Accessed September 9, 2003).

Bank Street. *About our awards*. URL: http://www.bankstreet.edu/ bookcom/about_awards.html (Accessed September 9, 2003).

Baxter, Kathleen A., and Marcia Agness Kochel. 1999. *Gotcha!: Nonfiction booktalks to get kids excited about reading*. Englewood, CO: Libraries Unlimited.

Baxter, Kathleen A., and Marcia Agness Kochel. 2002. *Gotcha again!: More nonfiction booktalks to get kids excited about reading*. Greenwood Village, CO: Libraries Unlimited/Teacher Ideas Press.

Baxter, Kathleen. Nonfiction booktalker. *School Library Journal* [Monthly column].

Children's Book Council. URL: http://www.cbcbooks.org (Accessed September 9, 2003).

Frontline: Inside the teenage brain. URL: http://www.pbs.org/wgbh/ pages/frontline/shows/teenbrain/etc/synopsis.html (Accessed September 9, 2003).

International Reading Association. *Children's book awards*. URL: http://www.reading.org/awards/children.html (Accessed September 9, 2003).

Jones, Patrick, and Dawn Cartwright Fiorelli. 2003. Overcoming the obstacle course: Teenage boys and reading. *Teacher Librarian* 30 (February). URL: http://www.teacherlibrarian.com/tlmag/v_30/v_30_3_ feature.html (Accessed September 9, 2003).

National Council for the Social Studies. *Notable social studies books for young people*. URL: http://www.socialstudies.org/resources/notable (Accessed September 9, 2003).

National Science Teachers Association. *Outstanding science trade books for students K–12*. http://www.nsta.org/ostbc (Accessed September 9, 2003).

The National Council of Teachers of English. *NCTE Orbis Pictus Nonfiction Award*. URL: http://www.ncte.org/about/awards/sect/elem/ 106877.htm (Accessed September 9, 2003).

Smith, Michael W., and Jeffrey D. Whelan. 2002. *Reading don't fix no Chevys*. Portsmouth, NY: Boynton/Cook.

Washington Post—Children's Book Guild Nonfiction Award. URL: http://www.childrensbookguild.org/awardnonfiction.htm (Accessed September 9, 2003).

Further Reading

Carr, Jo, comp. 1982. *Beyond fact: Nonfiction for children and young people*. Chicago: American Library Association.

Cianciolo, Patricia J. 2000. *Informational picture books for children*. Chicago: American Library Association.

Kobrin, Beverly. 1988. *Eyeopeners!: How to choose and use children's books about real people, places, and things*. New York: Viking.

Kobrin, Beverly. 1995. *Eyeopeners II: Children's books to answer children's questions about the world around them*. New York: Scholastic.

Pullis, Laura Turner. 1998. *Information investigation: Exploring nonfiction with books kids love*. Golden, CO: Fulcrum.

Wyatt, Flora, Margaret Coggins, and Jane Hunter Imber. 1998. *Popular nonfiction authors for children*. Englewood, CO: Libraries Unlimited.

Zarnowski, Myra, Richard M. Kerper, and Julie M. Jensen, eds. 2001. *The best in children's nonfiction: Reading, writing, and teaching Orbis Pictus Award books*. Urbana, IL: National Council of Teachers of English.

Chapter 9

Nonfiction Advisory Services in the School Library Media Center

Marcia Kochel

One of the great joys of being a school media specialist is helping kids find good books. By good books I don't necessarily mean award-winning, high-quality literature, but rather a book that they can't put down—one that they will stay up late reading and talk about with their friends. Maybe even one that they will remember as an adult or one that will change the course of their lives. If we are really lucky, those students will tell us about those important books. They will run into the media center and say, "This is the best book I ever read!" or "I never liked to read much before, but this book is good!" This doesn't happen every day, but those are the moments we live for the moments that get us through days of printer jams and network problems and broken overhead projectors.

School media specialists wear many hats. In addition to the major job components of teaching information literacy, collaborating with teachers, and providing reading guidance, they also administer a budget, handle cataloging and collection development, supervise and teach students, and distribute and repair computers and equipment. In my district media specialists also teach "prep time" classes, produce daily TV news shows, run book clubs, get up on ladders to clean LCD projectors, teach video editing classes, videotape band concerts, set up microphones and podiums, and troubleshoot computer problems of all kinds. Considering all of these duties, it is amazing that they have any time at all for helping kids find good books. But in spite of the demands of technology, most media specialists still see books and reading as central to their mission in the school.

A school media center differs greatly from a public library. In the school setting, media specialists work together with teachers, administrators, and parents to educate students and instill a love of learning. The overriding goal is to work as a team to deliver the school's curriculum. It is generally the media specialist's job to make sure reading and literature are promoted, and they have many ways of doing so. They do booktalks, make bibliographies, host guest authors, facilitate Accelerated Reader programs, celebrate Read Across America and Teen Read Week, make displays in the media center, recommend read-alouds to teachers, put up bulletin boards, and form book clubs. All of these techniques help build a school culture that values reading, but the most important method of reading promotion remains the most simple. It is the one-on-one guidance that media specialists give every day to students who say, "Do you know any good books?"

At its most basic, readers' advisory is simply recommending books, something media specialists do frequently, often without a lot of reflection on the process and results. But because it is so essential to the media specialists' job and to student learning, it is worthy of some reflection to ensure that young readers are fully benefiting from the process. This chapter focuses on nonfiction—how it is commonly overlooked by teachers and librarians, why it is so important for children, and how to promote it most effectively in a school media center.

No Respect

To quote Ed Sullivan (2001), nonfiction just doesn't get any respect from librarians and teachers. They tend to equate reading books with reading fiction and consequently to see nonfiction as less valuable than fiction (Carter and Abrahamson 1990). In Sullivan's experience, middle and high school students who come to libraries with reading lists assigned by teachers almost never have nonfiction on their lists. Class sets in English and language arts classes overwhelmingly tend to be novels. Little, if any, nonfiction is present on secondary teachers' bookshelves of paperbacks for self-selected reading. Fiction is also pervasive in elementary schools, where researchers find as much as 90 percent of what is read to be narrative in form (Dreher 1998). Well-meaning elementary school librarians sometimes require young readers to check out books only from the "Easy" section, thereby keeping them away from nonfiction. At storytime, librarians and teachers tend to read aloud from storybooks rather than to use informational picture books.

Penny Colman, a well-respected author of fiction and nonfiction, has been told that reading nonfiction is not "real reading" (Colman 1999, 217). She maintains that that in the world of children's publishing, powerful editors, educators, reviewers, and librarians have had a strong personal preference for fiction that has ultimately affected what literature is published and promoted for children and has created a bias toward fiction. Colman has made presentations at library conventions on myths about nonfiction and presented the following myths:

> Nonfiction is boring; nonfiction will not hook kids on reading; nonfiction is more appealing and appropriate for boys than for girls; nonfiction is for skimming or dipping in and out of, not for reading from beginning to end; and nonfiction books are not "real" books. (Colman 1999, 216)

Unfortunately, the majority of her audience members agreed that most people believe those five myths to be true.

One reason Colman cites for the negative perception of nonfiction is that it is often equated strictly with information or informational books, and this makes people think of encyclopedias or textbooks, not of the wide variety of nonfiction books available to children today. Ed Sullivan (2001) blames poor-quality series nonfiction for the perception that nonfiction is just about information. Sullivan describes these books as brief, superficial, poorly designed, cheaply made, and overpriced, with awful covers, and didactic or dull writing. Libraries do need these kinds of informational books for reports and reference, but they are not books that will turn kids on to reading and spark their imaginations. In my own experience in middle and elementary schools, series nonfiction on curriculum-related topics such at U.S. states, countries of the world, diseases, nutrition, biomes, and so on, almost never circulates outside of classroom assignments. As Sullivan puts it, they are books to be used, not enjoyed.

Fortunately, children are not limited to this dry, factual kind of nonfiction. In reality, nonfiction encompasses a broad spectrum of topics of great interest to kids of all ages, and many nonfiction books are captivating and well written. The next section explores the many reasons nonfiction should be valued, especially by school media specialists who have great potential to influence young readers.

Why Promote Nonfiction?

The premise of this entire book is that librarians who advise readers should be recommending nonfiction as well as fiction. But why should children's librarians, and in particular school librarians, be promoters of nonfiction?

Quality

Librarians traditionally are people who love books and the written word. They care about language and literature and have a desire to share their passion with others. When they find out about a good book, they want to promote it. Because librarians have traditionally equated "good" books with fiction, they may need to be convinced that nonfiction books can be well written and of high literary quality. In Penny Colman's opinion, the term "informational books" has limited people's understanding of the "complexity, richness, and literary nature of nonfiction" (Colman 1999, 217). She maintains that to write good nonfiction, it is necessary to utilize the same literary techniques used in fiction—including narrative, point of view, language, syntax, sequence, pace, tone, and voice. James Giblin, in an essay about the history of children's nonfiction, finds many examples of quality writing and notes that the best children's nonfiction encompasses a "topic of interest to young people, explored in depth, and presented with verve and imagination" (Giblin 2000, 424).

Awards can give nonfiction books added publicity and help librarians keep up with the best in nonfiction. Judging from some relatively recent changes in children's book awards, nonfiction appears to be gaining respect among publishers, teachers, and library professionals. While the highest honor in children's literature, the Newbery Medal, has rarely been awarded to a nonfiction book, several awards honor excellence in children's nonfiction and highlight the work of outstanding writers such as James Cross Giblin, Marc Aronson, Andrea Warren, and Jim Murphy, to name a few. At least two awards were established in the late 1970s, including the Boston Globe-Horn Book Award for Nonfiction and the Golden Kite Award for Nonfiction given by the Society of Children's Book Writers and Illustrators. In 1990, the National Council of Teachers of English instituted the Orbis Pictus Award for Outstanding Nonfiction for Children. It took the American Library Association until 2001 to award the first Robert F. Sibert Informational Book Medal, which is now annually awarded to the author of the most distinguished informational book for children published during the preceding year. In 2002, the International Reading Association revised its Children's Book Award categories and now honors an equal number of fiction and nonfiction books. Quality nonfiction books obviously exist, and there are now numerous organizations recognizing them for their literary merit.

Several recently published books help guide librarians and teachers to exemplary nonfiction books. Even very young children can enjoy informational picture books on an incredible array of topics. Patricia J. Cianciolo's *Informational Picture Books for Children* (1999) describes recommended books on the natural world (including animals, insects, reptiles, plants, ecology, and weather), numbers and arithmetic, the physical world (including inventions, technology, transportation, and astronomy), exploration, human growth and development, peoples and cultures, languages, and arts and crafts. *Gotcha! Nonfiction Booktalks to Get Kids Excited about Reading* (Baxter and Kochel 1999) and *Gotcha Again! More Nonfiction Booktalks to Get Kids Excited about Reading* (Baxter and Kochel 2002) recommend nonfiction titles for K–8 students about disasters, quests, poetry and wordplay, pets and other animals, ancient and modern history, immigration, unsolved mysteries, science experiments, vehicles, and many other high-interest topics.

Clearly, quality books are out there on a wide array of fascinating topics, and this alone makes them worth reading. However, this also leads us to perhaps the most important reason media specialists should promote nonfiction—because kids like it.

Pleasure and Enjoyment

Each year in June I survey the six hundred sixth- and seventh-graders at my school, asking them to list their favorite books. Harry Potter books always come out on top, as does *Holes* by Louis Sachar, the Princess Diaries books, and mysteries by Michael Dahl. The vast majority of the titles they write down are fiction (perhaps because that is what they think I want to hear), but when I look at the most circulated books in my library, the titles are different and they do not come from the fiction section. For girls, the most circulated book is *A Child Called It* and its sequels by Dave Pelzer, a man who writes about his survival of horrific child abuse. For boys the most sought-after books are comics, mainly Calvin & Hobbes and Garfield. Boys also spend a huge amount of time poring over the *Guinness Book of World Records* and Ripley's Believe It or Not books. Other areas of nonfiction also generate a lot of excitement and get heavy use from my students— most notably books in the art section (cartooning, how-to-draw, and graphic novels), books about crime and forensic science, sports books of all kinds, books about vehicles (e.g., muscle cars, lowriders, and BMX bikes), and funny books, whether jokes or poetry or word play. It is clear to me that when given a choice, middle school students often read about their personal interests, and that frequently leads them to nonfiction. They also read for entertainment—to laugh or to be grossed out or amazed, and this, too, leads them to nonfiction.

Nonfiction also appeals to younger readers. Even very young children often find nonfiction to be as exciting as the fictional stories they read (Carter 2000). Ray Doiron (2003) observed reading preferences among elementary students, finding that boys prefer books about sports, space, science, jokes, and vehicles, whereas girls choose picture storybooks as well as books about horses, cats, and crafts. Both boys and girls enjoy books about seasonal holidays and humorous stories, and both like animal stories, but boys tend to choose sharks, snakes and dinosaurs, while girls like pets, and animals such as deer, bears, and raccoons. Most of these favorite elementary school topics lend themselves perfectly to nonfiction reading.

Betty Carter and Richard F. Abrahamson have written two books about adolescents and nonfiction, in which they conclude young adults choose substantial amounts of nonfiction in their self-selected reading. They cite studies showing that interest in nonfiction emerges at about fourth grade and increases during adolescence (Carter and Abrahamson 1990). They also contend that much of this nonfiction is read for pleasure, diversion, and entertainment and found that the nonfiction books checked out by teenagers rarely corresponded to school assignments, but rather to personal interests. Sullivan concurs, noting that "for many young adult readers nonfiction serves the same purposes as fiction does for other readers: it entertains, provides escape, sparks the imagination, and indulges curiosity" (2001, 44). Noted nonfiction authors and Carter and Abrahamson strongly recommend that educators recognize and reward the nonfiction reading that teens do, because it is the literature that puts them on the path to lifetime reading (Abrahamson and Carter 1993). Nonfiction for young adults is currently a hot topic, so much so that a half-day program about booktalking nonfiction to teenagers was sponsored by YALSA (Young Adult Library Services Association) at the American Library Association conference in June 2003.

It is clear that children of all ages, from elementary to middle to high school, enjoy nonfiction and read it for pleasure. Ed Sullivan writes, "Because nonfiction is usually regarded in purely utilitarian terms, it does not seem to occur to some educators that a nonfiction work can simply be a 'good read'—something entertaining, fun, enjoyable, or just plain interesting" (2001, 43). It is time that media specialists recognize its value as pleasure reading and promote it through readers' advisory.

Achievement

From a purely practical perspective, providing readers' advisory for nonfiction reading may be a way of increasing student achievement, something every educator strives to do. Teachers today live with the reality of government mandated standardized tests and teacher accountability. Schools are carefully observed and teachers are judged on their students' scores. Although there is argument over how to assess student learning accurately, all educators know that students need strong reading skills. Reading is the building block of education, and it stands to reason that the more students read the better readers they will become. Jim Trelease, author of *The Read-Aloud Handbook* puts it this way: "The more you read, the better you get at it; the better you get at it, the more you like it; and the more you like it, the more you do it" (2001, 3). He strongly advocates reading aloud to children of all ages as well as incorporating sustained silent reading (SSR) into the classroom on a daily basis. He cites many studies showing that SSR increases student achievement. A key component to SSR is that students select their own reading material, whether it be magazines, newspapers, comics, fiction, or nonfiction. Given a broad selection of attractive and enticing nonfiction materials, many students would choose nonfiction for this kind of pleasure reading.

Research supports the idea the nonfiction reading increases student achievement. A major study of fourth-graders and literacy found that children who have experience only with fiction do not get the highest scores on national tests. Those students who have experiences with a wide variety of reading materials, including magazines and information books, showed the highest achievement on national reading tests (Campbell, Kapinus, and Beatty 1995). In addition, reading widely has been found to correlate with vocabulary development and general knowledge in elementary school students (Dreher 1998). It is clear that students benefit from reading a wide variety of materials and that encouraging them to broaden their reading habits would be worthwhile goal for school librarians. If our libraries are well-stocked with exciting and stimulating nonfiction, and we are promoting it to readers, they will undoubtedly read and achieve more.

Boys

When speaking of achievement, it is important to note differences between boys and girls. Trelease cites some sobering statistics: boys make up 70 percent of enrollment in remedial reading classes in the United States; boys are more likely to repeat a grade or drop out of school; boys are more likely to have learning disabilities; boys are more likely to be involved in criminal behavior; boys read less for pleasure; boys do less homework (2001). National reading tests over the past thirty years have shown boys consistently scoring lower than girls every single year (Scieszka 2003). Smith and Wilhelm, in a study of boys called *Reading Don't Fix No Chevys,* have compiled some compelling findings about gender, attitude, and reading. They found that boys provide lower estimates of their own reading ability than girls do, boys value reading as an activity less than girls do, boys have less interest in leisure reading and spend less time reading than girls, and that significantly more boys than girls consider themselves "nonreaders" (Smith and Wilhelm 2002). Based on these sobering statistics, it is clear that educators need to focus specifically on boys and reading achievement. As Jon Scieszka, founder of the Guys Read literacy campaign, writes, "something in the boys-and-reading equation isn't working" (Scieszka 2003, 18).

To get boys reading (and eventually achieving), Scieszka advocates providing book choice and finding the books boys like to read. These are two things that school media specialists are uniquely qualified to do. Smith and Wilhelm also list interesting findings about boys and book choices. They say that boys and girls express interest in reading different things and that boys are more inclined to read informational texts, magazine and newspaper articles, graphic novels, and comic books. Boys also like to read about hobbies, sports, and things they might do or be interested in doing. Doiron studied book circulation by gender among elementary school students and found that over two-thirds of the nonfiction books checked for pleasure reading were checked out by boys. Even at the young age of five or six years, boys begin to gravitate toward nonfiction (Sullivan 2003). Boys also appear to identify with their fathers' reading, which is likely to be utilitarian and nonlinear (and usually not fiction; Sullivan 2003).

If we are serious about providing book choice and finding books boys want to read, we must purchase, read, and promote more nonfiction. We must set aside our own personal preferences and give boys the books that they will like. This does not mean giving up on fiction, but rather treating nonfiction reading as equal to fiction reading. One of Penny Colman's myths about nonfiction is that it is more appropriate for boys than for girls. It would be a mistake to only promote nonfiction to boys—girls also enjoy it and benefit greatly from reading in a variety of styles. But based on what we know about guys and reading, it would be a grave mistake to neglect nonfiction when promoting books to boys.

How to Promote Nonfiction

A school media center is a unique library setting, one with a captive group of patrons who are in the building all day every school day of the year. Because of this unique setting and fixed clientele, media specialists are not limited to one-on-one readers' advisory to reach readers. They have many opportunities to guide readers to books that entertain, stimulate, and provide pleasure. Collection development, booktalks, teacher collaboration, displays, brochures, bibliographies, and one-on-one discussions are all methods that can be used for nonfiction readers' advisory.

Collection Development

A school media specialist develops the school's book collection and is largely responsible for what is contained in the school's media center. Budget constraints make collection development a challenge, but a current nonfiction collection that both relates to the curriculum and correlates with student interests should be a priority. Media specialists can't steer kids to books that they don't have or to books with which they aren't familiar.

Book reviews are, of course, one way to keep informed about new nonfiction. Media specialists should pay attention to nonfiction books that get starred reviews in *School Library Journal, Booklist, The Horn Book Magazine,* and other respected journals. *Voices of Youth Advocates* (VOYA) reviews books for young adults and rates books on quality as well as potential popularity among teens. Nonfiction books with high popularity scores are worth paying attention to.

Many titles that recommend books for children are short on nonfiction, but several sources mentioned previously can help librarians build a collection and keep up with new and excellent nonfiction. *Gotcha! Nonfiction Booktalks to Get Kids Excited about Reading* and *Gotcha Again! More Nonfiction Booktalks to Get Kids Excited about Reading* (Baxter and Kochel, 1999, 2002) list only high-quality and high interest nonfiction for K-8 readers. Bibliographies at the end of each chapter can be used for collection development. For teenagers, John T. Gillespie's *Best Books for Young Teen Readers, Grades 7–10* is a 1,066-page source that includes nonfiction as well as fiction divided into many categories. For younger readers, Patricia J. Cianciolo's *Informational Picture Books for Children* is a good place to start. *Great Books for Boys* by Kathleen Odean includes quite a few recommended nonfiction titles for ages two to fourteen (girls will also enjoy these books).

Current and past award winners of many nonfiction award winners are available online at these Web addresses:

- *Boston Globe Horn Book* Awards for Nonfiction, URL:http://www.hbook.com/bghb.shtml (Accessed December 7, 2003).

- Society of Children's Book Writers and Illustrators Golden Kite Award for Nonfiction, URL: http://www.scbwi.org/awards/gk_main.htm (Accessed December 7, 2003).

- National Council of Teachers of English Orbis Pictus Award for Outstanding Nonfiction for Children, URL: http://www.ncte.org/elem/awards/orbispictus (Accessed December 7, 2003).

- American Library Association Robert F. Sibert Informational Book Medal, URL: http://www.ala.org/Content/NavigationMenu/ALSC/ Awards_and_Scholarships1/Literary_and_Related_Awards/Sibert_ Medal/Sibert_Medal.htm (Accessed December 7, 2003).

- International Reading Association Children's Book Award, URL: http://www.reading.org/awards/children.html (Accessed December 7, 2003).

Also, the annual list of ALA Children's Notable Books (URL: http://www.ala.org/Content/NavigationMenu/ALSC/Awards_and_Scholarships1/ Childrens_Notable_Lists/Default1888.htm [Accessed December 7, 2003]), the YALSA Best Books for Young Adults (URL: www.ala.org/ yalsa/booklists/bbya [Accessed December 7, 2003]), and Quick Picks for Reluctant Young Adult Readers (URL: www.ala.org/yalsa/booklists/ quickpicks [Accessed December 7, 2003]) always include nonfiction and are worth looking at each year.

A good nonfiction collection will not include only award-winners—it will have plenty of light reading choices as well. Kids, just like adults, want to read for escape, for fun, or for a good laugh. One other source for nonfiction collection development is the *World Almanac Education Catalog* (available in print or online at http://www.worldalmanac.com [Accessed December 7, 2003]). The catalogs, featuring extensive nonfiction titles, show color book covers and highlight popular nonfiction books that do not necessarily win awards but kids love (such as books of fun facts, series books on popular topics, and DK Eyewitness Books). A listing in the catalog doesn't guarantee quality but can give librarians an idea of what is available.

Finally, media specialists should take suggestions from their students. I am always amazed at the topics they ask for, from BMX bikes to Shakespeare plays to remote-control cars to how to play guitar. Often their requests send me to Amazon.com or my local bookstores, where I find books both in the children's and adults' sections. The more media specialists cater to the real interests of their students and stock their libraries with enticing books, the more likely kids will be to want to hang out in the media center and to ask for advice about their reading.

Booktalks

Personally advising individual students, while rewarding and effective, is next to impossible in schools with hundreds of students. A librarian could never reach every single reader. But booktalking can be an incredibly effective way of introducing books to large groups of students. It is readers' advisory on a grand scale, and it has great potential for reaching readers of all abilities and interests.

School media specialists have an advantage over public librarians serving children—they have a captive audience available to them every day. Media specialists simply need to be proactive with teachers and offer their booktalking services. In my experience, both teachers and students enjoy booktalks. I regularly seek out teachers and ask if I can do a quick presentation either in the media center or classroom. I prefer the media center because then my talks can be more spontaneous, and I can gather up a good pile of books that students can check out immediately.

Some media specialists will have to make a conscious effort to include nonfiction in booktalk presentations. The tendency of educators and librarians to favor fiction can be deeply ingrained. Media specialists should make it a habit to always include some nonfiction along with fiction books. An advantage of nonfiction booktalks is that they don't take as much preparation as fiction booktalks. The goal is not to ramble on and on with every detail of a book—it is simply to whet kids' appetites for books and subjects they might not have heard of. The key is choosing books that appeal to your students. Media specialists should make every attempt to know their audience and choose books accordingly. Nonfiction books with photographs are particularly easy to talk about. A surprising, intriguing, or gross picture shown to a class can be all it takes to create a cluster of students wanting to take a closer look. *Mummies, Bones, & Body Parts* by Charlotte Wilcox is full of colorful mummy photographs. Likewise, the photos of the hundred-year-old frozen corpses in *Buried in Ice* by Owen Beattie and John Geiger have instant kid appeal.

Sometimes teachers want booktalks on a particular topic, but it is not usually necessary to have a theme. Many of my best booktalks have been on a complete mix of subjects. It keeps kids interested and allows me to talk about the most appealing books I have on hand at any given time. I might start with some examples of wordplay from *Jon Agee's Palindromania!* or *Elvis Lives and Other Anagrams,* then move on to a disaster such as the sinking of the U.S.S. *Indianapolis,* written about in *Left for Dead* by Pete Nelson. Then I would pull out *Rats! The Good, the Bad, and the Ugly* by Richard Conniff and show some of the photographs of rats on the endpapers. Next I would go on to science, discussing *While You're Waiting for the Food to Come: A Tabletop Science Activity Book: Experiments and Tricks That Can Be Done at a Restaurant, the Dining Room Table, or Wherever Food Is Served* by Eric Muller. I might include a biography such as *Spellbinder: The Life of Harry Houdini* by Tom Lalicki, then I would finish up with *Mystery on Everest* by Audrey Salkeld, a photobiography of George Mallory, who died trying to be the first to climb Mount Everest. As Kathleen Baxter and Marcia Kochel write in the introduction to *Gotcha! Nonfiction Booktalks to Get Kids Excited about Reading*, "I like to mix and match a hodgepodge of materials. It is very important to stay in touch with your audience. Kids today are raised on MTV and *Sesame Street,* and long attention spans are not part of their makeup. If they do not like the book I am talking about at a given moment, they won't have to wait long for a change; I will soon be talking about another" (Baxter and Kochel 1999, xiv).

Numerous books have been written on booktalking—both on how to do it and on specific titles to talk about. Most of these give tips and instructions that can be invaluable to inexperienced booktalkers. Some of the earliest (and most successful) books, written by Joni Bodart, focused exclusively on fiction. Many later titles have kept the same fiction-centered focus. A search of Amazon.com yields seventeen booktalking titles that are currently in print and available. Two of them, *Gotcha!* and *Gotcha Again!: More Nonfiction Booktalks to Get Kids Excited about Reading,* exclusively deal with nonfiction. The rest of the booktalking titles found at Amazon focus exclusively on fiction or contain a mixture of fiction and nonfiction. The more recently published titles (such as Chapple Langemack's *Booktalker's Bible*, a general guide to booktalking for all ages) tend to include a mixture, perhaps showing a growing recognition of the importance and popularity of nonfiction. For those booktalking to teenagers, Jennifer Bromann's (2001) *Booktalking That Works* provides excellent tips on how to write, organize, and deliver booktalks that will appeal to young adults (however, she does not include a great deal of nonfiction booktalks).

Media specialists should not underestimate the power of booktalking. It should be done often and with enthusiasm. It is the foot in the door that gives the media specialist access to all the students in the school, even the ones who think they hate to read. Students who encounter new and interesting books through a booktalking session will likely seek out the advice of the media specialist when they have future reading needs. When students know that the media specialist is available to help them find good books and that he or she knows what kids like, they may come back for individual readers' advisory services in the future.

Collaboration with Teachers

In the school setting, teachers and media specialists have many opportunities for working together in both big and small ways. Booktalking, as just noted, is a great way to build rapport with teachers. It lets them know what books the library has and shows them that the media specialist wants to take an active role in encouraging kids to read. Media specialists should take every opportunity to recommend books to teachers and, when they ask for read-aloud suggestions, should be sure to mention nonfiction titles. It may surprise them to find well-written and engaging nonfiction that students enjoy as much as novels. Teachers also may come to the media specialist for advice in choosing classroom sets of books. At most schools, these sets tend overwhelmingly toward fiction, but the media specialist shouldn't limit suggestions to just fiction. Perhaps a biography or memoir or history book would be the perfect balance to the fiction books already available. For example, the autobiographical *Guts* by Gary Paulsen makes a perfect complement to *Hatchet* and Paulsen's other fictional survival books. Students reading *Number the Stars* by Lois Lowry will also want to read *Darkness over Denmark: The Danish Resistance and the Rescue of the Jews* by Ellen Levine. Students will appreciate the variety provided by a nonfiction book, particularly those who resist reading fiction.

School librarians need to be proactive with teachers, letting them know about the resources they have to support the curriculum. If teachers don't come to the media center, media specialists can go to them with their best nonfiction in hand. If they study forensic science, the media specialist can stock up on books on crime solving and recommend good books or chapters to read aloud to the class. *The Bone Detectives* by Donna Jackson is one example of an outstanding title that tells about how scientists recreated a woman's face and solved a fascinating murder case. Media specialists can offer to do a booktalk for the class or to gather up the materials for a research project. Perhaps they can use nonfiction books to supplement a teacher's unit with a scavenger hunt or a hands-on project that utilizes the media center's resources. Efforts made in collaborating with teachers to promote nonfiction will have a ripple effect because teachers in turn influence so many students in the school.

Displays

There are many ways to promote books in the media center without saying a word. Bookstores know that to sell books, people want to see and touch their covers. Media specialists can use the same techniques to "sell" their nonfiction. First of all, media specialists should make sure the nonfiction section is an attractive and inviting part of the media center. The collection should be arranged so there is plenty of room for propping up books to highlight the most interesting and attractive ones available. Kids won't usually browse through books on the shelves that are hard to see. Shelf space should be tall enough so the oversized books can be seen and displayed. Book stands for each shelf can be purchased so there will be an attractive way to prop up books. Media specialists can invest in some sort of display shelving so new and interesting titles can be highlighted. No bookstore would keep the same displays in the windows for weeks on end, and neither should the media center. Frequently changing the books on display can create new interest among readers.

If the media center has a display case, it can be used to show off nonfiction that relates to curricular topics or to something in the news. If students are making models of pyramids, the media specialist can display books on mummies and ancient Egypt, such as the beautiful *Mummies of the Pharaohs: Exploring the Valley of the Kings* by Melvin and Gilda Berger or *Secrets of the Mummies: Uncovering the Bodies of Ancient Egyptians* by Shelley Tanaka. If the president gets a new dog, books on dog breeds and lives of the presidents can be displayed. Capstone Press has a series called Learning about Dogs that includes books on many breeds, and *Lives of the Presidents: Fame, Shame (and What the Neighbors Thought)* by Kathleen Krull contains great presidential gossip. When movies such as *Titanic* come out, it is a good time to showcase disaster books, both about the famous sinking, and other less well-known disasters. *Shipwreck at the Bottom of the World: The Extraordinary True Story of Shackleton and the Endurance* by Jennifer Armstrong is riveting. Almost anything can be an excuse to promote a nonfiction book. Nonfiction titles also go well with objects. Media specialists can use their own creativity or ask students to bring in their collections and treasures and display them with related books.

A more covert display tactic is to bring the books to where the students congregate. If students gather at the computer stations, media specialists can have some nonfiction titles casually lying on the tables nearby. If students read magazines in the beanbag chairs, good browsing books can be left there as well. Books on hot topics such as AIDS, mental illness, or human growth and sexuality can be left in strategic places. Middle school kids might not go seeking them but will of course take a look at them when they happen upon them.

Brochures and Bibliographies

Another way for media specialists to perform readers' advisory without saying a word is to provide booklists for their patrons. Some people take the time and effort to create attractive brochures complete with book covers and catchy annotations. Others make up lists of titles and print them out as bookmarks or lists. These lists help both students and parents and can be posted to the school's Web page or reprinted in school newsletters for wider distribution. When making bibliographies such as these, media specialists should be sure to include nonfiction titles along with fiction or make lists that include just nonfiction. A hot topic such as unsolved mysteries or amazing inventions or shipwrecks can be a great inspiration for a list of high-interest nonfiction. For an easy display media specialists can put their brochures together with some of the actual books—preferably colorful, attractive titles that will fly off the shelves.

One-on-One Recommendations

Booktalks, displays, and bibliographies can all promote reading and lead children to good books, but nothing can substitute for individual reading guidance, which is the theme of this entire book. Much has been written on general readers' advisory (usually for fiction) that also pertains to nonfiction readers' advisory, including techniques and tips for the readers' advisory interview. According to Shearer, readers' advisory involves an exchange of information between two people with the purpose of one suggesting texts for the other's reading enjoyment. The success of the transaction is subjective and is reflected in a reader discovering a book which is stimulating, entertaining, and enjoyable (Shearer 1996). This definition does not in any way limit itself to fiction reading. Whenever librarians recommend a fiction or a nonfiction book to a patron, they are performing readers' advisory.

Two main things make for a positive readers' advisory experience: relationships and knowledge. The school media specialist has frequent contact with students and has the opportunity to build a long-lasting relationship with the readers she advises. Positive interactions with students can lead to future interactions and to a level of trust that encourages them to approach the media specialist for advice on reading. At that point, it is crucial to ask questions sensitively and listen carefully to their responses.

The other component of readers' advisory is knowledge. Media specialists should do all they can to learn about the reading preferences of students. This can be done through informal conversations with students and teachers, observation of what they read, written surveys, and professional reading. They also must use their expertise to build a winning collection and become intimately familiar with it. This means stepping out of the fiction section and reading children's or adolescent nonfiction. The more the media specialist knows the nonfiction that is available, the better she can help a reader find an enticing book. The breadth of the media specialist's knowledge can lead to exciting connections. For example, when a student shows an interest in racecars, it may mean that he or she would enjoy a fiction book dealing with cars, but the media specialist should consider a wide range of formats. The student may enjoy a biography of a NASCAR driver, a drawing book, a guide to car repair, a book on futuristic cars, *Motor Trend* magazine, or a history of the automobile. Including nonfiction in the readers' advisory equation opens many doors, allowing students the opportunity to choose books that uniquely appeal to their interests.

Conclusion

To conclude, I return to my opening sentence. One of the great joys of being a school media specialist is helping kids find good books. For many media specialists, "good books" means fiction. But knowing what we know about the quality of nonfiction for children, the reading preferences of children (particularly boys), and the need to increase student achievement, it clearly is time to give children's and adolescent nonfiction the respect it deserves. As Ray Doiron concludes,

> Reading is reading and when we motivate people to read we need to be sure that we are helping them find materials they are interested in reading and that we are not telling them that fiction is "better" to read than information books . . . we must provide our students with the best quality examples of all types of texts and then celebrate everything they ever read. (Doiron 2003, 16)

It's time to expand our notion of "good books" and use our influence to guide readers to what they most want to read. For many young readers, that will be nonfiction.

References

Abrahamson, Richard F., and Betty Carter. 1993. What we know about nonfiction and young adult readers and what we need to do about it. In *Inspiring literacy: Literature for children and young adults*. Edited by Sam Sebesta and Ken Donelson, 159–72. New Brunswick, NJ: Transaction.

Baxter, Kathleen A., and Marcia Agness Kochel. 1999. *Gotcha! Nonfiction booktalks to get kids excited about reading*. Englewood, CO: Libraries Unlimited.

Baxter, Kathleen A., and Marcia Agness Kochel. 2002. *Gotcha Again! More nonfiction booktalks to get kids excited about reading*. Englewood, CO: Libraries Unlimited.

Bromann, Jennifer. 2001. *Booktalks that work*. New York: Neal-Schuman.

Campbell, J.R., B. A. Kapinus, and A.S. Beatty. 1995. *Interviewing children about their literacy experiences: Data from NAEP's Integrated Reading Performance Record (IRPR) at Grade 4*. Washington, DC: National Center for Educational Statistics.

Carter, Betty. 2000. A universe of information: The future of nonfiction. *The Horn Book Magazine* 76: 697–707.

Carter, Betty, and Richard F. Abrahamson. 1990. *Nonfiction for young adults: From delight to wisdom*. Phoenix, AZ: Oryx.

Cianciolo, Patricia J. 1999. *Informational picture books for children*. Chicago: American Library Association.

Colman, Penny. 1999. Nonfiction is literature, too. *The New Advocate* 12: 215–23.

Doiron, Ray. 2003. Boy books, girl books: Should we re-organize our school library collections? *Teacher Librarian* 30: 14–16.

Dreher, Mariam Jean. 1998. Motivating children to read more nonfiction. *The Reading Teacher* 52: 414–15.

Giblin, James Cross. 2000. More than just the facts: A hundred years of children's nonfiction. *The Horn Book Magazine* 76: 413–24.

Gillespie, John T., editor. 2000. *Best books for young teen readers, grades 7 to 10*. New Providence, NJ: R.R. Bowker.

Langemack, Chapple. 2003. *The Booktalker's Bible: How to talk about the books you love to any audience*. Westport, CT: Libraries Unlimited.

Odean, Kathleen. 1998. *Great books for boys*. New York: Ballentine.

Scieszka, Jon. 2003. Guys and reading. *Teacher librarian* 30: 17–18.

Shearer, Kenneth. 1996. The nature of the readers' advisory transaction in adult reading. In *Guiding the reader to the next book*. Edited by Kenneth Shearer, 1–20. New York: Neal-Schuman.

Smith, Michael W., and Jeffrey D. Wilhelm. 2002. *"Reading don't fix no Chevys": Literacy in the lives of young men*. Portsmouth, NH: Heinemann.

Sullivan, Ed. 2001. Some teens prefer the real thing: The case for young adult nonfiction. *English Journal* 90: 43–47.

Sullivan, Michael. 2003. *Connecting boys with books: What libraries can do*. Chicago: American Library Association.

Trealease, Jim. 2001. *The read-aloud handbook*. 5th ed. New York: Penguin Books.

Children's and Young Adult Books Mentioned

Agee, Jon. 2000. *Elvis lives and other anagrams*. New York: Farrar, Straus & Giroux.

Agee, Jon. 2002. *Jon Agee's palindromania!* New York: Farrar, Straus, & Giroux.

Armstrong, Jennifer. 1998. *Shipwreck at the bottom of the world: The extraordinary true story of Shackleton and the Endurance.* New York: Crown Publishers.

Beattie, Owen, and John Geiger. 1992. *Buried in ice: The mystery of a lost Arctic expedition.* New York: Scholastic/Madison Press.

Berger, Melvin, and Gilda Berger. 2001. *Mummies of the pharaohs: Exploring the Valley of the Kings.* Washington, DC: National Geographic Society.

Conniff, Richard. 2002. *Rats! The good, the bad, and the ugly.* New York: Crown Publishers.

Jackson, Donna M. 1995. *The bone detectives: How forensic anthropologists solve crimes and uncover mysteries of the dead.* Boston: Little, Brown.

Krull, Kathleen. 1998. *Lives of the presidents: Fame, shame (and what the neighbors thought).* San Diego, CA: Harcourt Brace.

Lalicki, Tom. 2000. *Spellbinder: The life of Harry Houdini.* New York: Holiday House.

Levine, Ellen. 2000. *Darkness over Denmark: The Danish resistance and the rescue of the Jews.* New York: Holiday House.

Muller, Eric. 1999. *While you're waiting for the food to come: A tabletop science activity book: Experiments and tricks that can be done at a restaurant, the dining room table, or wherever food is served.* New York: Orchard Books.

Nelson, Pete. 2002. *Left for dead: A young man's search for justice for the USS* Indianapolis. New York: Delacorte.

Paulsen, Gary. 2001. *Guts: The true stories behind* Hatchet *and the Brian books.* New York: Delacorte Press.

Salkeld, Audrey. 2000. *Mystery on Everest: A photobiography of George Mallory.* Washington, DC: National Geographic Society.

Tanaka, Shelley. 1999. *Secrets of the mummies: Uncovering the bodies of ancient Egyptians.* New York: Hyperion/Madison Press.

Wilcox, Charlotte. 2000. *Mummies, bones, & body parts.* Minneapolis, MN: Carolrhoda Books.

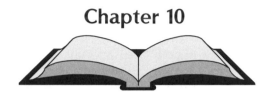

Chapter 10

Books That Inspire: Nonfiction for a Multicultural Society

Alma Dawson and Connie Van Fleet

The "Books That Inspire" project, created by the University of Oklahoma Libraries, showcases books that have inspired faculty and staff. The exhibit includes copies of the books, a description of each book and its impact, and a photograph of the person who nominated the title. In 2003, faculty and staff responded to the call for contributions to the "Books That Inspire" project with books that "offer spiritual and personal growth, new insights into everyday living, and have opened new opportunities for their readers. These books have helped readers overcome adversity and to live life more fully. They have provided solace for their readers; they have caused readers to change their minds about events and concepts, and had a liberating effect on many" (Lee 2003).

When people are asked to name books that have inspired them, that have shaped their lives and careers, it might be expected that the great works of literature will be represented. That is, after all, the stated purpose of great literature—to address important themes in texts that are memorable and inspiring, that shape the way people think and feel. What may be less predictable is that a substantial percentage of works mentioned (over half) will be classified as nonfiction, works we typically think of as factual and informative. That so many readers select nonfiction as works of inspiration and influence, books that are read in their entirety (as one would approach narrative fiction), is certainly support for Burgin's (2001) argument that readers' advisors should expand their scope beyond the current focus on fiction.

In addition, both fiction and nonfiction by authors of color and about multicultural themes are included in the "Books That Inspire" exhibit. In addition to fiction by Rudolfo Anaya (*Bless Me, Ultima*) and Barbara Kingsolver (*Prodigal Summer*), nonfiction titles as diverse as *Think and Grow Rich: A Black Choice* by Dennis Paul Kimbro and Napoleon Hill, *Farewell to Manzanar* by Jeanne Wakatsuki Houston and James D. Houston, and *Days of Grace* by Arthur Ashe are displayed and their impact on individual lives shared. Such selections demonstrate that authors of multicultural literature inspire others who are part of their society but may or may not share their ethnocultural origins. Their works celebrate self and community and give testimony to techniques of survival and strategies for success. Their words empower, mirror actions, affirm self, impact history, and show the common elements of cultures and of humanity.

The exhibit parallels the readers' advisory experience of many librarians. Those who serve in small libraries with a single reference desk or even a single public service point appreciate that determining the types of literature that recreational readers prefer is a good starting point in helping them find what they need. Most library staff, however, focus on finding books to satisfy the reader without consciously defining readers' advisory services in terms of a sharp demarcation between fiction and nonfiction. The crossover becomes even more evident when providing service to multicultural, multiethnic audiences. Whether or not one agrees with the practice, it is not unusual for libraries that serve diverse communities to create "African American" or "Native American" or other ethnic-specific sections, in which both fiction and nonfiction for the respective group are gathered.

Defining Multicultural Literature

While some scholars argue that even the notion of discrete, identifiable "cultures" in the United States is obsolete (Clausen 1997), most observers continue to use the term to denote an existing set of beliefs, perspectives, and practices that are distinct from other coexisting systems. In its broadest sense, a "culture" may be defined in terms of religion, race (although this concept is in dispute), sexual orientation, disability, ethnicity, profession, education, socioeconomic status, or even mode of communication (the culture of the Internet). Regardless of definition, the encompassing goal of multiculturalism is to create a society in which people from different backgrounds reflected in different ways can live together with respect and tolerance for each other. Multicultural literature is the manifestation of this approach. In essence, it is the written word that reflects a diverse society.

Although there are many aspects of diversity and although we recognize the value of an inclusive perspective, framing our discussion of multicultural nonfiction literature in ethnocultural terms seems most productive. This approach is congruent with discussions of multicultural literature in the fields of literary criticism, education, and library and information studies. We give attention, however, to world literature only as it relates to American audiences and concentrate on multicultural literature primarily as a reflection of U.S. society. Similarly, although books in languages other than English are worthy of consideration, in this chapter we have limited our attention to English-language materials.

In this chapter, the term "multicultural" refers collectively to people of color who comprise America's four major nonwhite populations: Latino, African American, Asian American, and Native American. The authors recognize that experience, heritage, perspective, and voice may vary within each of these umbrella designations and appreciate that each of these groups is distinct from the other and is diverse within itself.

Identifying groups in ethnocultural terms is not an attempt to categorize people by inherent identifiable ethnic differences. It is shorthand for a more complex recognition of the economic, regional, intellectual, social, and historical differences that have resulted from such categorizations and for the impact of the concept of "differentness" or "otherness" that Antonette (2003) explores in defining critical multiculturalism.

It is to be expected that communities whose experiences have not been acknowledged and whose sensibilities and perspectives have not been represented as an integral part of their own American culture would find it necessary to reclaim their history, celebrate their accomplishments, speak in their own voices, and define their place in that cultural frontier occupied by people who, in the words of Cuban-American scholar Gustavo Perez, "live on the hyphen" (Figueredo 1999, 23).

Nonfiction and Multicultural Audiences

Mainstream Literary Movements of Relevance

The literary nonfiction and literary journalism movements that have enjoyed increased critical attention and analysis in the past two decades are genres ideally suited to multicultural readers. The emphasis on real-world subjects and factual, verifiable authority lends credence to the author's world view while the narrative style increases readability and accessibility (Lounsberry 1990). Lounsberry asserts that literary nonfiction addresses itself to "the persistent themes of American imagination [including] conflicts between the individual and society, as well as the continued efficacy of the 'American dream' " (xvi). These central themes in multicultural fiction and nonfiction resonate with readers. The five specific narrative forms identified by Lounsberry as most representative of nonfiction—history, the sermon, travel writing, autobiography, and epic narrative—are those that traditionally have been employed by authors of color.

Literary journalism in particular deals with factual matter written in narrative prose, but the prose is spare and polished. Literary journalists immerse themselves firsthand in a community to present and report a holistic, complex view and typically look at daily lives as more revealing than noteworthy events (Kramer 1995; Sims 1995).

Kramer (1995) suggests that the popularity of literary journalism is the result of Americans' disenchantment and distrust with leaders and authorities in all walks of life and the desire to read widely to understand issues and form judgments independently.

> Literary journalism helps sort out the new complexity. If it is not an antidote to bewilderment, at least it unites daily experiences—including emotional ones—with the wild plenitude of information that can be applied to experience. Literary journalism couples cold fact and personal event, in the author's humane company. And that broadens readers' scans, allows them to behold others' lives, often set within far clearer contexts than we can bring to our own. The process moves readers, and writers, toward realization, compassion, and in the best cases, wisdom. (Kramer 1995, 34)

The distrust of authority and the emphasis on everyday lives are points of connection for multicultural readers. In short, literary journalism provides the same descriptive and interpretive role for multicultural and mainstream audiences that has been the provenance of fiction.

In addition to reflecting these narrative techniques, multicultural nonfiction has begun to find a niche in the sustained mainstream market for self-help books, consumer information, and political commentary. The place of such nonfiction at the top of best-seller lists is evidence of the popularity of this genre. Because such work ostensibly deals with universal procedure and fact, multicultural audiences have been neglected. It is only recently that there has been a recognition of the need to create guides that target specific populations.

Appeal to Multicultural Audiences

Nonfiction takes a central place in the recreational reading of people of color in the United States, and it is difficult to imagine effective readers' advisory services that do not take this into account. Consider the critical bibliography published by the editors of *Quarterly Black Review*. In compiling titles for *Sacred Fire: The QBR 100 Essential Black Books,* Rodriguez, Rasbury, and Taylor (1999) conducted a survey to identify books by authors from the African diaspora that had "the greatest impact" on the respondents. From these, they selected "a range of books that identified the issues and philosophies that we, as a people, felt were most critical and that were written by the artists who most eloquently and powerfully presented these issues to the world" (Rodriguez et al. 1999, 1). The genre index (pp. 226–28) lists sixteen titles in biography and memoir, nine in history, and twenty-four in unspecified nonfiction. That is, fully half of the artists (authors) chose to work in the realm of nonfiction.

As early as 1990, Lisa Lee observed that books by "Native American authors or on Native American themes have progressed beyond the occasional title by a small press and into the literary mainstream. Literary topics transcend their regionalism, and the breadth of subjects, themes, and publishing approaches is as varied as the numerous tribes across the nation" (Lee 1990, 80). Dahlin (1995) also observed a general resurgence of interest in Native American titles, primarily from the general population eager to learn about their cultural ways and traditions.

Evolution of Multicultural Nonfiction

Although each of the ethnocultural groups highlighted is unique, there are shared themes that appear in multicultural nonfiction. The evolution of such literatures in terms of a general thematic pattern parallels that of multicultural fiction.

Early writings tend to be grounded in a need for identity—an argument for recognition and respect. This self-definition is often phrased in terms of opposition to a dominant and unjust white society. It is an attempt to find one's place as the outsider, whether immigrant or native born. Authors move to the next phase, that of a person who balances between two cultures, the quintessential dilemma of those who live on the hyphen. This trend away from definition in terms of the other continues with an increased attention to self-reflection, to relationships within the culture itself. (Dawson and Van Fleet 2001, 252)

We see a move from description of original ethnic/cultural heritage, to interaction and conflict with other cultures, to shared themes and issues among people of all cultures. Earlier themes persist, new themes are added, and the literature becomes more diverse within itself. In addition, multicultural nonfiction has moved from the academy's scholarly texts to include easily accessible popular works, just as fiction by authors of color grew to embrace all levels of complexity and presentation (Dawson and Van Fleet 2001).

Implications for Libraries in a Multicultural Society

Multicultural nonfiction influences all segments of a diverse society, but it is particularly meaningful to members of identifiable ethnocultural groups. Librarians who wish to provide equitable and effective readers' advisory service will need to consider both fiction and nonfiction material by authors of color and works that reflect multicultural themes. An integrated approach to service will be characterized by attention to three aspects: mission, collection development, and readers' advisory.

Mission

A mission statement that articulates the library's vision of support for the information needs of a diverse clientele is a critical first step. Policies and action plans that evolve from such a shared vision will identify the "library as a place that encourages people to learn about each other and their cultures" (Jackson and Robertson 1991, 11).

Collection Development

Dynamic collection development provides the raw materials for the art of readers' advisory. Selection policies that give attention to nonfiction designed to meet the specific needs of diverse audiences develop naturally from an inclusive mission statement. While many collection development policies recognize the desirability of multicultural fiction, fewer specifically give attention to nonfiction targeted to various ethnocultural groups.

According to Jackson and Robertson (1991, 12), "building strong, varied collections with many worthwhile materials is the best way to be sure that all cultures are represented fairly." In addition to basic evaluation criteria, selectors will want to be aware of the popular forms identified in this chapter and relevant criteria for judging each in terms of its genre and its diverse audience.

Collecting nonfiction for multicultural audiences requires particular attention to certifying authorship or authority and assessing culture-specific content for accuracy, inclusiveness, and sensitivity. Furthermore, Jackson and Robertson (1991) urge librarians to evaluate materials for words with hidden demeaning implications. Libraries with populations who are not native English speakers may need to incorporate strategies for collecting in several languages. Consulting with community groups, readers, and public services librarians, conducting community analysis and user needs studies, and keeping current with professional and popular review sources are useful strategies for approaching unfamiliar literatures.

Public Service

Readers' advisory and reference librarians connect patrons with materials, and readers will benefit if the perspectives and knowledge of the two are merged to help find the right book. To connect readers with "books that inspire," readers' advisory librarians must understand the needs of diverse groups within the community and expand their vision to include nonfiction literature. The role of nonfiction in the lives of individuals or ethnic groups is powerful. Not only does nonfiction inform and entertain, it also affirms cultural identity for individuals and ethnic groups. In sum, users are empowered personally, and the information provided to them can form the basis for understanding the global community.

Readers' advisors may find it helpful to locate the readers' preferences in terms of the positioning of the individual and community within a scheme of sociocultural relationships. Three major perspectives emerge: relationship to the collective community; relationship to other individuals within that community; and relationship within the self as a member of the community.

Perspectives in Multicultural Nonfiction

Social History: Connecting with Community

Fleming (1999, 49) asserts that *"community* and *identity* are two of the most important criteria used to evaluate the humanity, potential, and spiritual worth of a people." Social history emphasizes the history and achievements of a particular cultural community. It gives readers a framework to understand the collective self and a foundation of pride and heritage from which to explore. How have my people shaped the world and themselves? How have they approached life, the arts, religion, and spirituality? Books such as *Indian Givers: How the Indians of the Americas Transformed the World* acknowledge the impact of a people who have too often been marginalized and whose contributions to world culture have too often been overlooked. These texts inform other cultures and help multicultural populations reclaim their heritages.

The expressed purpose of many authors of color is to reclaim history, to tell their own stories, to empower the collective. Frequently overlooked or misinterpreted by those who record history, these writers feel compelled to offer different perspectives and sometimes dispute interpretations or even matters of fact. Dee Brown's *Bury My Heart at Wounded Knee* is a classic reclamation of history by a Native American author. Arthur Ashe's *A Hard Road to Glory: A History of the African American Athlete* melds history and social criticism, chronicling the achievements of both famous and little-known athletes and analyzing the societal factors that influenced their lives, careers, and recognition (or lack thereof). His style is scholarly, his approach balanced, yet the book is persuasive and impels the reader toward an emotional response and social action. *The Chinese in America* is a scrupulously researched and vividly written account by Iris Chang that gives depth and scope to previously accepted knowledge of the subject.

Social criticism incorporates an evaluative and essentially political perspective to social history and typically explores the interaction of the group with other cultural groups and within itself. Literary journalism, whose "appeal has grown from the solid foundations of the form—immersion reporting, narrative techniques that free the voice of the writer, and high standards of accuracy" and which "pays respect to ordinary lives" (Sims 1995, 3), is ideally suited for social criticism. It "focuses on everyday events that bring out the hidden patterns of community life as tellingly as the spectacular stories that make newspaper headlines" (Sims 1995, 3). It is these everyday events and interactions that define the lives of Americans of color. This technique has been used to good effect to study the impact of political movements in Tom Dent's *Southern Journey: A Return to the Civil Rights Movement* and sociological phenomena in Walt Harrington's *Crossings: A White Man's Journey into Black America*.

Harrington's *Crossings* is literary nonfiction at its finest, addressing serious issues in all their complexity and reporting personal experience in a compellingly written narrative. He establishes a connection with the reader from the first sentence "My journey begins in the dentist's chair," a mundane experience to which all of us can relate. When he hears a racist joke denigrating African Americans, he suddenly, inexplicably, for the first time realizes that "those people" are—quite literally—his own children. Impelled by curiosity and the need to understand and protect his children, he heads "out into black America to learn something" and the reader is invited along on the voyage of discovery.

Helen Zia, an award-winning journalist and American of Chinese descent, combines her professional insights and personal experience in *Asian*

American Dreams: The Emergence of an American People. Her style is evocative, laced with personal anecdotes movingly told; her analysis is placed into a larger context of history, sociology, and psychology. The result is both intellectually satisfying and emotionally compelling. Frank Wu's *Yellow: Race in America beyond Black and White* places Asian Americans squarely in the center of discussions of America's approach to dealing with racial diversity.

Testimony is common to all cultural/ethnic groups, from the *literatura testimónio* of Hispanic and Latino populations to Native American testimony and African American slave narratives. Testimony focuses on eye-witness accounts and interpretations of events or phenomena and plays an important role in reclaiming history from the participant's perspective. Slave narratives, for instance, provide insight into the real meaning of slavery. The first-person stories, told in everyday language by ordinary individuals, are compelling in a way that no third party can replicate. Because they are the stories of real people, they take on a special aura of truth.

Native American Testimony: A Chronicle of Indian-White Relations from Prophecy to the Present, 1492–1992 (Peter Nabokov) is an anthology of firsthand accounts and stories that is as varied as the individuals whose words it contains. Reading the words of people who represent a variety of tribes and periods of history creates a sense of intimacy and an appreciation for actual human beings, some of whom are wise, some humorous, some ponderous, some ironic, some angry, some resigned, and some serene. No one who reads these vivid accounts will relegate Native Americans to stereotypical roles or consider them historical relics.

One House, One Voice, One Heart: Native American Education at the Santa Fe Indian School (Sally Hyer) mingles historical narrative and testimony in its approach to one of the most sensitive topics in Indian-Anglo relations: assimilation through education. For Japanese Americans, internment during World War II is one of the most painful and sensitive episodes in their history, and this is documented in *Only What We Could Carry: The Japanese American Internment Experience* (Lawson Inada). As with *Native American Testimony,* a wide variety of sources are included in this anthology, and the descriptions range from the poignant to the bizarre.

Criteria for Evaluating Multicultural Social History

- **Perspective.** Does the author offer a fresh approach? Is the point of view of the culture effectively presented?

- **Bibliographies and notes indicating extensive research and providing the opportunity to verify matters of fact.** Do the notes indicate that the author has provided solid information? Are titles given for readers who want to read further?

- **Contemporaneous testimony and eyewitness reports that provide a feel for the impact on real people.** Do the speakers come to life? Nichols's (1998, parag. 8) review of *To Be an Indian* found the brief comments ineffective, providing "the flavor of grievances but not enough detail to be useful." As a result, he found the book to be disappointing, of only marginal use to scholars and teachers and unappealing to the general public.

- **Factual accuracy.** Errors of fact tend to undermine credibility of the author, even when the errors are small or irrelevant. Gropman (2002), in his review essay of African American military history, found errors in all three of the books examined. He dismissed the first, wondering "why publishers would produce such erroneous material on blacks" (Gropman 2002, 336). In the second, he found "enough errors in this book to shake the confidence of any serious reader" (338). The third was better, but "not free from irritating errors," prompting a warning to handle with care (339). Fortunately, he was able to offer authoritative texts in substitution.

- **Contextualized descriptions.** Events do not take place in isolation; social history and criticism should establish meaning through a description of relevant contexts. Providing context avoids historicism and allows readers to make independent judgments about the events described.

- **Engaging literary style appropriate to the subject and the reader.**

- **Index.** Some readers prefer having an index; some don't care. Although people who prefer social history tend to read the entire text sequentially, many will want an index to check for topics covered, to revisit certain topics, or simply as an indication of quality of scholarship.

Personal History: Connecting with Other Individuals

Whereas testimony focuses on events, is usually recorded contemporaneously, and attempts to put observable facts into the record, memoirs focus on people. Memoirs and other forms of biography, although they reflect social and political circumstances, are essentially the recollections of individuals. For instance, *Having Our Say: The Delany Sisters' First 100 Years* certainly provides insight into changing mores, but it focuses squarely on the two women rather than on a specific event.

Life stories and memoirs are especially important for multicultural populations. It is a way of saying, "This is my world. This is what I have seen and done and felt. I do not need anyone else to speak for me." The appeal of biography is multilayered. It invites the reader to identify with the subject to recapture heritage and history, to gain a sense of community and belonging, and to share the lives of individuals.

While all forms of biography are expected to be factual, they are in actuality, interpretive. The author includes some details and omits others, thus shaping the life and his or her personal story as the reader perceives it. Most authors attempt to give a holistic view. Some biographies are limited to a specific area of a person's life, while others place lives in the context of events and juxtapose public and private life. Autobiographies are likely to include philosophical reflection and political commentary from the individual's perspective." (Van Fleet, forthcoming)

Readers who enjoy testimony are drawn to the political and social aspects of autobiography. Some autobiographies, such as *Farewell to Manzanar,* Jeanne Wakatsuki Houston's story of the treatment of Japanese citizens in World War II America, combine testimony, memoir, and biography in personalizing politics and revealing the people behind policies and stereotypes. *Bighorse the Warrior* (Tiana Bighorse) is the biography of Gus Bighorse, a young man during the Navajo's Long Walk of 1864 who tells his story in the context of the U.S. government's treatment of indigenous peoples.

Spiritual autobiography that explains the impact of religion on an individual's life is a popular form among multicultural audiences and was among the earliest writing of African Americans. Neurosurgeon Ben Carson's autobiography, *Gifted Hands,* is a moving account of his life in which he gives credit for his gifts and abilities to God and to his mother. Mason Betha, who gave up a lucrative career as successful rapper Ma$e to become a pastor, inspires readers with his life story and the sermon he weaves throughout the book, both delivered with sincerity and zest. Cissie Houston's story of her life as a gospel singer is a work of praise, and Patti LaBelle's autobiography is rich with the role that religion has played in her life. In *The Wind Is My Mother: The Life and Teachings of a Native American Shaman,* Bear Heart describes his life journey and religious precepts. Integrally woven throughout are descriptions of Native American–white political conflict and oppositional approaches to religion and environment.

It is very nearly impossible to tell the life story of a person of color in the United States without political overtones. The *Narrative of the Life of Frederick Douglass, an American Slave* (1845) is perhaps the best-known early example of an African American autobiography used for a decidedly political purpose. The accounts of slaves, many published in pamphlet form under the sponsorship of abolitionists, were very popular and overtly political in calling for emancipation (Andrews 1997). Current authors Nathan McCall (*Makes Me Want to Holler: A Young Black Man in America*) and Carl Upchurch (*Convicted in the Womb: One Man's Journey from Prisoner to Peacemaker*) describe the seeming inevitability of despair, violence, and imprisonment among young black men born in the inner city and shaped by social injustice and racial stereotypes.

Other authors use the stories of their lives to address other issues but evidence the same gender-focused approach. Faye Wattleton takes on reproductive choice and the accompanying political maelstrom in her autobiography *Life on the Line,* whereas in *Volunteer Slavery: My Authentic Negro Experience,* Jill Nelson analyzes the constraints faced by black women professionals. Wattleton's book is highly analytical, placing her life and ideas in the context of a richly described social and political environment. Readers will appreciate her attention to detail and encyclopedic knowledge of the political scene. Nelson's work is more limited in contextual observations but has a humorous and sly turn of phrase that is appealing.

Readers may also enjoy biographies in which the individual life story may be interpreted as a representation of the experiences of other group members. The feeling of community and identification is important to readers who prefer this type of biography. Although not overtly political in tone, such biographies cannot help but reflect the impact of society on their authors.

Although it focuses on his personal experience rather than that of a tribe or Native Americans collectively, Monroe's *An Indian in White America* is nevertheless representative, with his life story serving as an example of a life pattern followed by many Native American leaders (Nichols 1998). Esmeralda Santiago's *When I Was Puerto Rican* (also available in Spanish) is a personal autobiography, but many share her life experiences. While Maya Angelou's autobiographical works chronicle a life that is uniquely hers, they resonate with black women because they are in many ways representative of their lives as well. The language is rich, the emotions complex; the reader is invited to share horror, bemusement, sadness, and joy. There is also a coming-of-age element, a recognition that the author grows and changes over time. This intimacy, warmth, and humor are also characteristics of Debra Dickerson's *An American Story,* an autobiography in which the author effectively invites the reader to share her emotional and intellectual growth.

Other biographies recount the life stories of extraordinary individuals. These are people who have distinguished themselves in some way, whose names are familiar or should be. They are leaders, achievers, celebrities. Some of them represent "firsts." Although most readers can and will identify with them, they are models or ideals rather than representative everymen (and women). It is their difference that makes their stories noteworthy.

Particularly influential and well-known figures may be the subjects of numerous biographies which encompass all levels of scholarship, writing quality, and depth of character. Clayborne Carson's excellent *The Autobiography of Martin Luther King, Jr.,* commissioned by King's family after his death and based on Reverend King's personal papers and public record, is one of many but is recommended for its meticulous research and the effectiveness with which it captures its subject's intellect and vitality.

Readers who are interested in particular figures also may be interested in stories told from the family member's point of view. Reading *The Autobiography of Malcolm X* may or may not lead to a desire to read autobiographies by the civil rights activist's daughters (*Growing Up X* and *Little X*). Biographical works about Jackie Robinson run the gamut from scholarly texts such as Arnold Rampersad's *Jackie Robinson: A Biography* to a family album (and love story) by Rachel Robinson, *Jackie Robinson: An Intimate Portrait.*

People who lead the way are often recognized in biographies. It is especially important that the author effectively establish the social and political context of the times to give the reader a true sense of their accomplishments. Ada Lois Sipuel Fisher, the first African American to be admitted to the University of Oklahoma Law School, is exemplary in providing this sense of time and place in her autobiography *A Matter of Black and White: The Autobiography of Ada Lois Sipuel Fisher*, as are Rosa Parks in *Rosa Parks: My Story* and Charlie Sifford in *Just Let Me Play: the Story of Charlie Sifford, the First Black PGA Golfer.*

Te Ata: Chickasaw Storyteller, American Treasure, tells the life story of the first person ever declared an "Oklahoma Treasure." This scholarly work produced by University of Oklahoma Press, describes not just Te Ata's professional career and life but explores the way in which she brought the Indian world and Anglo society closer together through her work. This work is objective in tone and scrupulously researched, but the style carries the reader along and the author's admiration for Te Ata is obvious.

Autobiographies are engaging when they reflect the personalities of their authors. Joycelyn Elders autobiography, *Joycelyn Elders, M.D.: From Sharecropper's Daughter to Surgeon General of the United States of America,* captures her no-nonsense, straightforward style, her motherly wit, and her take-it-as-it-comes attitude. Blues great B. B. King's indomitable spirit and joi de vivre shine through as the story of his life unfolds through provocatively and humorously presented anecdotes and reflections in *Blues All around Me: The Autobiography of B. B. King.* Brent Staples's *Parallel Time: Growing Up in Black and White* exudes anger; Eddie Robinson's *Never Before, Never Again: The Stirring Autobiography of Eddie Robinson, the Winningest Coach in the History of College Football* leaves the reader with a sense of hope and an understanding of the impact of Robinson's positive attitude.

Ultimately, it is the personal story that draws readers—the intimacy of shared humanity, the individual spirit, the special characteristics and thoughts of unique individuals. Community and identity are built through shared experiences—the challenges and triumphs. There is the validation of recognition, the pride of shared accomplishment, or simply the feeling of connection with another human being.

Criteria for Evaluating Biography

- **Implicit scope and purpose.** Is this work about an entire life, birth to death, or adulthood only? Is it a sensationalized exposé, a critical analysis of the subject's impact, or an inspirational description? Is it a self-serving apologia or a balanced reflection?

- **Description of method.** Is this a biography or an autobiography? Did the author use interviews with the subject, primary documents such as letters, or secondary sources? Are these sources appropriately documented?

- **Context.** What were the influences on the subject's life? In what arena did the subject live and work? Is the biography imbued with meaning, or is it a simple chronology?

- **Factual accuracy.** While the most personal aspects of a life are not part of a public record, many events surrounding a person's life are verifiable and not open to interpretation.

- **Engaging literary style appropriate to the subject and the reader.** Is the style richly detailed, or is it a fast read? Is the tone angry, playful, wry, hopeful? Is the language eloquent and complex, or is it crisp and straightforward? Does the style reflect the personality of the subject?

- **Photographs, lists of achievements.** When photographs of subjects are included in biographies, they bring the subject to life for the reader. Discographies, bibliographies, athletic records, and other lists of achievement are shorthand for the subject's impact, and many readers enjoy these features.

- **Index.** Again, an index is a feature that some recreational nonfiction readers insist on and others never notice. Some readers will use an index to determine if key events and personalities are included in the biography. Some will use an index to determine depth of coverage.

Guidance and Self-Help: Connecting with Self

Although people of color develop a sense of community and identity through works that establish their history and tell stories of their communities and individuals with whom they share a common culture, they also need recognition of that identity as they go about their daily lives. Multicultural readers have demonstrated that guidance and self-help books are important to them as they face the world as unique individuals.

Researchers have demonstrated the impact that a clash of cultures can have on individual success. Recent reports have found that while Latinas and Asian American women are among the fastest-growing groups in the labor force, they are underrepresented in corporate offices. Many Asian American women, regardless of whether they grew up in the United States or came to this country as adults, "said their Asian cultural values are frequently at odds with their ability to successfully navigate the corporate landscape," echoing the earlier study of Latinas (Guido 2003, B5). Both groups reported that their status as women was as problematic as ethnic stereotyping, echoing the themes found in the Dickerson and Nelson autobiographies discussed earlier in this chapter. Books such as *The Maria Paradox: How Latinas Can Merge Old World Traditions with New World Self-Esteem* and *Leaving Deep Water: Asian American Women at the Crossroads of Two Cultures* help women deal with such acculturation problems on a personal as well as professional level. Women who want books on these topics but prefer a more assertive style may be more satisfied with *Dragon Ladies: Asian American Feminists Breathe Fire* (the cover is a good representation of the tone of this book) or *Warrior Lessons: An Asian American Woman's Journey into Power*, Phoebe Eng's autobiography cum advice book.

The repetition of themes across genres of nonfiction is not uncommon. For instance, the theme of Michael Datcher's autobiography, *Raising Fences: A Black Man's Love Story,* is the subject of the self-help guide, *How to Love a Black Man* (Ronn Elmore) and the inspirational *The Spirit of a Man: A Vision of Transformation for Black Men and the Women Who Love Them* (Iyanla Vanzant).

Publishers of self-help books are taking advantage of the multicultural market by targeting nonfiction works for people of color, with varying degrees of success, and reviewers and consumers are responding. Mainstream sources are recognizing the validity of nonfiction books geared to specific ethnocultural groups. *Consumer Reports* (2003, 24) included *Pay Yourself First: The African American Guide to Financial Success and Security* (Jesse Brown) among the seven titles reviewed in its analysis of best-selling personal finance books. This particular topic has proven enormously popular, with contributions such as a series of books published by *Black*

Enterprise, Latino Success: Insights from 100 of America's Most Powerful Latino Business Professionals, and targeted titles such as *The Black Woman's Guide to Financial Independence.*

Movies and television are evidence of the growing appreciation of the unique beauty of women of color. This recognition has led to the publication of a number of successful guides, among them *Asian Beauty, Latina Beauty* (from the editors of *Latina Magazine*), and *Fine Beauty: Beauty Basics and Beyond for African American Women.* Perhaps as evidence of the truth of Starletta Duval's observation, "White women worry about weight; black women worry about hair," a plethora of hair-care guides such as *Let's Talk Hair: Every Black Woman's Personal Consultation for Healthy Growing Hair* (Pamela Ferrell) are now available. Ayana Byrd and Lori L. Thorpe explore this theme in the cultural history *Hair Story: Untangling the Roots of Black Hair in America.* Written in a popular style and generously illustrated, *Hair Story* offers an opportunity for readers' advisory across nonfiction genres.

Inspirational nonfiction for multicultural audiences has followed the explosive lead of inspirational fiction, one of the fastest-growing markets in the publishing industry. Black authors "are making spirituality the hottest ticket in literature" (Starling 1998, 96). *Woman, Thou Art Loosed* by Reverend T. D. Jakes sold more than one million copies; Iyanla Vanzant's books of meditations regularly debut at the top of best-seller lists. Although a number of guides are equally relevant for men and women (Vanzant's *Acts of Faith: Daily Meditations for People of Color*), readers' advisors should be aware of gender-specific titles such as *Sister Wit: Devotions for Women* by Jaqueline Jakes and *40 Days in the Wilderness: Meditations for African-American Men* by Kwasi Issa Kena.

Christian releases continue to dominate African American inspirational work, but there is a continuing and slowly growing audience for books about Islam and African religions. Native American spirituality is being presented in some texts, such as *The Wind Is My Mother* (Bear Heart), but the essence of many Indian religions is closely guarded, often passed orally from generation to generation, and ceremonies and rituals are not open to those who do not belong to the tribe. Some authors, such as best-selling Yoruba priestess Vanzant, are open to any path to spirituality, and their works are accepted by Christians as well as those of different faiths.

Some guides offer inspiration without religion. Eric Copage's *Black Pearls: Daily Meditations, Affirmations, and Inspirations for African-Americans* is a compilation that includes quotes from such widely divergent sources as African proverbs, Sojourner Truth, Malcolm X, and Quincy Jones.

Criteria for Evaluating Multicultural Self-Help and Guidance

- **Tailored guidance.** Does the author offer advice that is special to the audience? *Consumer Reports* (2003) ranked *Pay Yourself First: The African American Guide to Financial Success and Security* seventh of seven best-selling personal finance books because the author "missed opportunities to offer tailored guidance" and "ignores minority scholarships when discussing college financing" (*Consumer Reports* 2003, 25).

- **Accuracy.** Does the author offer advice that is accurate, ethical, feasible, and appropriate? Does the advice conform to established norms in the field?

- **Form and features.** Burgin (2001) observes that nonfiction readers have expectations and preferences for features such as checklists, forms, and examples. A criticism of *Pay Yourself First* is its lack of forms. A strength of *How to Love a Black Man* is the inclusion of numerous self-tests and lists. The daily calendar format of many of the inspirational meditations collections works well for the reader and the subject matter.

Conclusion

Nonfiction literature takes many forms. Those described in this chapter are most popular with multicultural audiences and have been published in increased numbers in the past decade. Multicultural literature reflects our diverse society, helping each culture to understand itself and interpreting varied cultures to one another.

Nonfiction multicultural literature provides a new dimension to readers' advisory services, speaking in the accessible style of the narrative but endowed with the credibility of truth. It provides a sense of community, identity, and self. It allows its audiences to reclaim history, to define themselves and their culture, and to approach daily life through a unique lens. It acknowledges difference and oneness. Nonfiction multicultural literature also helps members of the dominant culture understand and appreciate differences of other ethnic and cultural groups. Readers' advisors who move beyond mainstream fiction to add multicultural and nonfiction titles to their repertoires enhance the opportunity to take the reader to the right book—the one that satisfies, amuses, teaches, or even inspires.

References

Andrews, William L. 1997. Secular autobiography. In *The Oxford companion to African American literature*. Edited by William L. Andrews, Frances Smith Foster, and Trudier Harris, 34–37. New York: Oxford University Press.

Antonette, Leslie. 2003. Liberal and conservative multiculturalism after September 11. *Multicultural Review* 12: 29–35.

Burgin, Robert. 2001. Readers' advisory and nonfiction. In *The readers' advisor's companion*. Edited by Kenneth D. Shearer and Robert Burgin, 213–27. Englewood, CO: Libraries Unlimited.

Clausen, Christopher. 1997. Welcome to post-culturalism. In *Multiculturalism*. Edited by Robert Emmet Long, 152–60. New York: H. W. Wilson. Reprinted from *The American Scholar* 65 (summer 1996): 379–88.

Consumer Reports. 2003. Best-selling finance gurus: Whose book is best? 68 (September): 24–26.

Dahlin, Robert. 1995. Native Americans ride to the fore: A significant resurgence of interest. *Publishers Weekly* 242: 50–53.

Dawson, Alma, and Connie Van Fleet. 2001. The future of readers' advisory in a multicultural society. In *The readers' advisor's companion*. Edited by Kenneth D. Shearer and Robert Burgin, 249–68. Englewood, CO: Libraries Unlimited.

Failde, Augusto, and William Doyle. 1996. *Latino success: Insights from 100 of America's most powerful Latino business professionals*. New York: Simon & Schuster.

Figueredo, Danilo H. 1999. The stuff dreams are made of: The Latino detective novel. *Multicultural Review* 8: 22–29.

Fleming, Robert.1999. Commentary. In *Sacred fire: The QBR 100 essential black books. Edited* by Max Rodriguez, Angeli R. Rasbury, and Carol Taylor, 49–52. New York: John Wiley and Sons.

Gropman, Alan. 2002. African-American military history: We can do better. *Armed Forces & Society* 28: 333–41.

Guido, Michell. 2003. Asian-American women face added business obstacles. *The Norman Transcript* (August 10): B5.

Jackson, Gloria, and Marilyn Robertson. 1991. Building multicultural-multilingual collections. *CMLEA Journal* 15: 11–13.

Kramer, Mark. 1995. Breakable rules for literary journalists. In *Literary journalism: A new collection of the best American nonfiction*. Edited by Norman Sims and Mark Kramer, 21–34. New York: Ballantine Books.

Lee, Lisa. 1990. Works by Native American writers find wider audience. *Publishers Weekly* 237: 80–81.

Lee, Sul H. 2003. Books that inspire III. URL: http://www.libraries.ou.edu/exhibits/inspire/inspire2003.asp (Accessed August 28, 2003).

Lounsberry, Barbara. 1990. *The art of fact: Contemporary artists of nonfiction*. New York: Greenwood Press.

Nichols, Roger L. 1998. Indian lives and history. *Journal of American Ethnic History* 17: 67 (4 pages). Retrieved September 1, 2003, from InfoTrac database.

Rodriguez, Max, Angeli R. Rasbury, and Carol Taylor. 1999. *Sacred fire: The QBR 100 essential black books*. New York: Wiley.

Sims, Norman. 1995. The art of literary journalism. In *Literary journalism: A new collection of the best American nonfiction*. Edited by Norman Sims and Mark Kramer, 3–19. New York: Ballantine Books.

Starling, Kelly. 1998. New directions in black spirituality. *Ebony* 53: 92, 94, 96, 98.

Van Fleet, Connie. Forthcoming. Life stories. In *The African American readers' advisor*. Edited by Alma Dawson and Connie Van Fleet. Greenwood, CT: Libraries Unlimited.

Books Used As Examples

Aranda-Alvarado, Belén. 2000. *Latina Beauty*. New York: Hyperion.

Ashe, Arthur. 1988. *A hard road to glory: A history of the African American athlete*. New York: Warner Books.

Ashe, Arthur. 1993. *Days of grace: A memoir*. New York: Knopf.

Bear Heart and Molly Larkin. 1996. *The wind is my mother: The life and teachings of a Native American shaman*. New York: Clarkson Potter.

Betha, Mason, and Karen Hunter. 2001. *Revelations: There's a light after the lime*. New York: Pocket Books.

Bighorse, Tiana. 1990. *Bighorse the warrior*. Tucson: University of Arizona Press.

Broussard, Cheryl D. 1996. *The black woman's guide to financial independence*. New York: Penguin.

Brown, Dee. 1970. *Bury my heart at Wounded Knee*. New York: Holt, Rinehart & Winston.

Brown, Jesse B. 2001. *Pay yourself first: The African American guide to financial success and security*. New York: Wiley.

Byrd, Ayana D., and Lori L. Thorpe. 2001. *Hair story: Untangling the roots of black hair in America*. New York: St. Martin's Press.

Carson, Ben, and Cecil Murphey. 1990. *Gifted hands: The Ben Carson story*. Grand Rapids, MI: Zondervan Books.

Cash, Joseph H., and Herbert T. Hoover. 1995. *To be an Indian*. St. Paul: Minnesota Historical Press.

Chang, Iris. 2003. *The Chinese in America*. New York: Viking.

Chow, Claire S. 1998. *Leaving deep water: Asian American women at the crossroads of two cultures*. New York: Dutton.

Copage, Eric V. 1993. *Black pearls: Daily meditations, affirmations, and inspirations for African-Americans*. New York: Quill/Morrow.

Datcher, Michael. 2001. *Raising fences: A black man's love story*. New York: Riverhead Books.

Delany, Sarah Louise, Annie Elizabeth Delany, and Amy Hill Hearth. 1993. *Having our say: The Delany sisters' first 100 years*. New York: Kodansha International.

Dent, Tom. 1997. *Southern journey: A return to the civil rights movement*. New York: Morrow.

Dickerson, Debra J. 2000. *An American story*. New York: Pantheon.

Elders, Joycelyn, and David Chanoff. 1996. *Joycelyn Elders, M.D.: From sharecropper's daughter to Surgeon General of the United States of America*. New York: Morrow.

Elmore, Ronn. 1996. *How to love a black man*. New York: Warner.

Eng, Phoebe. 1999. *Warrior lessons: An Asian American woman's journey into power*. New York: Pocket Books.

Ferrell, Pamela. 1996. *Let's talk hair: Every black woman's personal consultation for healthy growing hair*. Washington, DC: Conrows.

Fine, Sam, and Julia Chance. 1998. *Fine beauty: Beauty basics and beyond for African American women*. New York: Riverhead Books.

Gil, Rosa Maria, and Carmen Inoa Vazquez. 1996. *The Maria paradox: How Latinas can merge Old World traditions with New World self-esteem*. New York: G.P. Putnam's Sons.

Harrington, Walt. 1992. *Crossings: A white man's journey into black America*. New York: HarperCollins.

Houston, Cissy, and Jonathan Singer. 1998. *How sweet the sound: My life with God and the gospel.* New York: Doubleday.

Houston, Jeanne Wakatsuki, and James D. Houston. 1973. *Farewell to Manzanar: A true story of Japanese American experience before and after the World War II internment.* New York: Houghton Mifflin.

Hyer, Sally. 1990. *One house, one voice, one heart: Native American education at the Santa Fe Indian School.* Santa Fe: Museum of New Mexico Press.

Inada, Lawson Fusao. 2000. *Only what we could carry: The Japanese American internment experience.* Berkeley, CA: Heyday Books.

Jakes, T. D. 1993. *Woman, thou art loosed: Healing the wounds of the past.* Shippensburg, PA: Treasure House.

Jakes, Jaqueline. 2002. *Sister wit: Devotions for women.* New York: Warner Books.

Kena, Kwasi Issa. 1998. *40 days in the wilderness: Meditations for African-American men.* Nashville, TN: Abingdon Press.

Kimbro, Dennis Paul, and Napoleon Hill. 1991. *Think and grow rich: A black choice.* New York: Fawcett Columbine.

Kimura, Margaret, and Marianne Daugherty. 2001. *Asian beauty.* New York: HarperResource.

King, B. B., and David Ritz. 1996. *Blues all around me: The autobiography of B. B. King.* New York: Avon Books.

LaBelle, Patti, and Laura B. Randolph. 1996. *Don't block the blessings: Revelations of a lifetime.* New York: Boulevard Books.

McCall, Nathan. 1994. *Makes me wanna holler: A young black man in America.* New York: Random House.

Monroe, Mark, and Carolyn Reyer. 1994. *An Indian in white America.* Philadelphia: Temple University Press.

Nelson, Jill. 1993. *Volunteer slavery: My authentic Negro experience.* Chicago: Noble Press.

Nabokov, Peter, ed. 1991. *Native American testimony: A chronicle of Indian-white relations from prophecy to the present, 1492–1992.* New York: Viking.

Rampersad, Arnold. 1997. *Jackie Robinson: A biography.* New York: Knopf.

Robinson, Eddie, and Richard Labchick. 1999. *Never before, never again: The stirring autobiography of Eddie Robinson, the winningest coach in the history of college football.* New York: St. Martin's Press.

Santiago, Esmeralda. 1993. *When I was Puerto Rican*. New York: Vintage Books.

Shah, Sonia. 1997. *Dragon ladies: Asian American feminists breathe fire*. Boston: South End Press.

Shabazz, Ilyasah, and Kim McLarin. 2002. *Growing up X*. New York: One World/Ballantine.

Staples, Brent. 1994. *Parallel time: Growing up in black and white*. New York: Pantheon Books.

Tate, Sonsyrea. 1997. *Little X: Growing up in the nation of Islam*. San Francisco: HarperSanFrancisco.

Upchurch, Carl. 1996. *Convicted in the womb: One man's journey from prisoner to peacemaker*. New York: Bantam Books.

Vanzant, Iyanla. 1993. *Acts of faith: Daily meditations for people of color*. New York: Fireside Book.

Vanzant, Iyanla. 1996. *The spirit of a man: A vision of transformation for black men and the women who love them*. San Francisco: HarperSanFrancisco.

Wattleton, Faye. 1996. *Life on the line*. New York: Ballantine.

Weatherford, Jack. 1995. *Indian givers: How the Indians of the Americas transformed the world*. New York: Fawcett Columbine.

Wu, Frank. 2002. *Yellow: Race in America beyond black and white*. New York: Basic Books.

X, Malcolm; and Alex Haley. 1965. *The autobiography of Malcolm X*. New York: Grove Press.

Zia, Helen. 2000. *Asian American dreams: The Emergence of an American People*. New York: Farrar, Straus & Giroux.

Part IV

Practical Advice

The first three sections of this book have addressed the why, the what, and the who of nonfiction readers' advisory. This last section looks at the how, that is, the "nuts and bolts" of how to incorporate nonfiction into readers' advisory transactions.

In Chapter 11, Stacy Alesi (whose "Bookbitch" Web site offers book reviews, information on best-sellers and reading groups, and a Weblog of breaking book news) highlights the importance of communications in the readers' advisory process. In particular, she focuses on the importance of body language, listening skills, and knowledge of the resources in building a sense of trust between the user and the advisor while determining the user's interests and finding suitable reading materials. As with fiction readers' advisory, Alesi argues that the key is to find out what the user has read and enjoyed and to determine what those items have in common. Alesi's example (*Sixpence House* by Paul Collins) leads beyond the familiar nonfiction genre of "Travel Narratives or Essays" to a more specific subgenre, "Americans Living Abroad."

Vicki Novak provides further thoughts on "narrative nonfiction for recreational reading" in Chapter 12, suggesting that nonfiction readers have been ignored in the readers' advisory process because libraries equate nonfiction with informational needs and because our readers' advisory tools don't deal with nonfiction in any depth. She then cites reader reviews to show the importance of appeal factors to readers of narrative nonfiction and outlines some nonfiction genres. Novak lists several ideas for incorporating nonfiction into readers' advisory—from marketing recreational nonfiction to promoting cross-over works (true crime for mystery readers, biographical or historical works for readers of historical fiction).

The renaissance in advisory services for fiction readers has been one of the most exciting, energizing events in the profession's recent history. The chapters in this section of the book show that it is possible to bring that same excitement and energy to providing advisory services to readers of nonfiction. As Joyce Saricks says in her Introduction to this book, "It is time for librarians who work with nonfiction to join the fun."

Chapter 11

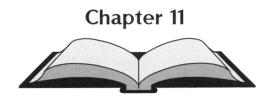

Readers' Advisory in the Real World

Stacy Alesi

Readers' advisory in the real world, in the library, revolves around one thing: communication. Communication is the cornerstone of readers' advisory, whether for nonfiction or fiction—everything else is just peripheral. It is infinitely helpful if the readers' advisor is well read and knowledgeable about what is available, but even the most well-read person will not be able to assist a patron unless she or he can communicate clearly.

Almost equally important is that the readers' advisor be aware of the available resources. There are many readers' advisory books as well as other sources for helping patrons find fiction, but print nonfiction readers' advisory reference materials are pretty much nonexistent. So what is the nonfiction readers' advisor to do? My advice is to be grateful for the technological advances made in the past few years and look to the Internet. The Internet has been a boon to nonfiction readers' advisory, making available an almost infinite amount of information. But before you can start searching, you need to know what you are searching for.

Fiction can be broken down into genres, and within each genre, you can get more and more specific about where a patron's interests lie. If the patron likes mysteries, you can move on to breaking it down further. For example, does the patron prefer American, British, or translated authors? How much gore can the patron tolerate? Does the patron prefer traditional mysteries, just some suspense, or thrillers? Male or female authors or protagonists? Amateur sleuths or police detectives or private detectives? The list really can go on quite extensively until you find that patron's "perfect mystery." Nonfiction works a little differently in that there really aren't any formal genre classifications other than "nonfiction," but if you think about the last bookstore you were in, you will begin to see a glimmer of the possibilities.

My local Borders devotes approximately 20 percent of their sales floor to fiction, 20 percent to children's, another 20 percent to music, and the remaining 40 percent or so to nonfiction. Interestingly enough, within the children's department, the same percentages apply, creating a mini-bookstore within a bookstore, if you will. Your library may have a similar breakdown, give or take a few percentage points either way. However, although Borders does classify works by subject (as the Dewey Decimal system does), "genres" are identified within these subjects.

There are several general areas that are broken down into smaller categories, much like fiction is divided into general fiction, romance, science fiction, mystery, and so on. Nonfiction encompasses the broadest categories of animals, art, business, health, history, math & science, religion, self-help, sports, travel, and so on, maybe a dozen or so in all. The goal of this type of division is to group books together in some semblance of order that the reader can understand. Even more important, the books are placed so that the reader can find what she or he likes and find similar books nearby. This is not usually the case in a library.

For instance, if a reader liked *A Year in Provence* by Peter Mayle, she could go back to the shelf where she found that book in the typical bookstore and find several more books like it. Will she find tour guides to Provence on that shelf? Not likely. The Mayle book is probably shelved in a section called "Travel Narratives or Essays," which is probably not too far from the tour guides to Provence, but more likely shelved alongside other books in that same genre—"Travel Narratives." There you can find books such as *A Walk in the Woods* by Bill Bryson, *Under the Tuscan Sun* by Frances Mayes, and *One Year Off* by David Cohen. These books have more appeal for the pleasure reader than the serious traveler. Taken at face value, the Mayle book is about Provence, the Bryson book about the Appalachian Trail, the Mayes book about Tuscany, and the Cohen book about world travel. Of course, they are all about those things, but they offer so much more than that. Bryson offers humor, Mayes offers recipes and advice on dealing with contractors in Italy, Cohen deals with the travails of traveling with small children, and so on. Yet they must have something in common because they are all shelved together, despite their diversity.

These books share a major commonality: they easily accommodate the leisure reader, the reader who wants to read a book for the enjoyment of it, with the educational aspects a nice bonus but probably not the main reason for the book's selection. In the library, however, you can't just send the patron off to the "Travel Narratives" shelf, because for the most part, there isn't one. Furthermore, the patron may not even realize that "Travel Narratives" is what she or he is seeking. It is up to the readers' advisor to ferret out that information and lead the patron to what she or he is truly seeking; something a little more specific than just "a good book."

Body Language

Readers' advisory starts at the most basic level: body language. A welcoming smile, eye contact, acknowledgment of the person standing before you—all this gets you off on the right foot. It's been my experience that there are two types of people who approach librarians for assistance: those who have unsuccessfully tried to find what they need on their own or are at a loss as to where to look for what they want, and those who simply crave attention. The attention seekers are hopefully a much smaller group.

In general, most people don't like asking for help, and if they are going to make the effort, it is up to the librarian to meet them halfway and acknowledge their presence. You need to make yourself accessible to your patrons or they won't bother you. For instance, if there are two librarians at the desk and one is busily typing away on the computer while the other is looking around and making eye contact with the patrons in the area, the one who is typing is less likely to be approached. The idea is to appear to want to help, and although there is nothing wrong with doing other things at the desk, it is important not to appear to be so involved in what you are doing that a patron would hesitate to interrupt you. Type away if you will, but look up fairly frequently. Make sure that there is no one standing a few feet away from the desk perhaps waiting for you to finish.

The same thing goes for reading—there are many libraries that frown on reading at the desk, but it can be a very good thing for the readers' advisor to do. Most of us simply do not have time enough to read everything we would like, and reading even twenty to thirty pages a day during downtime can give you an idea about a book and its merits. It almost always will provoke a patron into asking about your reading material and can make you seem more knowledgeable and even more approachable about books. But again, you have to be careful here. This is not the time to be totally engrossed in the latest thriller, because if you are too involved in the book, you undoubtedly will not be involved enough in what is going on around you. On the other hand, this can be a really good time to peruse the latest review journals or skim some of the new books so you can familiarize yourself with them. As with the typing, just remember to lift your head every couple of minutes and look around.

Listening

Now that you've made yourself approachable, it's time to move forward to the next important phase of communicating: listening. Sometimes patrons will have a clear idea of what they want, but more often than not, the patron just wants a "good book." *My* idea of a good book may not be the same as *your* idea of a good book, however, and least of all *the patron's* idea of a good book. So how do you determine what the patron really wants when she or he asks for a "good book?" By listening.

One of my earliest experiences with the value of listening was when a patron told me that she had just read the best book—*Adventures of a Psychic: The Fascinating Inspiring True-Life Story of One of America's Most Successful Clairvoyants* by Sylvia Browne—and asked if I could recommend any more books like that. I must have spent a good fifteen minutes with her discarding one suggestion after another, until a light bulb went off in my head. I finally asked her if she had read any other books by Sylvia Browne, and she looked at me like I was out of my mind. She insisted that she had asked me for books by Sylvia Browne to begin with and informed me that I hadn't been listening. She was probably right, and it was a good lesson to learn.

Sometimes the patron will simply ask for biographies or the latest political hot potato, but more often than not, the patron is approaching you because she or he not sure what to read next. It is the principal preoccupation of the readers' advisor to figure out what the patron truly wants. Put on your Sherlock Holmes hat and start by asking open-ended, nonthreatening questions. Asking yes or no questions gets you nowhere fast. Nonthreatening questions are exemplified by thinking about *how* you ask almost more than *what* you ask. It is absolutely crucial to appear nonjudgmental. Saying "You *liked* that book?" with the emphasis on the word "liked" conveys a more confrontational tone and a completely different meaning than saying, "Oh, you liked that book," in a more even, conversational tone. Bear in mind that you may be confronted by titles as diverse as *The Thief, the Cross and the Wheel: Pain and the Spectacle of Punishment in Medieval and Renaissance Europe* by Mitchell B. Merback; *Treason: Liberal Treachery from the Cold War to the War on Terrorism* by Ann Coulter; or *Stolen Lives: Twenty Years in a Desert Jail* by Malika Oufkir, but your reaction needs to be the same for any title that is presented as the patron's favorite. It may well be beyond your scope of understanding that someone would find a book on medieval torture a "good book," but remember that it is exactly this diversity that makes the job of the readers' advisory so fascinating.

Using the example of someone looking for a "good book," we need to find out what this patron considers good. Perhaps she or he starts out by asking for a good book, but "not a novel." So now you've determined that this individual is *probably* looking for nonfiction. And I stress the word *probably*—patrons don't always know the correct terminology, so one patron's "not a novel" could be "not a romance" or "not a horror novel," although usually "not a novel" will mean nonfiction.

By asking, "Did you enjoy *Tuesdays with Morrie*?" you can find whether the patron did or did not enjoy it or even whether the patron has never heard of the book. But then what? You could conceivably go through dozens of titles in this manner and not learn much that will help you. But assuming that you have already established that the individual prefers nonfiction, you can then ask that quintessential readers' advisory question, "What was the last book you read that you really enjoyed?"

Think of this approach as an upside down pyramid. You start at the top with a very broad question, and then as you listen, you can get more and more specific. For instance, if the last book the patron enjoyed was *Sixpence House* by Paul Collins, the next logical question is, "What did you like about it?" Sometimes you get lucky and get a definitive answer such as, "I love anything British." But more often than not, this question will invoke an answer such as, "It was good," and you're no further along than when you started.

If that is the case, then you will need to probe more carefully and with some finesse to avoid offending your patron. Asking too many questions can make people feel like they are being grilled, and your goal is to help, not to annoy. By asking more specific questions, you can determine where this person's interests lie and why she or he considers *Sixpence House* a good book. If you are not familiar with the book, your first step is to do a quick search on the database that is easiest for you to access and most likely to provide you with some information about the title, then to ask the patron for a brief synopsis. It is definitely helpful to know what the pundits at Amazon.com think the book is about, but it is more telling to hear what the patron thinks the book is about. By comparing the two descriptions, you gain your first glimpse into where this individual's interests lie.

Suppose this is the synopsis you get from your patron:

Sixpence House is about an American writer trying to buy a house in a small town in Wales called Hay-on-Wye. This town is famous for having a population of 1500, people and 40 bookstores. They never did buy a home though.

Even though you've only been given a couple of sentences, if you were listening carefully, there are several paths you can follow. A small town with so many bookstores ought to spark something about books or the publishing industry or even just retail sales. One avenue you could explore would be to inquire whether the patron enjoys reading books about books or the publishing industry or whether she or he has an interest in the retail industry.

Another point mentioned was that it was an American writer moving to Wales. You could inquire whether the individual enjoyed reading about the Collins's search for a home or the cultural differences Americans find when living abroad. You might further ask whether she or he enjoys reading about Americans moving abroad or if perhaps she or he is an Anglophile, enjoying anything British.

Taking this scenario to the next step, you can then do a search on Amazon.com for *Sixpence House,* explaining to the patron that you're trying to get more information about the book. It's all well and good to madly dash around the Internet to help a patron, but if she or he doesn't know what you're doing, the patron is liable to think you can't help and have gone on to something else. Keep the conversation going and keep the patron informed. Tell her or him that the first thing that comes up on Amazon is a review from *Publishers Weekly* and reassure the patron that *Publishers Weekly* gives a synopsis similar to the one you have just been given: "Collins can be quite funny, and he pads his sophomore effort with obscure but amusing trivia (how many book lovers know that the same substance used to thicken fast-food milk shakes is an essential ingredient in paper resizing?), but it's hard to imagine anyone beyond bibliophiles and fellow Hay-lovers finding enough here to hold their attention. Witty and droll though he may be, Collins fails to give his slice-of-life story the magic it needs to transcend the genre."

From this review, we learn that *Publishers Weekly* may or may not consider this a "good book." But we also learn that in their opinion, this book will probably only appeal to those who love books or are familiar with the town of Hay-on-Wye. Armed with this knowledge, you can then move on to a simple yes-or-no question like "Are you looking for additional titles about the book industry?" If you get a positive response (and often a relieved look), you are now ready to move ahead and suggest possible titles.

Resources

Where are you going to get these titles? If your idea of a good book is the latest James Patterson or Joyce Carol Oates novel, you may not have much to draw on for nonfiction. Even if you read a lot of nonfiction, you still may not be able to come up with a list of books about books. In fact, unless your reading tastes are completely diverse, chances are a patron will stump you daily. But there are lots of resources available, right at your fingertips, and the Internet should be your first stop for ease of use and speed in finding the information you need. Using Bowker's *Books in Print,* Amazon.com, or even your library's catalog (if it offers such information) will quickly and easily bring up the information you need.

Amazon.com is free and available everywhere there is an Internet connection, so let's start there. Most people are familiar with the editorial review section, which offers reviews by major publications such as *Library Journal, Kirkus, Publishers Weekly,* and *Booklist.* The customer reviews are usually available for most popular titles but sometimes lacking on the more esoteric ones. You should also be aware that the anonymity of customer reviews has called into question the veracity of these reviews. It is not unusual for authors to write their own reviews and to get their friends to do likewise, so bear that in mind (Harmon 2004). But you can also gain some interesting insight into what people who have read the book and who are not professional reviewers think about it. Everyone who reads a book brings her or his own history and point of view to it, which can make for some very interesting observations.

There are additional aspects to the Amazon database that you may not be aware of. Amazon provides suggested titles under the heading of "Customers who bought this book also bought," which in this particular case, is actually a helpful list including the following titles:

- *Out of the Flames: The Remarkable Story of a Fearless Scholar, a Fatal Heresy, and One of the Rarest Books in the World* by Lawrence Goldstone and Nancy Goldstone

- *A Book of Books* by Abelardo Morell (Photographer) and Nicholson Baker (Preface)

- *Speaking of Books: The Best Things Ever Said about Books and Book Collecting* by Rob Kaplan and Harold Rabinowitz (Editors)

- *Patience & Fortitude: A Roving Chronicle of Book People, Book Places, and Book Culture* by Nicholas A. Basbanes

- *Warmly Inscribed: The New England Forger and Other Book Tales* by Lawrence Goldstone and Nancy Goldstone

A word of warning here: this particular list is a good one, but more often than not, Amazon provides a peculiar list of titles, so tread carefully here. A better and more accurate resource is located near the bottom of the page under "Look for similar books by subject." This is a subject list broken down into various categories starting from the broadest point; for *Sixpence House,* the list starts with Travel, and then becomes more and more specific:

Subjects > Travel > Europe > Great Britain > General

Other subject headings include Wales; Biographies & Memoirs, then more specifically Travel or Memoirs; Literature and Fiction, then more specifically Books & Reading, then Booksellers & Bookselling; Travel Books on Europe, moving down to Great Britain or just Wales.

You can click on any of the subjects—working backward if necessary within each subject heading to get broader as needed—to bring up several titles that will hopefully appeal to your patron.

Bowker's *Books in Print* works a little differently but also offers a synopsis of most books, often includes the dust-jacket description, and offers authoritative reviews as well as links to review sources. *Books in Print* also lists subject headings (similar to those from Amazon.com), which are searchable within their database and may link back to the library's catalog. For instance, the subject headings listed for *Sixpence House* by BIP are as follows:

Bowker Subjects:

BOOKSELLERS AND BOOKSELLING

BOOK COLLECTORS

WALES SOCIAL LIFE AND CUSTOMS

General Subjects (BISAC):

ANTIQUES & COLLECTIBLES / Books

LANGUAGE ARTS & DISCIPLINES / Publishing

SOCIAL SCIENCE / Customs & Traditions

These appear as links to lists of titles, which, depending on your library's collection, you can then offer to your patron.

At this point you should have a better idea about what might please your patron. If the book industry was the wrong direction, then it's time to move in a different direction. Suppose you have ascertained that the patron likes reading about Americans living out of the country and doesn't particularly care about the book industry or where the book is set as long as it's not America. That will give you an entirely different set of criteria to work with.

As you may recall, one of the categories that Amazon listed under "Look for similar books by subject" was "Subjects > Biographies & Memoirs > Travel." Unfortunately, you generally won't find anything specific enough to what your patron wants, so you have to logically follow the steps until you get there. "Travel memoirs" is still a fairly broad description, but when you follow the link you are presented with a list of titles that may be just right. Some of the titles this list brings up are the following:

- *Into the Wild* by Jon Krakauer, about Christopher McCandless's journey and subsequent death in the Alaska bush.

- *The Road to Home: My Life and Times* by Vartan Gregorian, about the author's childhood in Iran and becoming president of the New York Public Library and then president of Brown University.

- *A Thousand Days in Venice* by Marlena De Blasi, about a professional chef (and writer) from Missouri, who travels to Venice on business, falls in love with a man and the city, and makes Venice her home.

- *Cuba Diaries: An American Housewife in Havana* by Isadora Tattlin, the diary of a housewife who spent four years with her family living in Cuba in the 1990s.

- *Braving Home: Dispatches from the Underwater Town, the Lava-Side Inn, and Other Extreme Locales* by Jake Halpern, in which (as described by *Publisher's Weekly*) Halpern toured "America's highways to report on stubborn stalwarts who defy eviction notices and cling to home despite floods, lava, fire and hurricanes."

There are many more to choose from, but even from just these few examples you can easily find a couple—*A Thousand Days in Venice* and *Cuba Diaries*—that should meet your patron's criterion of books about Americans living away from home, and in the process, you may spark an interest in something else. It is what all of these books have in common that may appeal to your patron.

Finding the Commonalities

All this questioning and research really doesn't take more than a few minutes, and most of the time that will be all it will take to have your patron happily leaving the library, book in hand. The key is finding the commonalities among the books your patron likes and then finding additional titles for her or him to read. The help patrons need in finding readable nonfiction for pleasure is similar to that which you would offer a patron seeking fiction and is completely different from that which you would offer a patron doing research.

It may help to think about it this way: good fiction should read like nonfiction, while good nonfiction should read like fiction. Fiction may be fantastic, but there needs to be something that draws the reader in so that she or he can feel empathy for the characters and somehow find their situations believable. Good nonfiction needs to have the pacing and drama of fiction because the truth is already there; it just needs to be presented in a way to draw the reader in and get the reader engrossed in that truth.

Nonfiction readers' advisory differs from fiction readers' advisory in that there are not nearly as many resources available for the nonfiction readers' advisor. It is important to be aware of the ones your library does have and to become familiar with them. Quiet time at the desk is a good time to check out some of these resources. Besides the aforementioned Bowker's *Books in Print* and Amazon.com, there are several other bookstores online that offer similar information and searchability. Here are a few to try:

- Barnes and Noble (URL: http://www.bn.com [Accessed December 8, 2003])

- Books-A-Million (URL: http://www.bamm.com [Accessed December 8, 2003])

- Powells Books in Portland, Oregon (http://www.powells.com [Accessed December 8, 2003])

Something that is helpful in keeping up with what's out there is the Powells review a-day, which offers reviews from a variety of sources on a variety of genres. This service can be accessed on the site or via subscription, URL: http://www.powells.com/review (Accessed December 8, 2003). Other online resources include:

- Book TV (URL: http://www.booktv.org/ [Accessed March 11, 2004]). This is the companion Web site to the television show "Book TV," which airs programs about nonfiction books on C-Span2 from 8 A.M. on Saturday mornings through Monday morning at 8 A.M. The Web site includes additional information such as best-seller lists, author chats, information on upcoming programming, and background information on authors and publishers.

- Nonfiction Reviews.com (URL: http://www.nonfictionreviews.com/cgi-bin/ae.pl [Accessed December 8, 2003]). Reviews divided by genres such as Medicine & Psychology, Biography, Religion, Paranormal & Fringe Science, Entertainment & Sports, Politics, and True Crime.

- *January Magazine* (URL: http://www.januarymagazine.com/nonfiction/nonfiction.html [Accessed December 8, 2003]). Reviews of popular nonfiction.

- *USA Today* (URL: http://www.usatoday.com/life/books/front.htm [Accessed December 8, 2003]). *USA Today* posts a list of the top 150 best-selling books. What makes this list unique is that there is only one list and it is based on actual sales, so the books reflect fiction, nonfiction, hardcovers, paperbacks, and adult's and children's titles.

- Booklist Center (URL: http://home.comcast.net/~dwtaylor1/ [Accessed December 8, 2003]). The Booklist Center bills itself as "The Web's Largest Collection of Book Lists" and includes lists of Book Awards and recommended books. There is a "general nonfiction" section at URL: http://home.comcast.net/~dwtaylor1/categorylist. html#NONFICTION%20(GENERAL) [Accessed December 8, 2003], but you can also peruse individual categories such as Politics & Government, Science and Technology, Humor, and History. The titles on these lists may be more esoteric than mainstream, so bear that in mind.

- Reading Group Choices (URL: http://www.readinggroupchoices. com [Accessed December 8, 2003]). Offers a mixture of fiction and nonfiction and includes reviews, comments, reading group guides, and discussion questions.

There are lots more out there, and new sites pop up every day, so daily surfing on the Web is always a good idea.

Another good idea is dearreader.com (URL:http://www.dearreader. com [Accessed December 8, 2003]). Suzanne Beecher started this site with the idea of getting people, especially busy people, to read by enticing them with a five-minute read every day—every week a different book. The original book club started and soon grew into a slew of book clubs, each with its own niche. It's a wonderful way to learn about books that you may not have the time or inclination to read. There is no cost to subscribe, and as Ms. Beecher points out, if you don't like the book that week, just use that delete button. There are so many choices available for people to spend their time on that reading often falls to the bottom of the pile, even for librarians.

The book club sends out approximately the first twenty-three pages of a book in five-minute-a-day segments, which will either hook you or not. There are several fiction clubs, but of most interest to the nonfiction readers' advisor are the Nonfiction Book Club and the Business Book Club. There is a team of readers searching out the most diverse nonfiction books with the best mass general appeal, while keeping away from controversy. The Business Book Club offers a plethora of popular business books, and by reading a snippet, you can easily get a feel for the book, which makes it that much easier to recommend it. This is a great way to keep up with what's new in popular nonfiction.

One cannot be a good readers' advisor without keeping abreast of the publishing industry. It is important to be familiar with the major print review sources like *Library Journal, Booklist, Kirkus, Publisher's Weekly,* and so on, but it is also important to be familiar with the more popular sources for book reviews—the ones your patrons use. Print sources include the *New York Times Book Review, USA Today, People* magazine, and your local newspaper. Television has become a major factor in determining which books become best-sellers, and one cannot overstate the influence of Oprah Winfrey, and to a slightly lesser extent, NBC's *Today Show.* Myriad book clubs abound, from *Good Morning America* to the *Washington Post* to Costco to local groups to perhaps groups in your own library. If you know what they're reading, it will be that much easier when a patron asks for "that book that was on TV, it has a really long name and there's a dog on the cover?" You will know that she or he means *The Curious Incident of the Dog in the Night-Time* by Mark Haddon, the August 2003 book club pick for the *Today Show* book club.

Fortunately, e-mail has made it much easier to keep up with all these periodicals. Here is a sampling of free e-mail subscriptions that are extremely useful:

- *USA Today* will send their books newsletter via e-mail every Thursday, which includes the "latest book gossip, best-sellers list, book excerpts and exclusive Open Book series excerpts." Sign up at URL: http://asp.usatoday.com/registration/newslettercenterlite/ newslettercenterlite. aspx?LOC=HPS002 (Accessed December 8, 2003).

- The *New York Times* will send their Books Update newsletter via e-mail every Friday (with a free membership) and includes book reviews, news, and features, plus links to exclusive author interviews, first chapters, and expanded best-seller lists. Sign up at URL: http://www.nytimes.com/mem/email.html (Accessed December 8, 2003).

- *Publisher's Weekly* offers a free daily (Monday through Friday) newsletter for paid print subscribers that is geared toward booksellers but is extremely useful for librarians as well. Their Web site offers this description: "Launched in May, 1997, *Publishers Weekly*'s e-mail Daily for Booksellers gives booksellers useful information to help them sell more books, including books and authors that are receiving media and review attention, news stories about independent and chain booksellers, bestseller lists from around the country, and changes in publisher policies that will impact booksellers. Most of the information is exclusive to the Daily and does not appear in the print *Publishers Weekly*." Sign up at URL: http://www. publishersweekly.com/index.asp?layout=eletters&industry=PW+ Daily (Accessed December 8, 2003).

Appearing Confident

Now that you are armed with the skills and tools you need to be of the utmost help to your patrons, it's time to point out one more important aspect of readers' advisory.

One of the best kept secrets of being a good readers' advisor is to appear confident.

Recently we had a patron come in who hadn't read anything for quite a while. He had some time on his hands and decided it was a good time to get back into reading. He wanted a "good book" but was unable to offer any insight as to what that meant other than the fact that he didn't want any fiction. He hadn't read anything in such a long time that he couldn't even answer that first question about the last good book he had read. The librarian assisting him tried offering titles in several areas, trying to find out where his interests were, but after about fifteen minutes of this, none of the titles she suggested pleased him, and they were both growing frustrated. Finally, she offered to get the readers' advisor librarian and came to me for some assistance.

Once she explained the problem she was having, I realized that he was going to have to be handled a little differently than most patrons. I approached him, introduced myself, and listened as he explained his situation. At that point, I took him to the new book area, selected a book—in this case, we happened to have a copy of *Positively Fifth Street: Murderers, Cheetahs, and Binion's World Series of Poker* by James McManus—and literally put it in his hands. I assured him that it was very popular with men and that it was a real page-turner (a phrase that entices many readers). I was so sure of myself, so positive that he would like it, that he didn't question me, and he left the library, book in hand, moments later.

Did I have some secret sixth sense that allowed me to ferret out what he really wanted? No, I left my crystal ball at home that night. Did the other librarian do anything wrong? Of course not, she bent over backward to help him. Sometimes just getting someone else—another body—to help is enough to make the difference; a different perspective, perhaps even the extra attention, may make it that much easier for the patron to make a decision. Patrons come to the library for a variety of reasons and getting lots of attention to find a book may be their priority. (Remember the attention-seekers?) But that wasn't the case here. In this case, it was simply my confidence that allowed the patron to feel that he was in good hands and that I wouldn't steer him wrong.

Self-assurance is a real plus in helping patrons find reading materials. If you're sure that the patron will like the book, she or he will generally be more willing to try it with an open mind. Conversely, if you appear to be indifferent or unsure about what you are recommending, the patron will also be unsure about accepting your suggestion. It almost sounds manipulative, but the goal is not just an attempt to grab the nearest book and convince the patron to read it. The goal is to ascertain her or his interests, find suitable reading materials, and hope that the patron likes it.

Readers' advisory in the real world, the library, encompasses three important factors: good communication skills, confidence in your ability to help the patron, and knowledge of the materials available. The most qualified readers' advisory librarians will excel at all three. But the reality is that a library that has one or two librarians who are so accomplished is indeed fortunate. Even then, the library is probably not fortunate enough to have the experts available every hour the library is open, which means that other librarians—who may very well be lacking in one or more of these three skills (and lack of knowledge of the material is the biggest hurdle)—are still going to be helping patrons. Having breadth and depth of knowledge of the materials is a wonderful, but not necessary, qualification for doing readers' advisory. If it was a requirement, however, a huge population of librarians would be unable to perform the readers' advisory function, and that simply isn't the case. All that means is that if you are not familiar with the latest in nonfiction, it is imperative that you be familiar with the resources available to you.

The most rewarding aspect of readers' advisory comes after the fact, when a patron returns with a glowing review and sincere thanks. Unfortunately, part of the process may also include a patron returning with a negative review on occasion. In fact, most of the time, you'll get no feedback whatsoever, so you'll have no idea whether the patron liked your suggestion. One hundred percent effectiveness, one hundred percent of the time isn't a reality; it's an unattainable goal. It's important to listen effectively, to be considerate, and try to fill your patron's needs, and in doing that, you will have achieved a realistic goal of being the best readers' advisor you can be.

References

Harmon, Amy. 2004. Amazon glitch unmasks war of reviewers. *New York Times* (February 14, 2004): section A, page 1.

Chapter 12

The Story's the Thing: Narrative Nonfiction for Recreational Reading

Vicki Novak

When public librarians think of nonfiction, they generally think of helping people locate books for informational purposes—for school projects, self-improvement, self-education, how-to, and the like. However, there is a whole crowd of patrons, whom we may not even notice, who are reading nonfiction for pleasure or recreation. For these patrons, the subject matter is not necessarily the most important determining factor in what they choose to read. For them, the most important factor is whether it's a good read, whether it tells a story that is absorbing, fascinating, and intellectually stimulating. Bill Ott writes that there are information people and there are story people (Ott 1997), and although he was referring to fiction readers, we can say the same thing about our nonfiction readers. Story people are looking for a compelling read, a book that will keep them up reading half the night, a book that makes them look at the world in a different way, a book that will teach them something they didn't realize they needed to know. They are looking for a vicarious experience that is just as enjoyable as reading a great novel.

Defining the Genre

There are many reasons for reading or consulting nonfiction books, but some recreational readers are specifically interested in nonfiction that tells a story. This type of writing has been called many names. In the late 1950s and early 1960s, some journalists began to write in a style that combined rigorous fact-based traditional journalism with the literary style of fiction. Truman Capote defined New Journalism as " 'a narrative form that employed all the techniques of fictional art but was nevertheless immaculately factual' " (Taylor 2002, 30). More recently, the Creative Nonfiction movement championed by Lee Gutkind has led to creative nonfiction programs at universities and a journal called *Creative Nonfiction,* founded by Gutkind. According to Gutkind, creative nonfiction techniques borrowed from fiction include "writing in scenes, using description, dialogue, specificity of detail, characterisation and point of view" (Brien 2000). This type of writing may also be called literary journalism, literary nonfiction, nonfiction stories, nonfiction novels, narrative nonfiction, nonfiction that reads like fiction, novelistic nonfiction, or narrative journalism, but what all have in common is that the writings "attempt to make drama out of the observable world of real people, real places, and real events" (Nieman Foundation 2000, 18).

Library patrons who like nonfiction stories may or may not be looking for books with a journalistic or a literary style of writing. Because some of the terms used for this literature focus specifically on these styles, for our purposes, let us use the broader term "narrative nonfiction." Narrative nonfiction tells a true story but the pacing, character development, and writing style may please even someone who normally reads only fiction. It can include such diverse genres as memoirs, stories of inventions, humor, medical suspense, true crime, survival stories, and others. Narrative nonfiction can be one linear story or shorter episodic stories, but it excludes nonfiction in which the story is less prominent than the informational content. Narrative nonfiction can be journalistic or literary, or it may instead have a light or comical tone, such as Bill Bryson's travelogues.

Where is the dividing line between narrative nonfiction and fictionalized biographies, novelizations of true stories, works that mix fiction with nonfiction, and even historical fiction? It is fairly common for memoirists to reconstruct dialogue, because they do not remember it verbatim. It is less accepted for authors to reconstruct scenes or use composite (combined) characters. However, creative nonfiction or literary journalism authors are generally strict about sticking to the facts and not making up events. Lee Gutkind writes, "Fiction, from a literal standpoint, is not true—or at least not totally true (not so as the writer is willing to admit), whereas creative nonfiction, if not completely true, is as true as the writer can make it. I am not unaware of the foggy gray line being drawn here, but one can't be easily literal about art and literature. The creative nonfiction writer tries to be as truthful and factual as possible. Making things up to enhance the narrative is unacceptable" (Brien 2000). Some authors do use some fictionalization and provide a statement to that effect in their books. Generally, if readers know that some parts of a book are fictionalized, they are then able to just enjoy it as literature. Authors who do not inform readers of fictionalization open themselves up to charges of unethical behavior.[1] To someone who is just looking for a good story, novelizations and mixtures between fiction and nonfiction may still be good choices, and we shouldn't hesitate to recommend good nonfiction stories that admit to some fictionalization.

Top Ten Reasons to Read Narrative Nonfiction

1. To indulge your curiosity.

2. Because real-life stories can be as exciting as fiction.

3. Because it "bridges those connections between events that have taken place and imbues them with meaning and emotion" (Nieman Foundation 2000, 18).

4. Because you have a personal or emotional connection with the subject matter.

5. To be inspired, touched, moved, or entertained (Goudsblom 2000).

6. Because it makes history come to life.

7. To learn something new, be challenged intellectually, or be exposed to new ideas.

8. Because it transports you to another time or place.

9. Because the quality of the writing often rivals the best fiction.

10. Vicarious experiences—you don't have to climb Mount Everest yourself![2]

Neglected Readers?

Readers' advisory service helps patrons find books that they will enjoy based on what they have read in the past. Why is nonfiction usually neglected in this process? Part of the reason that we are not serving our recreational nonfiction readers well is that our libraries are not structured to provide this service. Libraries that offer a separate readers' advisory desk often place it in the fiction room or even call it the "Fiction Desk." Patrons may be referred to the reference desk instead, but this can be confusing for both parties. The patron thinks of the reference desk as a place to ask informational questions, and the librarians working there may just think the patron is being too vague in the reference interview. They are expecting the patron to request a specific piece of information.

Another reason for our lack of service is that the readers' advisory tools available just do not cover nonfiction with any depth. From books to online databases to Web sites, readers' advisory tools overwhelmingly focus on genre fiction. The few nonfiction tools refer almost exclusively to the subject matter of the book, rather than also covering its appeal factors. Even our catalogs are not much help for readers, because the Library of Congress Subject Headings do not work well to find books of a similar nonfiction genre.

Subject versus Appeal Factors

One misconception about recreational nonfiction readers is that the subject of the book is the most important factor to them. In a discussion about nonfiction readers' advisory on the Fiction_L readers' advisory e-mail list, one librarian wrote, "In our library what we call readers' advisory is focused on fiction. I realize that some readers want non-fiction, but truthfully, we usually treat that as a reference question, by and large, not readers' advisory" (Fiction_L 2002). Another writes, "Most people, in my experience, looking for a non-fiction recommendation will have a subject area that they are searching for, which makes it a little easier" (Fiction_L 2002). Although it is appropriate to treat informational nonfiction requests as reference questions, nonfiction pleasure readers may be looking for something besides just the subject of the book. The subject may be important to some readers, but others are just looking for a good story. Did readers choose *Seabiscuit* (Hillenbrand 2001) because they were specifically interested in horse racing? Here are excerpts of selected reader comments from Amazon.com:

Let me say a few things up front: I have never set foot on a racetrack, I have watched the Kentucky Derby maybe twice on TV and I have little interest in jockeys, horse trainers or horses in general. For those who think this is a book about a racehorse, think again. It is a wonderful, descriptive work about the underdog, about triumph over adversity, about personality in animals and, most importantly, about a rarely discussed slice of America. (raygeo3 2001)

> I have no interest in horses. I rarely read non-fiction that is not work re-lated. This book, however, is such a wonderful and well-written history that I will have to read it again. The well-worn phrase that "history comes alive" in her prose sounds trite, but it is definitely true. (rawreader 2003)
>
> I'm not a big history buff or nonfiction reader, but I have to say that this is one of the most entertaining stories I've ever come across—it really reads like a good novel. The writing is superb, the characters are rich and lively and funny, the pace is quick and the level of detail in the research is truly amazing. (Rachel 2003)

These readers say that they did not read the book for its subject matter; instead, they talk about other aspects of the book that appeal to them. They like that it is descriptive, it is a story about an underdog, it is about a triumph over adversity, it is well written, it made history come alive, it read like a good novel, the characters are rich and lively and funny, the pace is quick, and it includes detailed research. These comments give us some idea of the book's appeal to readers who aren't interested in horse racing. As with fiction, "most readers are usually not looking for a book on a certain subject. They want a book with a particular 'feel' " (Saricks 1997, 35).

We should be careful to treat our nonfiction readers' advisory questions like our fiction ones, paying attention to the appeal factors along with the subject. Books that seem very different in subject matter can still be similar in their appeal. As an example, here are two books that seem to be very different. Let's compare the subject headings and appeal factors:

Fifty Acres and a Poodle: A Story of Love, Livestock, and Finding Myself on a Farm
By Jeanne Marie Laskas

A well-written account of a city-dweller journalist's fulfill-ment of her dream to live in the country. Told with humor and emotional resonance.

LC Subject Headings

Laskas, Jeanne Marie, 1958–

Journalists—United States—Biography.

Where Is the Mango Princess?
By Cathy Crimmins

The heart-wrenching, yet also humorous story of Crimmins's husband's recovery from a serious brain injury. Tells of struggles with an HMO and the changes in his personality and their relationship.

LC Subject Headings

Forman, Alan—Health.

Forman, Alan—Marriage.

Crimmins, C. E.—Marriage.

Brain damage—Patients—United States—Biography.

Personality change—Case studies.

From the descriptions and the subject headings, it seems that the only similarity is that they are both biographical. The subject headings aren't particularly revealing about who would like these books. Yet when we examine other common factors, we can see why the same person might enjoy both. They are both memoirs, written by female authors, with a story line that involves recovery from illness or injury. Both are episodic stories, and they are written in a contemporary literary style that also uses humor. We could recommend one to someone who liked the appeal factors of the other.

In her books *Now Read This: A Guide to Mainstream Fiction, 1978–1998* and *Now Read This II, 1990–2001,* Nancy Pearl uses setting, story, characters, and language as appeal characteristics to categorize fiction. In *Readers' Advisory Service in the Public Library,* Joyce G. Saricks and Nancy Brown define appeal characteristics as pacing, characterization, story line, and frame (which consists of setting, atmosphere, background, and tone). We can apply similar appeal factors to narrative nonfiction, using writing, setting, people, and story to categorize some of the ways that books appeal to readers. Here are some of the components that make up each appeal category.

Writing

- Pace (fast or slow; action driven or description driven)

- Use of language (poetic or straightforward)

- Tone (suspenseful, thrilling, humorous, inspirational, entertaining, motivating, encouraging, engrossing, informative, persuasive)

- Style (journalistic, literary, academic, casual, emotional)

- Point of view

- Amount of dialogue

- Award winners

Setting (Transports the Reader)

- Location

- Time period

- Atmosphere

People

- Level of "character" development
- Psychological insight into human condition
- Type of people (profession, gender, personality, heroes; celebrity or average person)
- Learning from other's experiences

Story

- Subject
- Possible plots: mystery/puzzle to solve, good versus evil
- Affects reader emotionally
- Intellectual challenge/new ideas
- Theme or message
- Fascinating, appeals to curiosity
- Vicarious experience
- One continuous story or episodic anecdotes

Narrative Nonfiction Genres

Narrative nonfiction can be further divided into genres. As with fiction, there can be overlap between genres and dispute about whether a particular one is a genre or subgenre. Here are some examples for each genre.

Biography, Autobiography, Memoirs, and Diaries

- *Angela's Ashes: A Memoir* by Frank McCourt
- *The Cat Who Went to Paris* by Peter Gethers
- *Fifty Acres and a Poodle: A Story of Love, Livestock and Finding Myself on a Farm* by Jeanne Marie Laskas
- *Having Our Say: The Delany Sisters' First 100 Years* by Sarah and A. Elizabeth Delany
- *A Heartbreaking Work of Staggering Genius* by Dave Eggers
- *The Liar's Club: A Memoir* by Mary Karr

- *Nine Lives: From Stripper to Schoolteacher; My Year-Long Odyssey in the Workplace* by Lynn Snowden

- *Roommates: My Grandfather's Story* by Max Apple

True Crime

- *Catch Me If You Can: The Amazing True Story of the Most Extraordinary Liar in the History of Fun and Profit* by Frank Abagnale

- *The Cuckoo's Egg: Tracking a Spy through the Maze of Computer Espionage* by Clifford Stoll

- *The Devil in the White City: Murder, Magic, and Madness at the Fair That Changed America* by Erik Larson

- *In Cold Blood: A True Account of a Multiple Murder and Its Consequences* by Truman Capote

- *The Stranger beside Me* by Ann Rule

- *Treasure Hunt: A New York Times Reporter Tracks the Quedlinburg Hoard* by William H. Honan

Travelogues or Books with a Strong Sense of Place

- *Going Back to Bisbee* by Richard Shelton

- *Midnight in the Garden of Good and Evil: A Savannah Story* by John Berendt

- *The Secret Knowledge of Water: Discovering the Essence of the American Desert* by Craig Childs

- *A Walk in the Woods: Rediscovering America on the Appalachian Trail* by Bill Bryson

- *A Year in Provence* by Peter Mayle

Medicine

- *The Blood of Strangers: Stories from Emergency Medicine* by Frank Huyler

- *The Hot Zone* by Richard Preston

- *Learning How the Heart Beats: The Making of a Pediatrician* by Claire McCarthy

- *The Man Who Mistook His Wife for a Hat and Other Clinical Tales* by Oliver Sacks

Journalistic Reportage or Exposés of Social Issues

- *A Civil Action* by Jonathan Harr
- *Fast Food Nation: The Dark Side of the All-American Meal* by Eric Schlosser
- *Newjack: Guarding Sing Sing* by Ted Conover
- *Our Guys: The Glen Ridge Rape and the Secret Life of the Perfect Suburb* by Bernard Lefkowitz

Essays or Short True Stories

- *Chicken Soup for the Soul* books
- *High Tide in Tucson: Essays from Now or Never* by Barbara Kingsolver
- *I Thought My Father Was God: And Other True Tales from NPR's National Story Project* edited by Paul Auster

Humor

- *Mama Makes Up Her Mind and Other Dangers of Southern Living* by Bailey White
- *Mirth of a Nation: The Best Contemporary Humor* edited by Michael J. Rosen

Overcoming Adversity

- *Nobody Nowhere: The Extraordinary Autobiography of an Autistic* by Donna Williams
- *Tuesdays with Morrie: An Old Man, a Young Man, and Life's Greatest Lesson* by Mitch Albom
- *Under the Eye of the Clock: A Memoir* by Christopher Nolan
- *An Unquiet Mind* by Kay Redfield Jamison
- *Where Is the Mango Princess?* by Cathy Crimmins

Adventure, Disaster, or Survival

- *Alive: The Story of the Andes Survivors* by Piers Paul Read
- *Endurance: Shackleton's Incredible Voyage* by Alfred Lansing
- *Into the Wild* by Jon Krakauer
- *Into Thin Air* by Jon Krakauer
- *The Perfect Storm: A True Story of Men against the Sea* by Sebastian Junger

History

- *The Professor and the Madman: A Tale of Murder, Insanity, and the Making of the Oxford English Dictionary* by Simon Winchester
- *Seabiscuit: An American Legend* by Laura Hillenbrand

Microhistories

- *Crying: The Natural and Cultural History of Tears* by Tom Lutz
- *Salt: A World History* by Mark Kurlansky
- *Zero: The Biography of a Dangerous Idea* by Charles Seife
- *Zipper: An Exploration in Novelty* by Robert Friedel

Science, Technology, and Inventions

- *Fermat's Enigma: The Quest to Solve the World's Greatest Mathematical Problem* by Simon Singh
- *Longitude: The True Story of a Lone Genius Who Solved the Greatest Scientific Problem of His Time* by Dava Sobel
- *The Soul of a New Machine* by Tracy Kidder
- *Where Wizards Stay Up Late: The Origins of the Internet* by Katie Hafner and Matthew Lyon

Providing Nonfiction Readers' Advisory Service

In many ways, nonfiction readers' advisory is similar to fiction readers' advisory. We need to create an environment that is conducive to discussions about books. However, libraries with a separate fiction desk need to make a special effort to see that nonfiction readers' advisory does not fall through the cracks. If the nonfiction collection is located close enough to the desk, it may be better for signs to say "Readers' Assistance," "Readers' Advisory," or "Reader Services" rather than "Fiction." Libraries with a single customer service desk or ones with a reference desk closest to the nonfiction section need to market the nonfiction readers' advisory services that they can provide. This includes providing passive readers' advisory services such as nonfiction booklists (paper bookmarks and online lists) and book displays. This sends the message that this library has noticed its nonfiction recreational readers and wants to serve them. Each booklist or display could include the line, "Do you like to read nonfiction stories? Ask at the ____ desk for other reading suggestions."

Some fiction readers may also be open to a nonfiction book that has similar appeal factors to novels they have liked. Historical fiction readers may like to try biography or history. Mystery readers might like true crime, and fans of medical thrillers might like to read about a true-life medical crisis. Although not all fiction readers are interested in nonfiction, by including an occasional nonfiction suggestion, we can show that nonfiction is not just for informational needs.

To prepare for doing nonfiction readers' advisory, pay attention to book reviews and the current nonfiction bestsellers. Pay particular attention to the nonfiction trade paperback best-seller lists, because many in this format are narrative nonfiction titles for recreational reading. When you examine a book, take a look at which authors have praised the book on the back cover. Recognized authors typically praise books that their own readers would also like (if someone were to compile a database of these author recommendations, we would have another tool to help us make connections between authors). Join or start a readers' advisory group that reads books in various genres. Be sure that nonfiction genres are included on a regular basis. When you receive a nonfiction readers' advisory question, don't panic! Remember to conduct a readers' advisory interview to find out if the patron is more interested in specific nonfiction subjects or if the genre or appeal factors are more important. Not every nonfiction question is a request for information. Finally, remember to consult nonfiction readers' advisory tools and colleagues who like to read nonfiction.

Selected Nonfiction Readers' Advisory Tools[3]

Although there are few print tools available to assist readers' advisors with nonfiction, there are helpful Web sites and online databases. A complete readers' advisory tool would offer these features: lists of author and title readalikes;[4] reviews of first-rate current titles for browsing, subject searching, and appeal factor searching; and lists of award winners. No current source offers all of these features in one place for nonfiction, but there are some that cover one or more features especially well:

AllReaders.com (URL: http://www.allreaders.com [Accessed December 8, 2003])

Along with fiction, covers "Biography" and "History." Features allow searching by subgenre or by some of the appeal factors (use the "Detailed Booksearch"). Provides computer-generated possible readalikes for each book.

BiblioTravel—for books that take you away (URL: http://www. bibliotravel.com [Accessed December 8, 2003])

Lists books set in certain locales, both fiction and nonfiction. Select "Advanced Search" to specify "History," "Memoir or Biography," "Travelogue," or other nonfiction genre.

BookBrowse.com (URL: http://www.bookbrowse.com [Accessed December 8, 2003])

Selects the best current fiction and nonfiction. For each title, provides the book jacket, excerpts from professional reviews, reader reviews, and an excerpt of the book. The genre section contains Biographies & Memoirs, *Chicken Soup* books, History, Travel, Adventure, and other nonfiction genres.

Booklist Center (URL: http://home.comcast.net/~dwtaylor1 [Accessed December 8, 2003])

Includes award winners in various fiction and nonfiction genres and lists compiled by subject experts. See Biography, Crime, History, Humor, Nonfiction (General), and other nonfiction genre categories.

Books 'n' Bytes (URL: http://www.booksnbytes.com/reviews_list.html [Accessed December 8, 2003])

Reader-submitted reviews. Nonfiction categories include True Crime and general Non-Fiction.

Christchurch City Libraries: If You Like … (URL: http://library. christchurch.org.nz/Guides/IfYouLike [Accessed December 8, 2003])

The Biography and Non-Fiction section includes several extensive lists of readalikes for authors, titles, and subjects.

Dear Reader (formerly Chapter A Day) (URL: http://www.dearreader. com [Accessed December 8, 2003])

The Nonfiction Book Club offers a five-minute portion of a book each day in via e-mail. A quick way to sample a new book each week to recommend to patrons.

Fiction_L e-mail list (URL: http://www.webrary.org/rs/flmenu.html [Accessed December 8, 2003])

Includes a booklist page (URL: http://www.webrary.org/rs/flbklistmenu.html [Accessed December 8, 2003]) and an archive page (URL: http://www.webrary.org/rs/FLarchive.html [Accessed December 8, 2003]).

This excellent readers' advisory resource also discusses nonfiction topics. Search the archives or the booklist pages for topics such as "Nonfiction That Reads Like Fiction," "Travelogues," "Recommended Biographies and Autobiographies," "Nonfiction Books for Discussion," "Favorite Biographies," "Sad but True," "Nonfiction Titles Dealing with Life Crises," "Good Memoirs for Discussion," "Biographies of Disabled People," "Nonfiction 'Real-Life Struggle' Books," and "Micro Histories."

The Lukas Prize Project Winners (URL: http://www.jrn.columbia.edu/events/lukas/winners/ [Accessed December 8, 2003])

Established in 1998 to honor the best in American nonfiction writing. Awarded by the Columbia University Graduate School of Journalism and the Nieman Foundation at Harvard University—winners tend to fall into the category of literary journalism.

National Public Radio Books Page (URL: http://www.npr.org/books/ [Accessed December 8, 2003])

Lists books mentioned on NPR by date. Features many thoughtful, current nonfiction titles.

NonfictionReviews.com (URL: http://www.nonfictionreviews.com [Accessed December 8, 2003])

Comprehensive, well-written reviews divided into several genres of nonfiction. Warning: unusually annoying flashing ads.

RatingZone (URL: http://www.ratingzone.com [Accessed December 8, 2003])

Rate books and receive a computer-generated list of recommendations. Works best to sign up for a free account and rate many items. Recommendations can be viewed by category, including Nonfiction, Biography, History, Law/Crime, and others.

Reader's Club: Non-Fiction Book Reviews (URL: http://www.readersclub.org/category.asp?cat=2 [Accessed December 8, 2003])

Reviews written by library staff divided into an exceptionally complete list of nonfiction genres, including Biography/Memoir, History, Humor, Science/Technology, Travel, True Adventure, True Crime, and others.

Reading Group Guides Nonfiction page (URL: http://http://www. readinggroupguides.com/findaguide [Accessed December 8, 2003])

    Select Nonfiction & Current Events, History & Politics, or Biography & Memoir to see nonfiction recommended for book discussion groups.

Sachem Public Library Reader's Advisor (URL: http://sachem.suffolk. lib.ny.us/advisor [Accessed December 8, 2003])

    See the right column for many wonderful nonfiction book lists from "The History of Stuff" to "True-Life Survival."

Skokie Public Library's Book Annotations (URL: http:// www.skokie. lib.il.us/Annotations/ListGenre.asp [Accessed December 8, 2003])

    Fiction and nonfiction reviews along with some readalike recommendations suggested by librarian reviewers. Doesn't include as many nonfiction books as some other sites, but the choices are good ones and the readalikes are more on target than computer-generated ones. Selecting the reviewer's name allows you to see other books reviewed by the same person.

What Do I Read Next?

    For more information, see *What do I read next?* URL: http:// www.gale.com/pdf/facts/wdirn.pdf (Accessed December 8, 2003). Subscription readers' advisory database that includes fiction and nonfiction and provides readalikes by searching similar subject headings. The Custom Search provides many subjects and can be limited to nonfiction books. Also includes lists of award winners.

Conclusion

    In a way, readers' advisory has come full circle. Kenneth Shearer writes, "The readers' advisory transaction, which in the early twentieth century was more involved in the provision of a course of studies related to a nonfiction subject, has changed to the present emphasis on a good book to read for personal satisfaction" (Shearer 1998, 115). Now, interest in memoirs and other types of creative nonfiction is higher than ever before, and libraries need to respond by including nonfiction in our readers' advisory service. We are no longer telling patrons what they should read for their betterment, but we have nevertheless returned to our roots by helping patrons find enjoyable nonfiction. Now, more than ever, there is a need for comprehensive nonfiction readers' advisory tools comparable to the excellent fiction tools we have. There is also a need to change the perception that a nonfiction request is always a request for pure information. By embracing nonfiction readers' advisory, we expand our services to our patrons and make the library an indispensable resource for entertainment and enrichment as well as information.

Notes

1. For an interesting discussion of alleged inaccuracies in popular narrative nonfiction, see the article by Doreen Carvajal, "Now! Read the true (more or less) story!" *New York Times* (February 24,1998): E1.

2. Instead, read Jon Krakauer, *Into Thin Air: A Personal Account of the Mount Everest Disaster* (New York: Villard, 1997).

3. Some of these and other sources are mentioned by Mary K. Chelton in her list *Readers Advisory Tools for Adults: A Five-Year Retrospective Selected Bibliography, with a Few Earlier Exceptions*, August 2003 (sent as an attachment to an e-mail with the subject "FW: resources list of websites (and print)" to the RA_Talk e-mail list by Maureen O'Connor on August 25, 2003) and by Maureen O'Connor in her message "Non-fiction readers' advisory" to the *RA_Talk* e-mail list on February 5, 2003.

4. "Readalike" may be a bit of a misnomer, because no book is an exact match for another one. However, the term is in common use in librarians' casual discussions about readers' advisory. These may also be called "similar reads" or "if you like ..." lists.

References

Brien, Donna Lee. 2000. Creative nonfiction: A virtual conversation with Lee Gutkind. *TEXT: The Journal of the Australian Association of Writing Programs* 4 (April). Available online at http://www.gu.edu. au/school/art/text/april00/content.htm (Accessed September 21, 2003).

Crimmins, Cathy. 2000. *Where is the mango princess?* New York: Knopf.

Fiction_L. 2002. Nonfiction RA (electronic mailing list discussion). (May 8 through July 29). *Fiction_L Archives*. URL: http://www.webrary. org/maillist/msg/2002/5/Re.NonfictionRA.html (Accessed September 30, 2003).

Goudsblom, Johan. 2000. Non-fiction as a literary genre. *Publishing Research Quarterly* 16: 5–12.

Hillenbrand, Laura. 2001. *Seabiscuit: An American legend.* New York: Random House.

Laskas, Jeanne Marie. 2000. *Fifty acres and a poodle: A story of love, livestock, and finding myself on a farm.* New York: Bantam Books.

Nieman Foundation. 2000. The state of narrative nonfiction writing. *Nieman Reports* 54: 18.

Ott, Bill. 1997. Story people. *Booklist* 94: 4.

Pearl, Nancy. 1999. *Now read this: A guide to mainstream fiction, 1978–1998.* Englewood, CO: Libraries Unlimited.

Pearl, Nancy. 2002. *Now read this II: A guide to mainstream fiction, 1990–2001.* Englewood, CO: Libraries Unlimited.

Rachel. 2003. Review of *Seabiscuit: An American legend*, by Laura Hillenbrand. *Amazon.com* (August 21). URL:http://www.amazon.com (Accessed September 26, 2003).

Rawreader. 2003. Review of *Seabiscuit: An American legend*, by Laura Hillenbrand. *Amazon.com* (September 10). URL: http://www.amazon.com (Accessed September 26, 2003).

Raygeo3. 2001. Review of *Seabiscuit: An American legend*, by Laura Hillenbrand. *Amazon.com* (March 6). URL: http://www.amazon.com (Accessed September 26, 2003).

Saricks, Joyce G., and Nancy Brown. 1997. *Readers' advisory service in the public library*, 2d ed. Chicago: American Library Association.

Shearer, Kenneth. 1998. Readers' advisory services: New attention to a core business of the public library. *North Carolina Libraries* 56: 114–16.

Taylor, Pegi. 2002. Creative nonfiction: Literary journalists use fictional techniques to tell a good story while sticking to the facts. *The Writer* 115: 29–34.

Conclusion

Beyond Fiction and Nonfiction

Robert Burgin

There are two problems with dichotomies such as those we deal with every day: true and false; right and wrong; madness and reason; fiction and nonfiction.

First, such dichotomies are not always as neat and clean as we assume. Even a dichotomy as basic as true-false is called into question by a masterful work of art, like Kurosawa's *Rashomon*. Novels like Twain's *Huckleberry Finn,* short stories like Melville's "Billy Budd," and works of nonfiction like Joseph Fletcher's *Situational Ethics* (not to mention Nietzsche's *Beyond Good and Evil*) cast doubt on the simple dichotomy between right and wrong. Philosophers like Foucault and psychologists like Laing point out that the dichotomy between madness and reason breaks down when we consider individuals like Van Gogh, Nietzsche, and Artaud.

Secondly, dichotomies are too often turned into hierarchies where one half of the dichotomy is given preference over the other. Not only is X different from Y, but X is better than Y in some sense. Good is better than evil. Light is better than dark. Reason is better than madness. Information needs are better, more legitimate than recreational needs.

In many ways, a central argument of the chapters in this book is that the familiar dichotomy between fiction and nonfiction has similar problems. Like the dichotomies discussed earlier, the one between fiction and nonfiction is anything but neat and clean. As Ken Shearer points out in his chapter in this book, some fiction is as "real" as nonfiction—Irving Stone's *The Origin: A Biographical Novel of Charles Darwin,* for example—and some nonfiction has elements of fiction—Truman Capote's *In Cold Blood,* for example. Some works seem to waver between the two poles. Catherine Ross reminds us in her chapter that Thomas Keneally's *Schindler's Ark* was published as fiction in Great Britain (where it won the Booker Prize for fiction) but was published as the nonfiction *Schindler's List* in North America. Carlos Castaneda's *The Teachings of Don Juan: A Yaqui Way of Knowledge* and Bruce Chatwin's *In Patagonia* are both acknowledged to be largely or totally fictional, but both are classified by libraries as nonfiction. Interestingly, in their chapters, both Kathleen de la Peña McCook and Ken Shearer use the richer metaphor of maps to discuss the intricate nature of fiction and nonfiction. The complexities of fiction and nonfiction clearly cannot be captured in a simple dichotomy.

Furthermore, like the dichotomies discussed earlier, the one between fiction and nonfiction evolved into a hierarchy in which nonfiction was somehow better than fiction. As Bill Crowley notes in his chapter, there was a strong bias against fiction among the intellectual elite in nineteenth-century America when the public library was coming of age; there was, for early library leaders, a "fiction problem." Fiction, as Duncan Smith puts it in his chapter in this book, was "cast out" of the Dewey Decimal system. For years, fiction titles were not given subject headings in library catalogs. Fiction and advisory services for fiction readers were ignored in schools of library and information science. (Shearer and Burgin 2001) Research on reading and readers was almost completely neglected in schools of library and information science (Wiegand 1997a, 1997b, 2000, 2001).

The fiction-nonfiction dichotomy is even more problematic because it gets tangled up with another dichotomy, the one between recreational and informational needs. Fiction is equated with recreational needs, which are somehow less important than the informational needs that are associated with nonfiction. Again, as Ross reports in her chapter (which examines interviews with almost two hundred adult readers), these distinctions are not clear-cut. Some fiction is informational, and some nonfiction is clearly recreational. As Carr states in his chapter, we read nonfiction for a number of reasons, for example, "to have mysteries explained, experiences recollected, questions answered, histories retold, and extraordinary experiences brought into the light of text." To use Shearer's examples, Michener's novel *Caribbean* is historically accurate, and Peter Mayle's *A Year in Provence* is entertaining with novel-like characters. Again, the value judgment that has been added to the dichotomy, the assumption that one's informational needs are superior to one's recreational needs, is baseless.

Looking at the Similarities

The fiction-nonfiction dichotomy does a disservice to libraries and their users. It degrades fiction and it ignores narrative nonfiction. Instead of focusing on the differences between fiction and nonfiction materials and fiction and nonfiction readers, librarians should look at the similarities.

For example, like fiction, nonfiction has genres and subgenres. Bookstores use some of these categories instead of Dewey or LC classification numbers to arrange their collections—biographies and memoirs, business and investing, travel, and other such categories. Within those genres we can find subgenres. *Outside* magazine, for example, divides its list of the best travel and adventure books into subgenres such as "The World's Great Places," "Journeys to Hell," and "Modern Masters and Young Turks" (Harvey et al. 1996). The online bookstore Bloodpage.com divides true crime titles into "Individual Cases," "Serial Killers," "Organized Crime," "Old West," "Trials," and other categories (URL: http://www.bloodpage. com [Accessed December 20, 2003]). Amazon.com divides its "Biographies and Memoirs" genre into "Arts & Literature," "Ethnic & National," "Historical," "Leaders," and several other categories. Even the "Management and Leadership" genre is divided into twenty-three topics, including "Motivational," "Negotiating," "Organizational Change," and "Teams."

Like fiction, nonfiction has appeal factors or what David Carr calls in his chapter "deeper dimensions." Elsewhere (Burgin 2001), I have noted that the appeal factors that Saricks and Brown (1997) outline for fiction— pacing, characterization, story line, and frame—can be applied to many nonfiction titles and that several other appeal factors—for example, reading level, the presence of checklists, the presence of tests, and the presence of illustrations—may also apply to nonfiction. In her chapter, Novak cites reader review's of *Seabiscuit* to show that the readers were more interested in appeal factors—that the book is the story of an underdog or the story of a triumph over adversity, that it is well written, that it makes history come alive, that the characters are rich and lively, that the pace is quick—than in the subject of the book. Even when nonfiction is tied to informational needs, these appeal factors may make the presentation of information more persuasive or more understandable to certain readers.

Even dictionaries have appeal factors. I remember being surprised to learn in my first Reference class that some dictionaries were prescriptive and some were descriptive. (Ironically, a work of fiction would have educated me along these lines if I had only read Rex Stout's novel *Gambit,* in which detective Nero Wolfe burns the 3rd edition of *Webster's New International Dictionary* page by page for threatening the integrity of the English language.) More recently, Chen-Josephson (2003) has outlined factors by which to judge dictionaries. Should the dictionary list meanings in order of most common definition or in historical order? How often does the dictionary have the word being sought? Are there illustrations or supplementary material? (I like the images included in *American Heritage Dictionary,* but a friend of mine finds them laughable.) Interestingly, Chen-Josephson's description of the dictionaries reads almost like the review of a work of fiction. *Merriam-Webster's Collegiate Dictionary* "exerts an intoxicating old-world authority [and] its illustrations are soulful." Some of the entries in the *Random House Webster's College Dictionary* are "decidedly less stirring" than others. He finds himself "exhausted and often exasperated by [the *Microsoft Encarta College Dictionary*'s] newcomer's efforts to please."

Cookbooks, too, have appeal factors. Readers' advisory guru Joyce Saricks recently reminded me that cookbooks differ in many ways apart from subject orientation. For example, there are cookbooks with political agendas (Frances Moore Lappe's *Diet for a Small Planet*), cookbooks associated with exercise programs (Bill Phillips's *Eating for Life*), cookbooks with photographs of each dish (Jamie Oliver's *Jamie's Kitchen*), cookbooks arranged by cooking method instead of the usual arrangement by type of dish (Alton Brown's *I'm Just Here for the Food: Food + Heat = Cooking*), cookbooks that illustrate techniques such as how to mince a shallot or string a pea (Mark Bittman's *How to Cook Everything*), cookbooks with separate illustrations for each step of each recipe (*The Good Housekeeping Illustrated Cookbook*), cookbooks with menu suggestions for each recipe (*Moosewood Restaurant Low-Fat Favorites: Flavorful Recipes for Healthful Meals*), cookbooks that list the nutritional analysis for each recipe and cookbooks that don't, cookbooks with spiral bindings, and on and on.

Just as there are many similarities between nonfiction and fiction materials, there are also many similarities between readers of nonfiction and readers of fiction. For example, the personal nature of the reading experience is extremely important for both nonfiction and fiction readers, a point made by McCook, Carr, and others in their chapters. Likewise, personal needs and learning styles may make some audiovisual formats more appropriate to some users, as Michael Vollmar-Grone argues in his chapter.

In his workshops for readers' advisors, Duncan Smith talks about a reader whose experience of *Prince of Tides* is so different from Duncan's own experience that it seems as if they are reading two different books. The same can be true of nonfiction titles. In his chapter, retired professor Ken Shearer writes eloquently about Thad Carhart's excellent memoir, *The Piano Shop on the Left Bank*. Based on Ken's recommendation, I recently read and thoroughly enjoyed Carhart's book. For me, the stories of the quirky Parisian characters were enjoyable, and the technical notes about the piano were enlightening. But the chapter on two master piano teachers (Peter Feuchtwanger and György Sebök) was the highlight of the book for me, perhaps because I also teach and am interested in the techniques that teachers of any subject use. To echo what Shearer points out, what appealed to me in *The Piano Shop on the Left Bank* was not exactly what appealed to him or his wife Ann or his friend Alan.

Advisors for nonfiction readers, viewers, and listeners need to focus on the personal nature of these nonfiction preferences, just as they do for fiction readers, viewers, and listeners. As Joyce Saricks notes in her introduction to the book, the same approach that has proved so successful with fiction readers' advisory services can work equally well with nonfiction readers. As Catherine Ross argues in her chapter, the readers' advisory interview and nonfiction appeal factors are keys to providing good advisory services for nonfiction readers.

Finally, like fiction, nonfiction may hold special appeal to specific groups of readers. Faris notes in her chapter that nonfiction can satisfy a child's curiosity or stimulate a preteen's brain development or excite a reluctant young reader. Kochel points out in her chapter that nonfiction appeals to young readers and can increase student achievement. Dawson and Van Fleet show in their chapter that multicultural nonfiction helps cultures understand themselves and understand one another.

Getting Past the Dichotomy

When readers' advisors recognize that the distinction between fiction and nonfiction is not hard and fast, they are free to recommend both fiction and nonfiction to readers in the readers' advisory transaction. A fine printed example of this is Peske and West's (2001) *Bibliotherapy,* which lists fiction and nonfiction recommendations side by side. For instance, Daniel Defoe's *Moll Flanders* and the Delany Sisters' *Having Our Say* are listed next to one another in a chapter on books "about unmanageable women who pushed the limits and stood their ground" (Peske and West 2001, 1). Carole Lieberman's *Bad Boys: Why We Love Them* ... can be found next to Emily Bronte's *Wuthering Heights.* S. E. Hinton's *The Outsiders* is wedged between Sylvia Plath's *The Bell Jar* and Anne Frank's *Diary of a Young Girl* in a chapter on coming-of-age books.

Or consider the list of pretrip reading compiled by travel writer Rick Steves (URL: http://www.ricksteves.com/news/0303/books.htm [Accessed August 3, 2003]), which mixes fiction and nonfiction. Hugo's famous novel *The Hunchback of Notre Dame* is recommended for travelers to

Paris, alongside nonfiction works such as Thad Carhart's *The Piano Shop on the Left Bank,* Adam Gopnik's *Paris to the Moon,* and Patricia Wells's *The Foodlover's Guide to Paris.* For those traveling to Italy, recommendations run from *Basilica* by William D. Montalbano (a murder-mystery set in Rome and Vatican City) to nonfiction such as Ross King's *Brunelleschi's Dome.* (Another example is *Outside* magazine's wonderful list of travel books, "The *Outside* Canon" [Harvey et al. 1996]. Nonfiction standards such as Harrer's *Seven Years in Tibet* and Paul Theroux's *The Great Railway Bazaar* are listed, but so are fiction works such as Melville's *Moby Dick* and Paul Bowles's *The Sheltering Sky.* In fact, the list includes a number of fiction titles in a category titled "*Outside* Lit 101.")

Or consider the possibilities surrounding the recent centennial celebration of flight and possible responses to a reader who is interested in books about women who fly airplanes. Biographies of Amelia Earhart might lead to other nonfiction about female pilots (Beryl Markham's wonderful *West with the Night*, for instance) or to works of fiction (Jane Mendelsohn's fine novel, *I Was Amelia Earhart*) or even to videos (Diane Keaton starring as the pilot in "Amelia Earhart: The Final Flight"). As Ross learned from her interviews with adult readers, even when subject is the important factor, readers often ignore the fiction-nonfiction distinction and want to read "everything" on the topic.

In *The Act of Creation,* Arthur Koestler (1964) argues that creativity is the result of juxtaposing two seemingly dissimilar things. This act of "bisocation," as Koestler terms it, explains both artistic creativity ("O, my luve's like a red, red rose") and scientific creativity (stellar gravity is like terrestrial gravity). Making these kinds of connections is part of what readers' advisors help readers do. To use the example that Stacy Alesi discusses in her chapter, seeing the connections between Paul Collins's *Sixpence House,* Marlena De Blasi's *A Thousand Days in Venice,* and Isadora Tattlin's *Cuba Diaries: An American Housewife in Havana* is an inherently creative act. One takes place in Wales, one in Venice, and one in Cuba; one involves a writer, one a professional chef, and one a housewife. But they are all about Americans living away from home, and the latter two may appeal to a reader who enjoyed *Sixpence House.*

It is important to remember that finding these connections is not just what reader's advisors do. Finding connections is what librarians do. Classification is all about connecting items, all about determining that one set of items is enough alike to have the same subject heading or that another set of items is enough alike to have the same classification number. Information retrieval is also about connecting items; like reader's advisory, retrieval is about finding "more like this." (Google, after all, is just an advisory service for Web pages.)

Breaking down the traditional fiction-nonfiction dichotomy benefits both readers' advisory services and the field of librarianship in several ways. Among other things, it broadens the arena in which readers' advisory can be practiced, enabling us to satisfy a greater number of users and enabling us to learn more about the acts of reading, listening, and viewing. The lessons learned from understanding why individuals read and enjoy nonfiction titles can be applied to our understanding of why individuals read and enjoy fiction titles and vice versa. The lessons learned from understanding why nonfiction audiovisual formats are more effective for some users, as Vollmar-Grone argues in his chapter, can help us understand why those formats are more effective for fiction and vice versa. Developing best practices in readers' advisory for nonfiction readers will help develop best practices in readers' advisory transactions for fiction readers and vice versa.

Going beyond the fiction-nonfiction dichotomy brings the profession closer to its roots in education by recognizing that both fiction and nonfiction have educational value, a point that Crowley makes in his chapter. Breaking down the dichotomy raises the status of discretionary or leisure reading by showing that it can involve nonfiction as well as fiction, and this helps remove the stigma that relegates the majority of users (those with recreational needs) to a second-class status. It helps move the profession closer to recognizing that schools of librarianship should educate students in readers' advisory and related topics. It provides a greater impetus to the development of better tools to support the readers' advisory process.

Finally, transcending the dichotomy brings readers' advisory closer to other core issues in librarianship (as noted earlier, both classification and retrieval deal with the same kinds of connections that lie at the heart of readers' advisory) and closer to the core issues in other fields, as we recognize that the issues of interest to readers' advisory for both fiction and nonfiction are related to the issues of interest to a number of other disciplines. As Wiegand (1997b, 2001) points out, there are potentially fruitful connections between librarianship and literacy studies, reader-response theory, the ethnography of reading, and the social history of books and reading. It is easy to see fruitful connections to areas as diverse as marketing, psychology, classification theory (Bowker and Starr 2002), and the study of social networks (Barabási 2002). In a similar manner, as Kathleen de la Peña McCook points out in her chapter, nonfiction readers' advisory can also forge an important link between libraries and other institutions such as local history societies, museums, botanical gardens, aquariums. Likewise, Marcia Kochel's chapter notes that nonfiction provides opportunities for school librarians to collaborate with teachers.

There is a subgenre in philosophy that involves the philosopher describing a dichotomy and then showing that the dichotomy doesn't hold. Philosophers from Socrates to the present have written in this subgenre and have used the technique to shed light on a number of issues. For example, Kant worked in this subgenre by examining the dichotomy between empiricism and rationalism; Nietzsche, the dichotomy between good and evil; Foucault, the dichotomy between madness and reason; and Hilary Putnam, the dichotomy between fact and value. Those of us who value readers' advisory services can do something similar and go beyond the traditional dichotomy between fiction and nonfiction—a dichotomy that has not served us well, a dichotomy whose resolution opens up tremendous possibilities.

References

Barabási, Albert-László. 2002. *Linked: The new science of networks.* Cambridge, MA: Perseus Publishing.

Bowker, Geoffrey C., and Susan Leigh Star. 2002. *Sorting things out: Classification and its consequences.* Cambridge, MA: MIT Press.

Burgin, Robert. 2001. Readers' advisory and nonfiction. In *The readers' advisor's companion.* Edited by Kenneth D. Shearer and Robert Burgin, 213–27. Englewood, CO: Libraries Unlimited.

Chen-Josephson, YiLing. 2003. Word up: Which dictionary is the best? *Slate* (December 4). URL: http://slate.msn.com/id/2091949/ (Accessed December 8, 2003).

Harvey, Miles, et al. 1996. The outside canon: A few great books. *Outside* (May). Also available at URL: http://www.outsidemag.com/magazine/0596/9605feo.html (Accessed December 20, 2003).

Koestler, Arthur. 1964. *The act of creation.* New York: Macmillan.

Peske, Nancy, and Beverly West. 2001. *Bibliotherapy: The girl's guide to books for every phase of our lives.* New York: Dell.

Rick Steves, "Booked for Adventure." URL: http://www.ricksteves.com/news/0303/books.htm. Accessed August 3, 2003.

Saricks, Joyce G., and Nancy Brown. 1997. *Readers' advisory services in the public library.* 2d ed. Chicago: American Library Association.

Shearer, Kenneth D., and Robert Burgin. 2001. Partly out of sight; not much in mind: Master's level education for adult readers' advisory services. In *The readers' advisor's companion.* Edited by Kenneth D. Shearer and Robert Burgin, 15–25. Englewood, CO: Libraries Unlimited.

Wiegand, Wayne A. 1997a. MisReading library education. *Library Journal* 122: 36–38.

Wiegand, Wayne A. 1997b. Out of sight, and out of mind: Why don't we have any schools of library and reading studies? *Journal of Library and Information Science Education* 38: 316–26.

Wiegand, Wayne A. 2000. Librarians ignore the value of stories. *Chronicle of Higher Education* 47 (October 27): B20.

Wiegand, Wayne A. 2001. Missing the real story: Where library and information science fails the library profession. In *The readers' advisor's companion.* Edited by Kenneth D. Shearer and Robert Burgin, 7–14. Englewood, CO: Libraries Unlimited.

—

Index

About the Editor and Contributors

Stacy Alesi is a library associate at Southwest County Regional Library in Boca Raton, Florida, where she created a Readers' Advisory program utilizing volunteers, assisted in creating a short Readers' Advisory "cheat sheet," maintains the Mystery page of the Readers' Advisory section of the Palm Beach County Web site at www.pbclibrary.org, recommends new titles for the branch collection, gives monthly booktalks at local nursing homes, and is the Volunteer Coordinator for more than one hundred volunteers each month at her branch, in addition to her circulation duties. She has worked for Borders Books & Music for seven years, in every capacity from bookseller, trainer, and manager to her current position as facilitator of a contemporary fiction reading group. She created and maintains a Web site at www.bookbitch.com. This enlightening site offers book reviews, information on first time authors, best-sellers, reading groups, and everything in between; a weblog of breaking book news; a resource of links to dozens of book-related Web sites; and monthly promotions. She is a regular contributor to *Library Journal* of reviews in general fiction, legal fiction, suspense, and chick-lit. She is currently an undergraduate student majoring in English at Florida Atlantic University.

Robert Burgin is a Professor at North Carolina Central University's School of Library and Information Sciences. He holds a BA from Duke University and a Master's and PhD from the University of North Carolina at Chapel Hill. He served in public libraries for ten years and served as the Assistant State Librarian for Information Technology with the State Library of North Carolina for two years. His publications include articles in readers' advisory, management, and information retrieval. He coedited, with Kenneth D. Shearer, *The Readers' Advisor's Companion* (2001) and contributed two chapters to that book: "Partly Out of Sight; Not Much in Mind: Master's Level Education for Adult Readers' Advisory Services" (with Kenneth D. Shearer) and "Readers' Advisory and Nonfiction." He also contributed two chapters to *Guiding the Reader to the Next Book* (1996): "Readers' Advisory in Public Libraries: An Overview of Current Practice" and "Readers' Advisory Resources for Adults on the Internet." Burgin is currently Vice-President/President-Elect of the North Carolina Library Association.

David Carr teaches at the School of Information and Library Science at the University of North Carolina at Chapel Hill, where he specializes in collections, reading, and reference work in the humanities and social sciences. As a scholar and consultant, he also addresses learning outside schools, especially in public cultural institutions such as libraries and museums. His work emphasizes self-directed inquiry and critical thinking, adult curiosity, informal learning, and independent scholarship. As a scholar, he is most interested in the unfinished issues of adult life and the processes that help human beings to become deeply informed over time. David Carr has consulted at the following institutions among others: Brooklyn Museum of Art, Children's Museum of Indianapolis, Cooper-Hewitt National Design Museum, Historical Society of Pennsylvania, The Jewish Museum, Museum of Fine Arts—Houston, Museum of Jewish Heritage, National Endowment for the Humanities, Rhode Island School of Design, Strong Museum, and the W. K. Kellogg Foundation. In recent years, he has lectured and written on the passion of reading in adult life. A collection of David Carr's essays, *The Promise of Cultural Institutions*, appeared in 2003.

Bill Crowley worked for twenty-three years in New York, Alabama, Indiana, and Ohio in many capacities. He earned a BA in history from Hunter College of the City University of New York, an MA in English from Ohio State University with a thesis in occupational folklore, an MS in library service from Columbia University, and a PhD in higher education at Ohio University in Athens, Ohio. Crowley has published in both the higher education and library and information science literatures, addressing diverse topics, including the competition between "library" and "information" in graduate education. He served as Chair of the State Library Agency Section of ALA's Association of Specialized and Cooperative Library Agencies. In 1996, Bill joined the faculty of Dominican University's Graduate School of Library and Information Science, where he is now a Professor.

Alma Dawson is Assistant Professor in the School of Library and Information Science at Louisiana State University, where she teachers courses that include collection management, library user instruction, and foundations of library and information science. She also worked in school and academic libraries in Louisiana and Texas. She is an active member of ALA, the Association for Library and Information Science Education, and the Louisiana Library Association. A graduate of Grambling State University, she received her MLS from the University of Michigan and her PhD from Texas Woman's University. Dawson's contributions to the library and information science literature include two publications related to readers' advisory services: an

African American Readers' Advisory (with Connie Van Fleet) and a special issue of *Louisiana Libraries* on "Enhancing Information Literacy for Diverse Populations."

Frank Exner, Little Bear, is a Squamish Indian from British Columbia, Canada. With articles and book reviews in *Journal of the American Society for Information Science* and *Bulletin of the American Society for Information Science*, he indexed *The Readers' Advisor's Companion* and *Guiding the Reader to the Next Book* and created a master index for twenty years of the State Library of North Carolina's Summer Reading Program Manuals. Exner, Little Bear, is currently a doctoral student at South Africa's University of Pretoria Department of Information Science by distance education, having received MIS and MLS degrees from the North Carolina Central University School of Library and Information Sciences. His current research focuses on the authority control of American Indian personal names.

Crystal Faris is the Youth Services Manager of the Nassau Library System, Long Island, New York. She is also an adjunct instructor at the Graduate School of Library and Information Studies at Queens College. Previously she was a branch manager and youth services librarian for the Indianapolis-Marion County Public Library. She holds a BA in Communication Arts from Judson College in suburban Chicago and an MLS from Indiana University, where she was a recipient of the Evelyn Ray Sickels Award for outstanding academic achievement and high potential for success in the field of children's librarianship. She wrote the manual for a cooperative reading program between the Association for Library Service to Children, a division of the American Library Association, and the PBS television show *Reading Rainbow*; the reading program was titled *Math Is Everywhere, Read All about It!*

Marcia Kochel is currently the media director at Olson Middle School in Bloomington, Minnesota. She has previously worked as a media specialist with K–8 students in Chatham County, North Carolina, and Bloomington, Indiana. She received a BA in American Studies from the College of William and Mary and a Master of Science in Library Science from the University of North Carolina at Chapel Hill. She is the coauthor of two books published by Libraries Unlimited, *Gotcha! Nonfiction Booktalks to Get Kids Excited about Reading* (1999) and *Gotcha Again! More Nonfiction Booktalks to Get Kids Excited about Reading* (2002).

Kathleen de la Peña McCook is Distinguished University Professor at the University of South Florida where she teaches courses on public libraries, adult reading, and cultural heritage in the School of Library and Information Science. She currently serves on the Notable Books Council of the ALA Reference and User Services Association and has been honored with that Association's Margaret E. Monroe Adult Services Award.

Vicki Novak is an Adult Services Librarian at the Maricopa County Library District in Phoenix, Arizona, where she has worked for twelve years. She received a Bachelor of Arts Degree in English from Northern Arizona University and a Master of Library Science degree from the University of Arizona. She first became passionate about readers' advisory after taking a class called Reading Interests of Adults, taught by Dr. Wayne Wiegand. She leads a book discussion group that discusses both fiction and nonfiction, and she loves to promote nonfiction through book displays and bibliographies. With the assistance of the Fiction_L e-mail list, she compiled a bibliography called "Good Reads from the Real World: Nonfiction that Reads Like Fiction." She served on Arizona Library Association's Arizona Adult Author Award committee in 2001. In the past, she wrote a column for her library's staff newsletter called "InterNetWorking @ the Library."

Catherine Ross (MA, MLIS, PhD) is Professor and Dean of the Faculty of Information and Media Studies at the University of Western Ontario, where she teaches in the MLIS program, the MA program in media studies, and the LIS doctoral program. Recent publications include coauthored books *Communicating Professionally* and *Conducting the Reference Interview* as well as scholarly articles on the reference transaction and on readers' advisory. For some time, she has been involved in a research project on reading for pleasure based on open-ended interviews with some two hundred avid readers. She was awarded the Reference Service Press Award in 1996, 2000, and 2002. She has also written four nonfiction books for children and in 1996 won the Science Writers of Canada Award for best science book written for children for her book *Squares: Shapes in Math, Science and Nature*.

Joyce G. Saricks has worked as Coordinator of the Literature and Audio Services department at the Downers Grove (Illinois) Public Library since 1983. She joined the library staff as a reference librarian, after receiving her MA/MAT in Library Science from the University of Chicago, and she has also worked as head of Technical Services at Downers Grove. She has written two books on readers' advisory – *Readers' Advisory Guide to Genre Fiction* (2001) and, with Nancy Brown, *Readers' Advisory Service in the Public Library* (1989, rev. 1997). She has written several articles on readers' advisory, presented workshops on that topic for public libraries and library systems, and spoken at state, regional, and national library conferences. In 1989, she won the Public Library Association's Allie Beth Martin Award, and in 2000 she was named Librarian of the Year by the Romance Writers of America.

Kenneth D. Shearer is a retired Professor of Library and Information Science at North Carolina Central University. An honors graduate of Amherst College, he earned the MLS and PhD degrees from Rutgers University. He worked at Peninsula Public Library in New York and Detroit Public Library in Michigan. He edited *Public Libraries* from 1978 through 1988, wrote approximately fifty articles and scholarly papers, and edited or coedited several books, most recently *The Readers' Advisor's Companion* (with Robert Burgin 2001) and *Guiding the Reader to the Next Book* (1996). One of his three sons, Timothy, is an academic librarian concurrently working on his PhD at the University of North Carolina at Chapel Hill and has therefore become his most successful recruitment effort.

Duncan Smith is an Assistant Vice-President for EBSCO Industries. He is the creator and founder of NoveList, EBSCO Publishing's electronic readers' advisory service. Smith is currently the Product Manager for NoveList and EBSCO's new Book Index with Reviews database. Prior to NoveList, he was the Coordinator of the North Carolina Library Staff Development Program, a statewide continuing education initiative housed at North Carolina Central University's School of Library and Information Sciences. Smith is a nationally recognized trainer and researcher in the area of readers' advisory services. He has published widely in this field and in 1997 received the Margaret E. Monroe Award from Library Adult Services from ALA's Reference and User Services Division for his teaching and writing in this area.

Connie Van Fleet is Professor, School of Library and Information Studies, University of Oklahoma. She holds a BA in Psychology (University of Oklahoma), an MLIS (Louisiana State University), and a PhD in Library and Information Science (Indiana University). She has been recognized for distinguished teaching at the university level (Louisiana State University) and significant contributions to library adult services (ALA/RUSA Margaret E. Monroe Library Adult Services Award) and is the recipient of the 2004 ALISE Teaching Excellence Award. She is currently coeditor (with Danny P. Wallace) of *Reference & User Services Quarterly*. Her work on library services in a multicultural society has appeared in a number of publications and focuses on older adults, people with disabilities, and ethnically diverse populations. She has taught readers' advisory courses at three universities. "The Future of Readers' Advisory Services in a Multicultural Society," coauthored with Alma Dawson, appeared in *The Readers' Advisor's Companion* (2001). Van Fleet and Dawson are currently collaborating on *The African American Readers' Advisor: A Guide for Readers, Librarians, and Educators*.

Michael Vollmar-Grone is the Audiovisual Librarian of the Amos Memorial Public Library in Sidney, Ohio. For more than a dozen years, he has developed and defined the Audiovisual Department, which includes the movies, music, and audiobook collections. He holds a Master of Library Science degree from Kent (Ohio) State University and a Bachelor of Science in journalism degree from Bowling Green (Ohio) State University. His latest published contribution is the "Public Library Video Collections" chapter of *Video Collection Development in Multi-type Libraries: A Handbook* (2d ed., edited by Gary Handman, 2002). Prior to joining the library, Vollmar-Grone earned his living as an award-winning photojournalist and corporate photographer.